FRENCH ROOTS

JEAN-PIERRE MOULLÉ & DENISE LURTON MOULLÉ

FRENCH ROOTS

Two cooks, two countries &
the beautiful food along the way

FOREWORD BY PATRICIA UNTERMAN

Photography by Jan Baldwin

TEN SPEED PRESS
Berkeley

We write to taste life twice,
in the moment and in retrospect.
—ANAÏS NIN

to Maud & Elsa

CONTENTS

ACKNOWLEDGMENTS

Cree LeFavour has been our guardian angel during the making of this book. David McCormick, our agent, had the good intuition of having us meet, and we are so grateful. Cree guided us through the process of writing a cookbook, was patient reading our stories, and thoughtful when correcting our nonnative English. She understood our bicultural lives and helped us share the things we sometimes take for granted. We have become close friends and look forward to other projects together.

Jan Baldwin came from London and visited us for a week to capture our home and lives in Bordeaux. Jan's photographs represent perfectly the blend of country rustic and sophistication we strive to maintain, in our food, and in our everyday life. She always shot with curiosity, good spirits, and impeccable taste. Stylist Alice Hart, along with our daughter Elsa were very helpful that week, as many pictures needed to be taken in so little time. We are also grateful to Don Hicks for contributing some of the beautiful pictures he has taken of the ranch and garden in Healdsburg.

It was a pleasure working with Jenny Wapner at Ten Speed Press. She subtly found the way to keep us on the right path while letting us explore our diverse ideas. Toni Tajima made it all come together with her creative designs, finding just the right way to combine earthiness with elegance.

We are thankful to our parents, who instilled in us a deep sense of earth's preciousness. They taught us how to respect and receive the land's bounties, and how grateful we should be of it. We took these lessons for granted, but after having put them down in a book, it is very clear they are responsible for our "bon sens" which is to be down to earth and unpretentious.

Friends shared their recipes with us: Evan Shively, Natasha Landau, and Sybille de Brosses.

My sister, Christine Bazin de Caix, as well as Helen Calen and Bernadette Donascimento are to thank for the beautifully decorated tables at Chateau Bonnet.

Our dear daughters were fantastic helpers. Maud took care of our ranch and its abundant vegetable garden during our months away in France. Elsa helped us tremendously with recipes and much of the cooking while in Bordeaux. Alban, Elsa's husband, as a gourmet, was the perfect critic for his wife's testing recipes. Maud and Elsa are both excellent cooks and an inspiration.

We thank all of you who entice us to put these words down. We hope it will bring more conviviality to all of our lives, as well as respect for the beautiful planet earth we all share.

We can be contacted at: www.twobordelais.com

FOREWORD

by Patricia Unterman

"Alors, we are having our picnic now," announced Denise.

She unfurled a tablecloth over some wet logs in the middle of a meadow in the foothills of the French Pyrenees. Jean-Pierre pulled bread, charcuterie, cheese and fruit from a wicker basket. The Americans, kids and adults in sweatshirts and jackets, actually thought it was raining. The French, in shirt sleeves and shorts, sipped wine from tumblers and admired the scenery. We picque-niqued for exactly forty-five minutes and damply piled back on the tour van, which headed straight up the mountain to an encampment of Basque shepherds in their late spring stage of transhumance, the annual migration of pastoral animals with their human and canine caretakers.

The mountain pastures dotted with tiny yellow wild flowers looked like psychedelic green velvet. Misty bare peaks and forested slopes enveloped us. Our French-American contingent set up tents amidst outcrops of rock. We shared the meadow with woolly white sheep on impossibly skinny legs and monolithic reclining dun cows in leather necklaces strung with tin bells. The ruddy shepherds in serge jackets and black berets lived in a crumbling stone building with a tiny stove. There Jean-Pierre heated up his *garbure*—a thick soup of ham, cabbage and vegetables enriched with stale bread and mountain cheese—our dinner.

I had never been anyplace as profoundly beautiful as this, and I have never spent a more miserable night. At dawn we watched the sheepdogs corral ewes for milking, guiding them one by one into the hull of a gutted car, its open doors creating a stall. The cheesemaker, in white coat and hat, heated an aluminum pot of sheep's milk over a burner on the stone floor of the house, added a few drops of rennet, and gently stirred it with his hands until he was able pull out a soft, poofy basketball of curd—the birth of a wheel of tome de pyrenees. Draining the whey, he gave us the warm solids, sheep's milk fromage frais, to eat with wild berry preserves, and cooled the rest in a pail anchored in the icy stream that meandered through the pasture. I have never tasted anything more delicious, or more intimate with nature. Jean-Pierre and Denise had taken us Americans by the hand and dragged us to experience the wonder of the traditional food they grew up eating. We would never be the same.

This happened twenty years ago. As I read *French Roots,* more memories flooded back—being with Jean-Pierre and Denise in Peyraud and Arcachon, and in Berkeley and Healdsburg. The two of them taught me, and a whole generation of northern Californians, how to eat and drink and cook and live.

Now, reading this evocative joint autobiography, I discover what great storytellers they are. They describe the evolution of their unique, multi-cultural sensibility in a moving coming-of-age story with benefits: it includes an inside look at the Chez Panisse kitchen, a wonderfully personal collection of recipes (some so simple and homey I started cooking them for dinner; others I'm aspiring to take on) and a lifestyle primer. Most of all, they've written a love story—their own—rooted in provincial France and nurtured by the social freedom of America.

I didn't want this book to end.

INTRODUCTION

Denise

Nearly every day of our more than thirty-three years of married life, Jean-Pierre and I have sat down together to eat lunch. It's not a heavy meal: We have a large green salad from Jean-Pierre's garden, a French cheese, bread, and a glass of wine. In winter, we might make soup, a frittata, or an omelet for a heartier meal. On occasion we take a light dessert—fresh fruit with crème fraîche or, in winter, a slender slice of cake with an espresso.

Whatever happens to be ready to pick in the garden usually determines our lunch—perhaps it's December and the leeks are all that survive. Instead of the usual green salad, we'll have blanched leeks with anchovies, egg, and vinaigrette. In spring we might have cauliflower, cabbage, or another winter vegetable that has survived the heavy frosts. In summer we'll dress the just-picked green beans in vinaigrette, a plate of brandade, and a small green salad.

The ritual of sitting down to eat a meal, whether it's just the two of us for lunch or twelve friends and family for dinner, reveals something about the pace and focus of our lives. The table, and what occurs at it, is central to the vitality of our lives; it's there that our relationships and our work coalesce around food, wine, and conversation. The food we cook and the wine we offer and consume at those meals grounds us, linking us to its diverse sources. Through those sources we engage our culture and community as well as to the natural world we share.

What we hope *French Roots* offers is a sense of the connection between the Old World food and practices of rural France and the way we, as quasi-Americans, eat, drink, and live today. With recipes for simple preparations for vegetables, fruit, meat, and fish set alongside classic French dishes, we hope to link what many people think of as California cuisine and what we know is, more often than not, the simple—even elemental—cooking of rural France. We hope these connections show through the stories and adventures that accompany our recipes. We hope to offer some insight on how the many differences between French and American culture shape not just the ways we approach cooking, eating, and drinking, but also the small and large ways that we love, marry, raise children, entertain, and generally engage with the world. We see ourselves as a bridge between what can be the vastly divergent cultures and practices of France and the United States.

It is no accident, of course, that I met Jean-Pierre in Berkeley, a city simmering with creativity and a lively spirit of rebellion. In our own ways, Jean-Pierre and I have long been restless rule-breakers. We escaped the traditions, limitations, and safety of France for the alluring social and professional freedom California offered. We ended up in that particular paradise because we rejected tradition-loving France; yet in no small part, it's an Old-World approach that informs the food and wine included here.

This book is our attempt to capture the most meaningful old traditions cross-pollinated by the freedom to improve and improvise that California has allowed. We are truly hybrid, and this book represents that mixed heritage. That so many of the values that the food revolution brought to California were founded on rural French values and practices is no great surprise. One of the qualities that I hope makes our book worthwhile is the way these two elements are integrated in the food and ingredients we choose.

Flexibility and creativity in the kitchen are just a couple of the qualities that make Jean-Pierre the chef he is. His innovations and the breadth of his creativity yield the results they do because of his insistence on the integrity of his ingredients. For Jean-Pierre, this often means hours spent in the garden and orchard, tilling, planting, weeding, pruning, watering, composting, harvesting—all the hard outdoor labor of producing your own food. Whether it's the green garlic he keeps growing year round outside the door or the vinegar he ferments using our leftover wine, his attention to detail as well as his upbringing are what make his food as clean, pure, and truly remarkable as it is.

Our refusal to waste food is one of the most telling signals of our rural French sensibility, a sensibility that is tied up with frugality as much as it is tied to a deep respect for food as a valuable, nearly sacred, part of life. Whether it's a handful of slightly soft strawberries left over from making a tart or a half-bushel of overgrown green beans from the garden, we'll find a way to put it to use.

When Jean-Pierre creates a new dish, it is not infrequently the result of his desire to use the last, valuable bit of some ingredient that awaits his attention. From Seafood Sauerkraut (page 190) to Rabbit Rillettes (page 235), the real cooking of France is founded on a belief in using every last bit of what has been harvested or slaughtered. In the spirit of preserving, are the assorted preparations we call Mini-Recipes around the Duck (page 140). These recipes originate in a ritual of communal butchering that still takes place in the French countryside. Neighbors gather and for three days pluck and scald and gut and cut to preserve the meat for the year ahead. The practice arose in a time when refrigeration was nonexistent and survives today out of an attachment to the flavors and traditions of meat and fowl preserved this way. The products—duck confit, terrines, duck fat, smoked breast, duck prosciutto, and rillettes—are testaments to the purity of flavor and simplicity that have made French culinary traditions so influential.

What is included here is the food, culture, and influence of Berkeley through the lens of our rural French roots. It is French cuisine as practiced by a couple who have become, however incongruously, Californians. From this perspective, we hope to strengthen the food and culture of France and California.

After thirty-some years in the United States, I'm not American, nor am I entirely French. I have an American passport and driver's license, and Jean-Pierre and I raised our two daughters, Elsa and Maud, in the United States. While I prefer living in the United States to living in France full-time, I remain more French than American. Why is that? I have never shed my strong French accent despite my fluent English. Maybe it's my way of holding onto and signaling that my manners, values, and perspective remain rooted in the French countryside—in its food, wine, and culture and its affection for older, slower ways of being in the world.

Despite my accent and my enduring attachment to France, I revel in how direct and free the English language and American social practices enable me to be. I find English more linear than French; it gives itself to informality and ease in a way that the circuitous *politesse* of French does not. The freedom of the language matches the ease in America to do as you like, take risks, think for yourself, and make new friends outside your inherited social circle. This is a very un-French way of being in the world. Despite my seemingly intractable French sensibility in certain things, I find Americans and their laws, customs, and manners refreshingly uncomplicated.

I am the product of a wine family—whatever affected the vineyards and the wine determined the prosperity of the family. The cultivation of the grapes, the wine we produced from them, and whether that wine was good, great, or indifferent were all that mattered.

I've recreated much of what I most value from my rural childhood in the life I live with Jean-Pierre. We live country lives—our converted stone barn at Peyraut in Bordeaux is situated on ten acres amidst the vineyards, and our house in California sits nestled in the hills surrounded by pristine land populated by wildlife—coyotes, bobcats, mountain lions, ducks, geese, and cranes. Some of these animals live on the property, some stop by to refresh themselves in the pond. Whether we're at Peyraut or in Healdsburg, this life in the countryside is the life we envisioned for ourselves after many years amidst the urban bustle of Berkeley.

In Bordeaux and in Healdsburg, we work toward as much self-sufficiency as possible. Each property has its limitations and strengths. We keep bees for honey and tend mature apple, pear, fig, and hazelnut trees in Bordeaux; in Healdsburg we enjoy an extended growing season for herbs and vegetables, our pond is stocked with fish year-round, and we cultivate olive trees.

Wherever we are, most of the wine we drink comes from friends or family. Jean-Pierre keeps a magnificent vegetable garden at both of our houses. In season, he supplies the bulk of the vegetables and all of the lettuce for our table. For the first time this year, Jean-Pierre cured green, Tuscan-style olives and pressed his own olive oil. We gather cèpes (porcini), chanterelles, and morels from the woods, and Jean-Pierre hunts deer, boar, and game birds when given the opportunity.

I don't want to pretend we don't go to the store—of course we do. I often buy bread and shop for fruit, fish, meat, and staples at the farmers' market or health food store. In Bordeaux, Jean-Pierre shops at the farmers' markets in Libourne and Branne, not far from our house. The point is not to go "back to the land" for the sake of a wild experiment in natural living—the point as we see it is to live and eat well by staying as connected as possible to where our food and wine come from and to those who grew it or caught it or slaughtered it before it arrives in our kitchen. This matters to us because that's the way we grew up—buying strange produce from halfway around the world, bringing it into the kitchen, and trying to make sense of it doesn't appeal to either of us. Certainly, we buy cheese from France when we're in California, but in France we prefer to drive down the road to buy goat cheese and eggs from the neighbor who has been a friend of the family for two generations.

Jean-Pierre and I feel most at home when we're in sync with the seasons through eating what we grow, shoot, catch, and forage. It's not only to eat well that we do this—although we do, of course, eat well. For my part, I'm at my best and most grounded in the world when I regularly notice the color of the sky or the vivid green threads of fine grass sprouting by the pond after the rain. The staggered arrival of fruits and vegetables as they come into season again each year is my ultimate calendar, just as the mournful lowing of the cows at feeding time is the best sort of clock for me. Simple as these rhythms are, like a lucky glimpse of a red bobcat slipping through the grass, they are prescient reminders of nature and its power.

Jean-Pierre

Denise and I were married only six months after our fateful sidewalk meeting on Shattuck Avenue in front of Chez Panisse. The depth and longevity of our marriage—thirty-three years and counting—might have something to do with the food we shared on our first date. The meal Denise prepared was pure seduction. She'd managed to smuggle into the country an amazing foie gras from her Tante Anne's geese, along with an exceptional duck confit the likes of which I hadn't tasted since I'd left France nearly two years earlier. For dessert Denise made the best cherry *clafoutis* I'd ever tasted—the whole cherries, stones intact, making it quintessentially French. We ate the meal slowly at the table in her tiny apartment, first savoring the buttery foie gras on crisp toast, before starting on the rich saltiness of preserved game in the shredded duck confit on a bright, peppery salad of barely dressed arugula. There was ample—extremely good—Champagne. It would have been difficult for me not to fall for Denise: The effortless ease of a native language in common paired with her beauty conspired to seal my fate.

Our shared sense of exile in Berkeley, the language, and the food she prepared with such exquisite taste and attention turned a date into a lifetime. She's been my ideal partner; our commitment to our rural French roots has always mingled effortlessly with our desire to take risks, explore, and shake some of the nonsense out of the dullest parts of our traditional French heritage. I guess that's how we've forged such a charmed life: by cobbling together our mixed desires into our own ideal version of new and old.

When I met Denise I had been working at Chez Panisse for just a few years. It was during the somewhat chaotic reign of the talented, rowdy chef, Jeremiah Tower, when all the excesses of Berkeley in the seventies made their way quite naturally into the kitchen. It was an exciting time to be a chef in California. What I discovered at Chez Panisse—along with the chaos—was a passionate group of chefs, cooks, and visionaries who welcomed a dose of the professional kitchen discipline I brought in the form of my formal French training.

Alice Waters never wavered much in her vision for Chez Panisse. Despite many changes over the years, she remained committed to certain principles. My loyalty followed; the integrity of the ingredients I had to work with and my freedom to do what I liked with them, paired with the general spirit of experimentation, kept me attached to the restaurant. I brought my formal culinary training to Chez Panisse but learned there, in turn, that I'm at my best as a chef when I am loose, open, and experimental. Creativity and risk-taking were ever-important elements amid the slightly reckless impulses that launched Chez Panisse. What I did in the kitchen couldn't be solely defined by French or even European values, no matter how powerfully those traditions shaped the food and menus that have made the restaurant so famous. For the most part, although it was hard work, as any kitchen work is, I loved the joyful, creative cooking I had the freedom to put into practice at Chez Panisse for so many years, and a great deal of it is included here.

Like most French men and women of my generation who were raised in the countryside, what was on the table each day was foraged, picked from the garden, or bought from a neighbor. Without a freezer or supermarket, it was impossible not to eat whatever was in season—not just vegetables and fruits, but meat, dairy, and seafood. In this sense, the recipes I developed over the course of my many years at Chez Panisse reflect the food of my childhood.

To organize the wide range of material here, Denise and I decided to present the chapters and recipes in a loose chronological order that makes explicit how our cooking has evolved over the course of more than sixty years. We begin with our respective mothers—both named Elizabeth and each a terrific cook in her own right—in a chapter on the traditional food they cooked for us. The recipes in this chapter, "French Family Life," are mixed. Some are fairly refined and would have been reserved for the expansive, multicourse, multigenerational Sunday afternoon lunches that my mother worked for days to prepare, but most stick closer to the unassuming food of the French countryside. The second chapter, "Life in Berkeley in the Seventies," takes its name from the decade that defined us personally and professionally as we made our way in a foreign country. These recipes are from those early days at Chez Panisse, as well as from our lives as we began them, independently, in that bristling, bustling time and place. Chapter three, "Back to Bordeaux," is focused on the food that we cook and eat in France and includes many of the recipes I have taught over more than twenty-five years during our tours through our company, Two Bordelais. Approachable but sophisticated, these recipes most closely represent the way we eat and cook today—a sort of hybrid California-French cuisine that changes each season—really, each month—as fruits ripen, vegetables mature, and animals are caught, hunted, or slaughtered. Chapter four, "Denise in the Kitchen," are mostly Denise's recipes for the simple, mostly French foods that she makes so often. During my years in the kitchen at Chez Panisse, Denise cooked when I arrived home late to finally relax with a glass of wine and a bite of whatever she had cooked earlier for the girls—usually an uncomplicated meal much like you might make from the recipes in this chapter. Chapter five, "In the Kitchen at Chez Panisse," is a return to Chez Panisse, representing some of the recipes I like best from that era. The recipes in this chapter are the most modern and the most challenging—although by no means out of reach for any home cook willing to take them on. Chapter six, "Aperitifs and Toasts," is focused on a crucial French ritual, the *aperitif*. The hors d'oeuvres and liqueurs here are deeply familiar to us after years of marking the end of the day with the ritual of a glass of rosé or white wine and a small bite as we talk and sit around together before sitting down to the table. Before this final chapter is a piece on how Denise approaches wine, her thoughts on pairing wine and food and some of the history of her rather famous father, the wine maker André Lurton.

As you'll see as you read *French Roots*, I take great pleasure in working with my hands. I enjoy weeding almost as much I like harvesting a big bunch of radishes for our aperitif. Tinkering with equipment and taking on building projects—a duck pond, a garden shed, an irrigation system—all of these things get me outdoors. Physical labor is somewhat cathartic for me. Although I'm now retired and have less of a need to wind down from the pressures of the kitchen than I once did, I work as hard as I do because I can't seem to accomplish enough to satisfy myself. My ambition is to make my own balsamic vinegar, start a barrel of hard cider made from apples grown on the property, cure the hams of the wild boar I shoot, expand my charcuterie repertoire, produce more of my own wine and olive oil, keep a cow for experiments in cheese making, and plant ever more fruit trees. My latest project: Pick all the wild plums on our ranch in Sonoma and make *eau-de-vie de prune*, plum alcohol, for all the aperitifs and cocktails I make. I'll eventually get around to it. For now, I'm pleased to offer here a few of the recipes and techniques I've learned over the years. I hope you find the book useful and rewarding.

GETTING STARTED

Writing and Executing a Menu

Whether you're cooking two courses and a dessert for an intimate dinner party at home or putting out food for one hundred expectant diners at a restaurant, the significance of the process that goes into planning what to cook and how can't be overstated. A menu does not mean, of course, an array of choices as we know the term in common restaurant parlance; a menu in this context is the cook's own plan for the food he or she will prepare, including each dish's ingredients, style of preparation, and sequence within the meal as a whole. Setting a menu, even in your head, is the only way to prepare for a meal before it appears at the table.

In a great restaurant or for an ambitious meal at home, the unfolding of an outstanding menu will surprise, challenge, and satisfy. In the best of cases, a truly outstanding menu is a shared experience, bringing everyone at the table together by evening's end—something like the way people might feel who, together, have glimpsed a remarkable but ultimately inexplicable sight that has faded from view. A menu can fail or succeed in the kitchen, but no matter how talented the chef, the food he or she cooks cannot surpass the limitations the menu sets.

There are no mysterious secrets or magic formulas for planning a menu—practice, imagination, and a little dedication to the work and effort required will take you most of the way. My advice is to tackle your menu with energy and enthusiasm—you'll never find the effort wasted. The work you do on paper at the planning stage will lead you into the natural flow of the meal as you get down to the physical work of shopping, prepping your ingredients, and cooking. Like most work worth doing, the more frequently you do it, the easier and more satisfying it becomes.

Contrast and balance are the central principles of a menu. Don't think of this simply in terms of ingredients—think about texture, temperature, richness, color, and strength. I'll explain all these in more detail, but for now remember that each plate has its own place in the whole and that each plate is sequential or in some way in conversation with the previous one. Good menus flow, progressing from one point to another the way a good story unfolds.

At Chez Panisse, I had a loose format. More often than not, the first course was a composed salad. In winter, the salad would often be warm or would contain both cooked and raw ingredients. Although there are virtually infinite variations when it comes to such salads, my standards often involved wild mushrooms, duck confit, and quickly seared fish or scallops over endive, watercress, or wilted chicory. In summer, the cold salads I liked best were arugula and mixed garden lettuces, complemented by smoked fish, summer vegetables, or eggs.

The second course was almost always a soup, a vegetable ragout, or a pasta—if it wasn't fish (which it might well have been if there was no fish in the first course salad). I might have followed a first course of green asparagus salad with fresh pasta with smoked black cod and peas, but I followed warm dandelion salad with goose rillettes with chestnut soup, especially in winter. As you'll find when you read the recipes here, I believe there's no such thing as too much seafood. Most of the fish I served at the restaurant was baked and served with a sauce, such as local halibut roasted and served with black olive salsa or poached and served with a concentrated seafood stock or an unassuming Meyer lemon butter.

While putting the first two dishes together I'd have been thinking about trying to move from a lighter dish—a salad, say—to a heavier dish (but not too heavy because the main course was still to come). This was often where the fish came in because it's rich and versatile but not overly heavy. If the first-course salad was warm and on the heavy side, I would follow it with a much lighter fish, while at the same time thinking about which textures I'd offered thus far. If I had a contrast of sour and bitter in my salad, I'd more likely follow it with a rich, sweet fish dish such as wild king salmon with herb butter.

My next task would be to fit the main course in with the first two courses so that it balanced them out and worked with them as a continuum, ideally moving the meal forward to another level as the menu took on momentum. At Chez Panisse, the main could be squab, quail, chicken, guinea hen, pork, veal, beef, or lamb, but it was almost always cooked in the fireplace, either grilled or spit-roasted.

A rich stock gives dimension to most savory dishes, even if you don't really know it's there, so I usually served meat and game with a reduction that suited the dish. If I served beef, I'd make a concentrated beef stock and then mount it with red wine and aromatics to finish the sauce. For venison, I'd start with something lighter, like veal stock, and add a stronger flavor to the reduction at the end—maybe juniper berries or green garlic. The main-course plates were usually finished with plenty of vegetables and a simple starch. If I served a fairly rich marrow risotto for my second course, I might serve fish for the main to keep the meal from feeling too heavy; but if I'd served a pasta dish for the second course, I would not serve a risotto as the starch on my main dish, or potatoes, yams, or other starchy vegetables either. If I'd served mussels with fingerling potatoes for the first course salad, you wouldn't find potatoes on the main-dish plate or, for that matter, potatoes in any form on the remainder of the menu. Whether it's fish, meat, or poultry for the main course, I'm a bit of a traditionalist; rather than a forlorn portion of meat, game, or poultry on the plate by itself, I prefer the classic balance of textures and flavors that a range of ingredients give a plate.

Whether it's at the level of writing the menu, shopping, or getting everything done on time, the limitations on the chef are not only technical or conceptual, they're practical. If I have poached fish for the second course, my burners will be occupied. That means cooking my main course anywhere but on the grill is out of the question. If I have two chefs and an intern putting out a starch and a vegetable on the burners for the main course, I need to keep both components fairly simple. If the starch is going on the grill with the meat—say potatoes that have been parboiled but must be finished on the grill—then I know I can push my cooks to do something more challenging with the vegetable.

It's about the space I have and the balance I'm trying to maintain. You and your kitchen will determine these factors—do you have four, six, or eight burners? A competent daughter, son, spouse, or friend to help you put out the meal? At home if I have meat on the grill, I'll plan a simple starch that I can make ahead—usually a gratin. That way the gratin is in the oven while I'm out at the grill. I know when I plan the menu that I can't be standing at the stove stirring mushroom risotto while the fat on my lamb chops flares the fire into great flames outdoors. When I throw a big party at home, I adjust the menu according to the help I have available. Sometimes I'm on my own, but sometimes I have my daughter Elsa, an excellent chef and the best possible sous-chef. When I have her I know I can do more and do it better no matter how many plates we're putting out. I also know she loves to bake and make dessert, so I plan for her to take on that part of the menu—a bit like the pastry chefs did at Chez Panisse.

Dessert, important as is it to the menu as a whole, must accommodate itself to the main menu. That doesn't mean it's an afterthought—far from it. It simply means that as the last statement of the meal, it must put an exclamation on the menu, giving it its final flourish, completing its last turn to the finish. It is, in the end, part of a whole and ultimately determined by what precedes it. I met with the pastry team on Thursdays, menus for the week in hand. In advance of the meeting I asked them to prepare a list of available ingredients that they were hoping to work with that week. Maybe the first cherries of the summer have ripened, and they want nothing more than to make clafoutis to serve with brandy ice cream. Maybe quince are on their list, but I had my eye on them to use in a duck breast salad. We'd then juggle the days to make the use of the best ingredients in turn.

Let's say it was September, and I had as a starter a tomato salad with mozzarella, black cod with wild fennel oil for a second, and a main of quail, caramelized apples, and an apple vinegar and demi-glace reduction for the sauce. At the pastry meeting, the chefs saw that there were apples in my main so they would not do an apple tart with Calvados ice milk; just as if I've done white shrimp with Meyer lemon salsa for the first course, they would not have a lemon sorbet for dessert. It's really fairly simple on this level: You don't want to repeat key elements; rather, you want to extend the motion and tenor of what has come before.

At Chez Panisse I tasted everything that left the kitchen twice, once from the first service and again for the second seating. I also walked the kitchen throughout the afternoon, observing, commenting, correcting, tasting. Judging when a dish has reached its right point is delicate. As with a painting, doing too much can impart a self-conscious affectation that is as unappealing as the dullness that results from doing too little. Sometimes the flavors of a dish are muddled because they're competing with one another: Some part needs to be omitted for the clarity of the ingredients to come through. At other times a dish is overly simple or just not very interesting; it needs another element of flavor or texture. Maybe it's as simple as a pinch of salt to bring the essential flavors of the dish to the fore, maybe it's a squeeze of lemon or a drop of vinegar to brighten a dish that is too subdued, maybe it's a drizzle of olive oil or butter to round out the feel of the food on the palate and to impart the unctuousness that so many of us crave.

One of the most common mistakes beginners make is settling on a menu in the abstract without thinking about ingredients. Once an item makes it on the menu—say a strawberry tart for dessert

despite the January snows piling up on the windowsill and the sterile Chilean strawberries forlornly waiting in the produce section—nothing changes. Ignoring the realities of the hard, white-cored berries they tote home, they proceed with that tart. It will not be particularly good. Flexibility is essential.

Wherever you are and whatever time of year it is, get in the habit of buying ingredients that are in season and as fresh and local as they can be. As most cooks know by now, choosing strawberries from the next hemisphere that resemble that fruit in name and looks only is not the way to make a memorably delicious tart. A strawberry tart is only true to its kind when served in June, July, or August, using berries that exude their sweet, distinctive fragrance of field and forest with each bite.

If you have to change your menu at the last minute because you can't find the ingredients you need in peak condition, you adapt. The sauce you had planned for the salmon might work with halibut if the salmon for sale that day looks mushy and dull, and if the sauce won't work with halibut, buy the halibut if it's the best thing you see on ice and then dream up—or look up—a sauce to go with it.

Sourcing your ingredients is one of the most crucial parts of cooking—mass-produced fruits, vegetables, meat, and poultry are not grown for flavor. At Chez Panisse I worked with supply lists from more than thirty farmers, cheese makers, fishmongers, ranchers, and foragers. These offerings, faxed or called in each week, included a daily catch of the fish from the Monterey Fish Market, seasonal meats and poultry from Bill Niman Ranch, and, of course, a vast range of fruits, vegetables, and herbs from, among other places, Chino Ranch, Cannard Farm, Star Route, and Full Belly Farms. After many seasons, the rhythm of items that appeared on these lists—down to the week—imprinted itself on my consciousness. Well before this information arrived, I'd sit alone in my study writing that week's menus knowing precisely when the first artichokes would arrive, when the morello cherries were at their peak, and when the cream was at its richest and most flavorful. It was a little uncanny, even to me.

Paying close attention to where your food comes from will put you in tune with when ingredients are at their best. Composing menu upon menu, year after year and coming to instinctively anticipate the arrival of the green garlic, the first asparagus, the ripening of the white peaches, and the running of the wild king salmon wasn't magic—it was the result of practice. Without consciously thinking about it, I intuitively worked these briefly available prizes into the week's menus as they unfolded on the pages before me.

Most people who cook regularly have some sense of seasonal ingredients, and many use that knowledge to guide them when planning a menu. If you're not one of these people, get in the habit of noting the country of origin for everything you buy. Depending on where you live and where you shop, you may be surprised at just how far food travels even when local varieties are available. Why buy an apple flown in from New Zealand in October when local apples are at their peak in all but the coldest climates? Paying attention to the origin of the food you buy naturally extends into considering who produced it. At the restaurant, I was fortunate enough to know with incredible precision where the ingredients I cooked came from. This was in no small part because I maintained personal relationships with the purveyors. Over the years many became friends as I came to know them as well as their spouses and children—even their dogs. As many of our farmers, fishmongers, cheese makers, and foragers moved, died, gave up farming, or simply grew old and retired, I built new relationships, discovering unfamiliar varieties of fruits and vegetables, breeds of meat and poultry. I gained immeasurable knowledge from the hardworking people who cultivated, caught, or gathered the food I cooked. Knowing that the ricotta on the plate that night was made by hand from local sheep's milk produced by a herd freshly put to pasture or that Jim had trapped the Dungeness crab in one of his impossibly rickety cages and that Frank had delivered and nursed the young lamb mattered. It changed not just the way I perceived the flavors of the food, but how I handled it, what I paired it with, and how I presented it. These influences were subtle but real.

On a smaller scale, you can foster relationships like these through farmers' markets, at farm stands, and even through specialty stores that do some of the hard work of careful sourcing for you. I haven't mentioned the loyalty you build by buying from people you know. This loyalty works both ways: They'll sell you the best of what they have because they know you understand and appreciate it, and you can trust the freshness and integrity of everything you buy.

COOKING

Once you've finished shopping and settled on a menu, the rest is relatively uncomplicated. Put together a serious prep list and get to work with your *mise en place*. You know, of course, that this means getting every ingredient you'll need to execute your menu as close to ready as possible: washing lettuce and wrapping it in a damp towel; filleting and boning fish; making stock and other reductions; measuring ingredients and combining what you can; cooking any part of the meal that benefits—or at least doesn't suffer—from being prepared ahead. When I'm in the kitchen doing this work, I'm frequently struck by how fortunate I am to be there, turning a wealth of premium ingredients into a meal.

If I can get the prep work in order, when my guests arrive I can enjoy them rather than finding myself exiled from all the pleasure. Every cook has his or her own talents, skills, and preferences. By experience, you know what does and what doesn't work for you. Be respectful of your limitations, but don't be timid. Pushing yourself to try new techniques and explore flavors is no small part of the pleasure of working with food. When I was a young chef in the seventies, the restaurant asked me to come up with something special for a fundraiser. I decided to make a huge platter of different stuffed birds in aspic—partridge, guinea hen, duck, goose, chicken, quail. It took two days of steady labor to execute this extraordinarily challenging dish, but I couldn't have been more pleased with the results, not just because it was spectacular to look at and eat, but because I learned so much in the process. In sum, don't be afraid to apply the force of your energy and intelligence to your cooking.

If you decide to stretch yourself in a slightly different way—say by preparing a five-course meal for twelve guests for the first time—get some help. I'm never sorry to have someone in the kitchen washing pots and putting the menu in action while I'm settled at the table. All the work of putting together an ambitious meal is well worth it—I have many pleasures in life, but a lively evening with outstanding food and memorable wine ranks high among them.

The Art of the Table

A meal is a sensual experience unlike any other; the smells and tastes, and the look of both food and table all contribute to the pleasure of the evening. Even sound is important—not so much music, but the fine clatter of silver and crystal meeting amidst dinner table conversation. Real elegance never comes across as fussy or self-conscious. Unfortunately, achieving it is anything but effortless.

When it comes to throwing a dinner party, Jean-Pierre and I are a well-oiled dining room-kitchen team. We've thrown a great many dinner parties over the years—professional events, entertaining friends and cozy family gathering. Fron there we instinctively follow the natural sequence of preparation, I would sooner argue with Jean-Pierre over the menu than he would second guess the linens I've chosen or how I plan to seat the tble. I reserve antique linen napkins and tablecloths for parties and formal meals, ironing the beautiful old fabric to a crisp, smooth sheen. Food not only looks better but it tastes better when it's eaten off of a porcelain or glass plate. The same is true of wine—a beautiful, thin crystal glass shaped to optimally release the wine's essence makes an immense difference in how we perceive it. Use your very best linens, glasses, plates, and silver no matter how old or precious they might be. I've learned the hard way that place cards save many awkward moments if there are eight or more people to seat at a table. Seat the table with as much care as you take in setting it—a party is easily made or spoiled by the careless arrangement of your guests. When at home in California, I seat according to the personalities and interests of each individual. The pleasure of the table as a whole is my guide. In France, however, I have rules to follow. There, I seat the female guest of honor on the right side of the man of the house and her husband on the right side of the lady of the house. The French know their position right away by their seat. I play by these rules in France but not in the United States, where marking hierarchy in this way would be entirely lost on my guests.

Careful preparation in the dining room no less than in the kitchen signals your guests to relax, folding them into the comfort of your hospitality from the moment they arrive.

—Denise

Kitchen Essentials

A cook's ideal is to always have the best ingredients on hand. Although I take pleasure in producing my own food for its own sake and for its superior quality, I also grow herbs and vegetables, and make vinegar and regularly stick garlic in the ground so that I have these key ingredients handy when I need them. Keep potted herbs on the windowsill if you don't have a garden or if it's cold outside. Make your own vinegar by stashing a small oak barrel and pouring your leftover wine into it whenever you don't finish a bottle (see page 19 on making vinegar). Harvest and preserve whatever you can from summer to winter. I stick cloves of garlic in the ground year-round in France and California. The stalks that readily sprout provide me with a steady supply of green garlic, which I prefer to the bitter heads that are available at the market in winter. I also grow my own garlic and store it by hanging it in a cool, dry place. If you don't have a garden you can buy fresh garlic at the farmers' market and store it the same way. Beyond herbs and garlic, there are some basic ingredients you want to always have in your pantry. As you'll see, I have strong opinions about salt, herbs, spices, oils, and vinegars because these ingredients make a profound difference to the final quality of even the simplest dish.

Shopping

I doubt anyone who has read this far needs to be reminded of the importance of seeking out the highest quality, freshest ingredients. This truism, virtually the mantra of the food revolution, need not be expanded on here. The following section is simply meant to provide practical clues for putting this principle into practice whether you're making stock or shopping for fresh kidneys.

SALT

I keep three kinds of salt in my kitchen. One is coarse sea salt with grains as large as small hailstones, which I use to season the cooking water for vegetables and to preserve fish, meat, and poultry, including Duck Confit (page 144). When you salt cooking water to blanch vegetables or cook pasta the water should taste like the ocean. When the water is quite salty, vegetables and starches absorb plenty of salt during cooking, eliminating the need to add additional salt either before serving or at the table. When I do add salt to a dish before serving I use unrefined sea salt, or *fleur de sel*. It's slightly gray and tends to stick together as it retains moisture from the air. Normal, superfine table salt is too fine; even when used in moderation, it coats food and dominates flavors. Use it for baking, if at all. Sometimes I use flaky salt to finish, usually Maldon from England. The fine, thin crystals impart a little texture if used sparingly on the right foods.

Chefs have a tendency to oversalt. As soon as you taste the salt in a dish, it's too salty. Salt should bring out the flavor of your ingredients without asserting itself or being noticeable on the palate. It's always better to cook with the proper amount of salt so that it cooks into the food rather than adding salt on top of the finished dish—you're sure to taste it if it's sprinkled on top.

SPICES

When I cook I rely on a small, classic repertoire of spices. I like a little black pepper to give food a finished taste, but I don't want to know it's there unless, of course, I'm making *steak au poivre* or another dish that is meant to be assertively peppery. White pepper has a sharp, slightly bitter taste to my palate, so I don't use it.

My dislike of spicy food was something of a running joke at Chez Panisse. Mark Miller, a talented chef I worked with in the seventies, was the king of spices. He'd make something really wild and offer me a taste just to see me react. Miller believes that spices and chiles add flavor, and I'm sure they do. I guess I'm just not all that interested. What's the point? Good food should be simple and clear. I want to taste the meat, the fish, the vegetables without the distraction of alien flavors. When I eat truffles, I eat them with eggs or plain pasta and butter because I want to focus on the flavor of the truffles. I feel the same way when I have a beautiful chicken or green beans from the garden—I want to taste them, not something I've added to them. An exception to this practice is Monkfish in

Spicy Tomato Sauce (page 57), a dish my mother made, which does have a mildly spicy dimension. For it I rely on my favorite chile pepper, ground piment d'Espelette from the Basque country; its flavor is subtle and goes very nicely with fish. I will add a pinch of cayenne when I make something very rich like hollandaise, but you'd never know it's there.

Other spices you'll find in my basket by the stove are cloves, which I sometimes stick into an onion when I make an old-fashioned stock, and nutmeg, which makes its way into potato dishes, cheese soufflés, and other classic French preparations—again, you'll hardly know it's there but its presence would be missed if you left it out. I keep coriander seeds to add to marinades of fish and poultry and juniper berries for game and choucroute. Saffron is excellent in classic mussel dishes, such as Baked Mussels with Saffron and Cream (page 53). I also add saffron to rice when I make paella or risotto. Fennel seed is mostly for fish stock, although sometimes I add it to my curing salt when I preserve fish. Although they're popular with many cooks, I never use paprika, cinnamon, turmeric, or hot chiles.

VINEGAR

If I am circumspect when it comes to spices, I am expansive with vinegar. When I cook, I keep five vinegars at hand: Champagne vinegar; one good and one excellent balsamic vinegar; an apple cider vinegar; and a red wine vinegar (I like to make my own—see below—it's better than commercial red wine vinegar but serves the same purpose). Often I combine my homemade red wine vinegar, a little port, and a splash of sherry vinegar: the results are complex, with a soft acidity and a note of sweetness that's excellent on most salads.

Making Your Own Vinegar

There really isn't much to making your own vinegar—of course, you could go take a course or a read a whole book on fermentation which is a fascinating subject. Compared to making other fermented foods, vinegar is safe and easy given its high acidity. All you need to begin is a small wooden barrel that will hold about 3 gallons, a bottle of unpasteurized vinegar containing live culture (Bragg's makes a good one) and plenty of leftover wine. (If the wine fails to ferment, you can buy a culture (called a mother) online or in any winemaking supply store.)

Simply pour your leftover red, white, or rosé wine into the barrel along with a cup or two of bottled, cultured vinegar. I use wine we don't finish and wine we don't like, but never wine that's corked or otherwise undrinkable. Continue to add wine to the barrel over time, and after three to four months you will have your own wine vinegar. Once it's established, you can continue to add wine to the barrel, although each time you do, you dilute the acidity. This can be a good thing, giving you mild, fruity vinegar.

Once you've gotten a little practice, start a barrel with white wine only. If you're really good at it (and you drink a lot of champagne), you can start a champagne vinegar as I did thirty years ago at Chez Panisse when I saw so may bottles of champagne returned to the kitchen unfinished. (This is a rare occurrence at our house!)

VERJUS

Verjus is the juice of the unripe grapes culled from the vines in midsummer to improve the quality of the grapes for the final harvest in October. I get mine from Château Bonnet—Denise's family's winery in Bordeaux—where they've made it for decades. In the United States, Navarro and several other producers make it and sell it in specialty stores. Denise's family introduced me to verjus, and I first began using it at Chez Panisse in the eighties. I was a latecomer, particularly for a French chef; in the wine-producing regions of France, it has been a staple for centuries. You'll see evidence of this in old French cookbooks where it's called for in place of vinegar.

I like verjus because it's softer than vinegar with a hint of fruit; its acidity is far less aggressive than that of vinegar but can take its place in most applications. It's a particularly good substitute for vinegar in any sauce for fish, including classic beurre blanc. I use it frequently at Château Bonnet when Denise's father serves very old wine because it doesn't spoil the palate for the subtle nuances of these extraordinary bottles. I highly recommend it when you're cooking a menu you plan to pair with outstanding wine, old or new.

OILS

I use grapeseed oil or sunflower oil for high-heat cooking. I'm not a fan of flavored oils (or vinegars, for that matter), and I actively dislike truffle oil. Excellent olive oil is probably one of the most essential ingredients in any kitchen. I have decent olive oil that I use to cook at low temperatures, such as when I sauté vegetables. This oil is extra-virgin oil, usually from Italy or California. For salads or for drizzling on fish or vegetables before serving, I use a high-quality, relatively unrefined olive oil that's greener and more pungent than the oil I cook with. Plenty of good olive oil is commercially available these days. Look for a date and origin on the bottle as you would when buying wine. I buy the best I can find and press my own from olives growing on Denise's cousins' ranch in Healdsburg. I've planted my own olive trees on our property, but they're too immature to yield much oil.

HERBS

I have a fairly limited repertoire of herbs, but I use them in virtually everything I make. I couldn't cook without fresh thyme, parsley, bay leaf, tarragon, chives, basil, and sage. I could get by without rosemary, although I do use it on occasion. I have no use for cilantro, and I very rarely use marjoram or oregano. Dill I like for a few fish dishes and fennel fronds are subtle and useful in moderation. I'm lucky enough to live in a climate where I can grow virtually any herb year-round.

Storing herbs once they're picked is a challenge. I often keep them in a jar with water like a bouquet; at the restaurant, where we needed great quantities of herbs, I stored them in a tub loosely wrapped in damp towels. The tub was stored in the walk-in or in the coolest spot I could find in the kitchen.

A Note on Bouquet Garni

This is my standard mix of herbs and aromatics that I use for a wide range of recipes—you'll encounter it frequently throughout the book. You'll see that my natural frugality mixed with practical reality leads me to call for what might be considered by many to be the leftover, useless parts of the plant like parsley stems and the green part of leeks. The truth is, these parts contain the flavor but in a less pretty, tougher form. We generally don't eat leek tops, but that's not because they're not flavorful. The same might be said of parsley stems. I call for celery as an optional ingredient because the flavor is so subtle. If you have it, use the tough outer ribs for your bouquet garni and save the tender core for eating. As for the thyme, it's fresh. The bay leaf should be fresh as well, but dried is fine if that's what you have. Make a little bundle of the ingredients with kitchen twine so that you can easily fish them out of the pot before serving.

1 leek, green part only
6 to 8 parsley stems
1 (4-inch) celery rib with leaves (optional)

2 bay leaves
3 sprigs thyme
Garlic and shallots

I like the taste of garlic but I don't use old garlic, which develops a strong, bitter flavor. This is the kind of garlic you will find at the grocery store in winter and even sometimes in summer; often it's grown in China and has been stored for months in gas chambers to keep it from sprouting. Avoid this stuff at all cost. Use garlic when it's in season during the summer and fall. Buy a big bunch at the farmers' market in September or October and hang it in a cool spot. When it's gone, wait until spring when the green garlic arrives. You'll find it sold in single stalks or in bunches; look for a stiff, woody stem with flat, narrow leaves at the top attached to a white, tube-shaped stalk, often with a tinge of purple, at at the base where the immature bulb forms. Green garlic has a subtle flavor and a beautiful, bright color. Finely chop the stems for marinades, pound them into a paste with a mortar and pestle, or lightly sauté them with chicken, eggs, or vegetables.

Shallots are crucial to my cooking, but I don't touch the oversize elephant shallots that have become popular in recent years. Real shallots are the gray shallots or *échalote grise*. They have a fairly thick skin but a subtle taste. They're difficult to find, in part because they're so delicate and difficult to grow. I buy them whenever I see them in France at farmers' markets. I've tried, unsuccessfully so far, to induce farmers I buy from in California to grow them.

FISH, CRUSTACEANS, AND MOLLUSKS

When I call for seafood, I mean fresh. I never buy frozen fish except to use as bait. If frozen is all you can get, cook something else. Fresh fish has firm, moist flesh. If it's whole, it has bright eyes, glistening scales, and feathery gills. It's not easy to find truly fresh fish like this for sale. Sometimes the lighting at the grocery store or fishmonger can trick you into thinking fish looks fresh when it's not. Many fishmongers have ways to conceal the age of a week-old fish. Befriend the person you buy fish from, building mutual trust. You will be rewarded with honest advice about the freshest fish in the case. Some supermarkets sell high-quality fish and shellfish, but most do not. If you must shop at a supermarket, choose your seafood carefully.

When you buy mollusks, tightly closed shells are a must. The origin of shellfish—whether it's oysters, clams, or mussels—is also important because water temperature, salinity, and minerals affect the flavor, size, and texture. We eat a lot of mussels in France during the summer because they're small, plump, and delicious, but I have a hard time finding good mussels in California.

MEAT, GAME, AND POULTRY

More and more in this country, we have access to high-quality beef and poultry. For the beef, try to find grass-fed animals, ideally finished on a little organic grain (this isn't politically correct, but it marbles the meat and mellows the flavors). I've been talking to ranchers for the past twenty years, trying to help them improve their grass-fed meat so it's juicy, fatty, and generally tasty. I think that the answer is to have the animals slaughtered when they are three years old, instead of at the usual eighteen months. In France, the older butchers buy cattle raised exclusively on grass but the

animals aren't slaughtered until they're older which, they claim, produces better meat. I know from experience that their meat is excellent.

Buy poultry that is USDA certified organic or, alternatively, naturally raised on small farms. I often buy birds in the United States and in France that are not certified organic, but I only do this when I know and trust my source. I want a bird that has been fed a varied diet while living a healthy existence with access to the outdoors. I'd also like to be sure the bird has been handled properly before I bring it home.

As for game, I have just four words for you: Go shoot your own!

Americans are not as fond of offal as Europeans seem to be. This is a shame because there's nothing quite like fresh sweetbreads, kidneys, or calves' liver. One taste of these delicacies, fresh and well prepared, and I think you would agree. Pork liver can be tricky to prepare. I have had excellent pork liver dishes in China, but at home I stick to parts from chicken, veal, and lamb.

Stock

Making your own stock is something you may not want to deal with at home, and I don't blame you. Even if you have a good vent over your stove, your whole house is going to fill with the smell of chicken, fish, or beef. The larger the batch, the more pervasive the smell will be. Buying high-quality stocks is becoming more of a viable option, although they can be relatively expensive.

Whenever I roast a chicken at home, I throw the leftover bones in a pot with an onion, a few bay leaves, and a sprig of thyme, and cook it for an hour or so. Denise and I love fish soups and sauces so I make fish stock frequently, using parts from the fish we eat or requesting heads and other discarded bits from the fishmonger.

Cooks are passionate and opinionated when it comes to stock, beginning with how long a stock should cook. My rules are pretty simple: half an hour for fish stock, three hours for poultry stock, and eight hours for beef stock. There are two ways to make stock. The simplest way is to throw chicken or fish carcasses in plenty of cold water with vegetables and herbs and then bring the mixture to a simmer. The more complicated method requires sautéing or roasting the chicken or fish bones, then adding the vegetables and cooking for another ten minutes and only then adding water.

For beef stock, always roast the bones and vegetables in the oven before putting them in the stockpot. Vegetable stock is very useful for many dishes, especially soup or for poaching fish. The process is similar to a chicken or a fish stock, without the proteins. Onions, leeks, carrots, celery, and bouquet garni are the main ingredients, but you certainly can add other ingredients like mushrooms, turnips, or even tomatoes. Coarsely chop the vegetables, cover with cold water, and bring the water to a boil along with a good bit of salt to help the flavors develop. Skim any impurities from the surface, turn the heat down, and simmer for forty-five minutes to an hour. Strain out the solids through a fine-mesh sieve, cool down to room temperature, and refrigerate. Most stocks will last for at least a week refrigerated and for several months in the freezer.

For court bouillon, simply add a splash of white wine or vinegar to your vegetable stock.

CHICKEN STOCK
Bouillon de Poulet

Chicken stock is precious because of its versatility and its potential to improve the depth of flavor in a surprising number of dishes. Use it for a soup, for a reduction to add to a sauce, as a hot bowl of plain bouillon when you're tired or sick, or just keep it in your refrigerator in case inspiration strikes. Chicken stock freezes well. You can portion it however you want—in small containers, in an ice-cube tray, or in plastic bottles. I keep very little food in my freezer other than ice and ice cream, but I do store stock there so that I have it when I need it. —JEAN-PIERRE

Makes 6 cups

2 pounds chicken carcasses or bony parts

8 cups water

1 onion, quartered

2 carrots, peeled and cut in large pieces

1 celery stalk

1 leek, white and light green parts, washed and halved top to bottom (green top reserved for bouquet garni)

Bouquet garni: 1 leek, green part only, 6 to 8 parsley stems, 1 (4-inch) celery stalk, 2 bay leaves, 3 sprigs thyme (see page 21)

Put the chicken parts and the water in a large stockpot or soup pot set over high heat. Bring to a boil, reduce the heat, and skim off any scum that rises to the surface. Add all the vegetables and herbs and simmer over low heat for 2 to 3 hours, skimming periodically. Strain and cool quickly. Refrigerate or freeze in a tightly sealed container.

BEURRE BLANC

Beurre blanc is one of the most versatile of the classic French sauces. Although traditionally made with white wine, you can change the sauce's character by using different kinds of wine. A beurre blanc made with Champagne is a delicate sauce that's excellent on fish while sweet wine gives fullness and body ideal for sole or scallops. Although it contradicts the name—blanc, of course, meaning white in French—you can make the sauce with red wine. I do this when I want a rich sauce for dry aged steak or grilled striped sea bass with young leeks. —JEAN-PIERRE

Makes about ³/₄ cup

2 or 3 medium to small shallots, diced

¹/₂ cup white wine

2 tablespoons white wine vinegar

³/₄ cup (6 ounces) salted butter, cut into small pieces, at room temperature

In a small pot set over medium heat bring the shallots, white wine and vinegar to a boil. Simmer until the liquid is almost reduced. Remove the mixture from the heat and slowly whisk in the pieces of butter one by one, making sure each one completely melts before adding the next. If the mixture gets too cold and the butter is not melting, briefly set the pan over very low heat and continue to add the butter. Once all the butter is incorporated the sauce should be silky, smooth and thick enough to coat the back of a spoon. Taste and adjust the seasoning with a pinch of salt once all of the butter is incorporated. You can either strain the sauce to remove the shallots or leave them for a more rustic sauce.

Sauces

Many home cooks are nervous when it comes to making sauces. I don't blame them—some can be quite difficult even if you've made them many times. Let's be frank: Sauces belong in restaurants for the very good reason that it's almost impossible to get a sufficient quantity of juices from chicken or beef that you roast at home. Compound butters, however, are fairly simple to make. Spread on a hot meat, poultry, or fish, they mix with the cooking juices to give an excellent final result.

Cold sauces such as mayonnaise and salsa verde are far more approachable than cooked sauces. From a basic recipe for a fresh sauce of chopped tomatoes you can go in any number of directions; simply add chopped herbs, black olives, Meyer lemon juice and zest or, best of all, your pan juices.

Hollandaise, béarnaise, or beurre blanc are good additions to fish, meat, or vegetables. They need more technical skill than cold sauces, but are not really difficult to make. Just a little practice and a few failures, and you'll be a pro in no time.

Cooking Methods

Whether you choose to sauté, braise, poach, or grill depends on your goals and equipment. I choose grilling over most any method when I can because I like the flavor as much as I enjoy the simple pleasures of building a fire and watching the elemental process of transforming raw meat, fish, or poultry into a meal. Maybe I feel this way because I spent more than thirty years of my life at Chez Panisse, where grilling was the quintessential cooking method. As much as I like to grill, I couldn't do without sautéing, frying, braising, and poaching. Each method has its advantages. Mastering them all calls for the right equipment and a few simple techniques. Whatever method you choose, don't cook meat or poultry that's still icy from the refrigerator; season it and let it sit out to temper for a half hour or so on the counter before you begin to cook. Seafood is the exception to this rule; it's best left on ice or in the refrigerator until you begin cooking.

SAUTÉING

Many the recipes in this book call for olive oil. It's usually my first choice but certainly not the only one. When I'm in France I often use duck fat; it's what most people in Bordeaux use to cook at home, because they often have it stored away from processing many ducks at once (see page 140). In the south of the country, they use olive oil for almost everything. In Normandy and Brittany, they would think it absurd to use olive oil when, of course, they have ample supplies of rich butter! If you think olive oil is too strong for a dish, use vegetable or grapeseed oil instead. If it's appropriate, use butter or, as I often do, a mix of butter and oil. Butter doesn't burn quite as quickly when mixed with oil but you still have its rich flavor.

I like copper sauté pans lined with stainless steel. Unfortunately, most of the copper pans made today are much lighter than they used to be; not at all like the excellent, heavy cast-iron pans I use in California. One word about nonstick pans: I like them for cooking fish but if you use one be sure it's "green" (ceramic is best) and safe to use.

If you have a decent oven with a relatively even distribution of heat, that's all you need to bake, roast, or braise. I prefer a wood oven but regulating the heat can be complicated. Roasting is a fairly simple process—a piece of seasoned meat, poultry, or a whole fish bakes on its own without much fuss. If you want to roast a garnish or accompaniment alongside, like garlic, onions, or potatoes, add them according to the cooking time of each ingredient: I like whole garlic cloves with chicken and parboiled potatoes with a rib roast. My preference when it comes to roasting pans goes to terra-cotta dishes or Le Creuset pots, but often a regular baking sheet works best. Braising is simply roasting in liquid—often stock or wine. Whether you cover the pot or not depends on your goals: Leave the lid off to reduce the liquid and concentrate the flavors; leave the lid on if you want to keep the meat, fish, or poultry submerged in liquid throughout the cooking process and if you want to prevent browning.

POACHING

Poaching is submerging an ingredient—an egg, a duck leg, a fillet of fish—in liquid and simmering it gently on the stove or in the oven. Duck confit is made by slowly poaching duck legs in simmering fat. Poaching a whole stuffed chicken is an excellent example of the merits of this process. The combination, or I should say the exchange of flavors between the chicken, the stuffing, and the poaching liquid (chicken stock) makes it one of my favorite dishes. The distinction between braising and poaching is so fine that in the end it comes down to pure semantics.

FRYING

Grapeseed, sunflower, and peanut oils are among my favorite frying oils. The temperature of the oil is crucial; check it frequently as you cook by submerging a thermometer in the hot oil. You can fry pretty much anything. My favorites are vegetables dipped in batter, herbs like parsley or sage, and, of course, potatoes. Try frying some very thin slices of unpeeled Jerusalem artichoke to serve as an aperitif with a little fleur de sel. They're better than potato chips!

GRILLING

I kept this technique for the end because it's the ultimate, most natural way to cook. Whether you're working over mesquite charcoal, oak or fruit tree wood, vine cuttings, or fig twigs, the distinctive flavor of the fuel will affect the taste of your food. Seek out the best fuel you can and do not use chemically processed briquettes. Lump charcoal is the best substitute for real wood.

The preparation of good coals before you begin to cook is an essential step for successful grilling. Starting with newspaper and kindling and then adding small pieces of oak or fruit wood, I build a good-size fire, adding larger pieces of wood as the kindling begins to burn. I rarely use a chimney starter, but they work fine if that's what you're used to.

The whole process takes probably almost an hour, but at the end you are sure to have extra coals if needed. Adding fresh wood while you're cooking is never a good idea not just because of the flames but because the sap and other combustibles in the wood can give your food a strong flavor. When you have a thick layer of hot coals, you can push aside the unburned wood (if you have any) and start grilling, but first scrub the grill and give it a gloss of oil if it's not well cured. I try to avoid gas grills, but if that's all you have, heat it up in advance on the highest setting, adjusting the heat lower only if you don't have the space to move your food off to the side. If your wood-fired grill has a lid, you may want to use it to retain heat and infuse your meat with more of the flavor from the smoke but don't get carried away: You should keep your eye on the cooking process, moving the meat or poultry to prevent flare-ups, turning it, and moving it from hot to cooler areas for even cooking. (Fish should not be moved frequently because it's so fragile and prone to sticking.) Your goal is to brown meat and poultry without overcooking it. This is a trickier job when it comes to pork and a relatively simple one if you're cooking a steak. Pork does best when cooked slowly at lower temperatures; depending on the cut, it can dry out quickly over a very hot fire. Like pork, chicken is best cooked over more mellow coals or indirect heat because it requires more time to cook through. A fire that's too hot will burn chicken skin but leave the interior raw. Steaks and whole fish can handle a hotter fire—you want to brown the exterior quickly while preventing the interior from cooking through. (Unless, of course, you like your steak done "well.") Rest pork, chicken, duck, fish, and beef in a warming oven (180°F/80°C) for five to ten minutes before carving or serving. This allows the heat from the exterior to penetrate the meat or fish while allowing the juices—no matter what you're cooking—to coagulate.

Learning to relax into the pleasures of grilling takes time and practice. Every grill is different and every time you grill you'll need to observe the process carefully because a range of variables can alter the results. The temperature of the air outdoors, the depth and heat of the coals, and the beginning temperature of the protein you're grilling are a few of the factors that will determine your cooking time and your ultimate success. Once you've gotten comfortable with the process, there's nothing quite as pleasing as cooking over fire.

recipes

FRENCH FAMILY LIFE
France en Famille

I grew up in the eastern part of France, in the mountainous Jura region, and to this day I love the mountains. As a child, I spent my summer vacations in Normandy, leaving me with an enduring affinity for the ocean. Those years shaped the way I cook today in other ways as well. I absorbed the old, disappearing ways of rustic French farm life in the process of coming to grasp the rhythm of the seasons as the summer months unfolded. My mother, a talented cook no matter what she had to work with, made the summer harvest come to life in her expert preparation of the freshest vegetables, fruit, and dairy.

My parents had lived in Normandy before my father took a job with a large dairy manufacturer, and the family moved to a village near Bayeux. When they moved, they held onto a large house in Montfiquet, and this is where I spent my summers until my twenties. My most vivid memories of childhood come from those months by the sea. These months were pure relaxation and pleasure for everyone in the family—less so for my hard-working father who could only come for a short, two-week vacation.

A local couple in their seventies, formerly servants in a big château in Vaubadon, lived in the house year-round. Their work as caretakers and gardeners for my family was done with the greatest precision. Arriving road-weary and irritable after a two-day car trip spent squabbling with my brothers as we vyed for space in the tiny car, we'd find the house open and thoroughly aired, each room immaculate, beds neatly made with freshly pressed linens, bouquets from the extensive gardens brightening every room, the pantry stocked with food. It was paradise to pile out of the car on arrival, my brothers and I running through the house to see it all again after so many months away, the familiar scent of the sea air evoking the freedom of the beach and the uninterrupted weeks of summer to come.

We ate well throughout those idyllic months, our hunger never so great as it was after long summer days spent tiring ourselves out playing at the beach and in the woods. Our first task on arrival was gathering our special tin milk cans and galloping with them in hand, a clatter of excited voices and banging tin, across the pasture to the woman next door. She filled our containers with fresh milk to bring to our mother back at the house.

This hearty dairywoman's farm and pasture, supporting about a dozen Normandy milk cows as well as healthy rows of apple trees, abutted our property to the south. The rhythm of my day was set by her schedule. I watched and listened to her each morning while it was still cool and each evening after the heat of the day, when she walked onto the pasture, calling to gather her small herd. She milked the big gentle animals right there in the grass where they grazed, sitting on a compact three-legged wooden stool she moved from cow to cow. She worked purposefully and unhurriedly, gathering what she took in a tin bucket, a clean white linen cloth always at hand to wipe the udders. Once a bucket was full she poured the milk into a larger container, which she set beside the road to be picked up by truck and delivered to the *laiterie*, or dairy, for bottling. She kept some of the raw milk back for herself and to sell to her neighbors. I remember best how peacefully she sat in the pasture, the light of the sun angling to begin or end her day as well as mine, her presence there as certain and regular as the days themselves.

It's not easy to find milk so fresh and rich. The milk we bought from her had so much fat that after only one day in the refrigerator (we had an old General Electric model left behind by the U.S. Army, a relic of D-day!), the cream that rose to the top of the jar formed a layer so thick that we could stick our fingers in it and scoop out a big blob—there was nothing quite like it. My brothers and I licked it from our fingers, a forbidden treat we indulged as often as we could get away with. It wasn't that my mother didn't want us to have the cream she used for desserts, piling it on her lovely cakes and on the fresh berries we gathered as they ripened over the course of the summer. It was simply that, quite understandably, she didn't want our grubby fingers in the clean, fresh cream.

Beyond the pasture were woods—mostly wild and ideal for a pack of adventurous boys. Normandy is not the Riviera. It rained more days than not. On those days, we stayed away from the beach, instead spending long afternoons scrounging the forest floor beneath the massive oaks for mushrooms, returning again and again to our special, secret spots, sometimes richly spotted with the soft orange blur of chanterelles, the craggy, almost primitive brown tops of morels, or the almost invisible brown-gray of cèpes pushing up from the leaf mold and decomposing remains of the previous year's acorns. The forest was ours—for hours we'd walk without getting lost, each spot imprinted by memories of years past.

Of course, much of the time we spent in the woods was pure play—whether we were supposed to be mushroom hunting or not. Building forts became a serious endeavor for us over the years. We began with logs, leaves, and sticks as any respectable kids might, only to get carried away building larger, more ambitious structures. By the end of the summer one year we had managed to erect a rather beautiful three-room "house." I'm proud to say it was so large and imposing that a forest ranger, having discovered it while on patrol, demanded we dismantle it, as the land we'd built on was a park.

Our thirst for spending endless hours behaving like savages in the forest—all under the pretext of mushroom hunting—was crowded out at times by other work. My father, ever the scientist, ana-lyzed the purity of the water bubbling up from a natural spring not far from the house. When the water was cer-tified to be as pure as it tasted, we were enlisted to fill and tote large vessels of it to the house for drinking and cooking. As onerous as hauling water was, it wasn't our most hated job—that honor we reserved for the tedium of picking wild blueberries. My mother's tarts were so extraordinary that we protested, but did it anyway. To keep the duty fair, and to prevent us from consuming more than we brought home to her in the kitchen, she set a quota of one cup for each of us. If one of us didn't meet the quota there was no tart that day for the laggard. Tasting my mother's blueberry tart is the only way to appreciate just how harsh this punishment was.

On sunny, warm days we invariably went to the beach. When we were still babies, my mother put us down to nap and when we woke she'd drive us to the beach in the family's banged-up 403 Peugeot. With the addition of stray cousins we often managed to cram as many as nine kids in the car, all of us wearing the anachronistic itchy wool swimsuits that chafed and itched wet or dry. (I think my grandmother may have been responsible for knitting those tortuous woolen suits, which never seemed to dry no matter how strong the sun.)

The beaches around Saint Laurent remain relatively unchanged even today, their extraordinarily fine white sand stretching for miles uninterrupted by beachgoers. At low tide, the water can be as much as half a mile away from the high tide mark, a distance we'd run, gleefully racing to be the first to reach the foaming remains of a receding wave. Normandy at the end of the fifties remained the theater of a large-scale clean-up operation, as the marks of the events beginning June 6, 1944, still scarred the vast sands of Omaha Beach. For a gang of kids, the big holes where the bombs had hit a dozen years earlier were pure magic. Filled with warm, sun-heated seawater, these giant pits served as our private, heated swimming pools on a beach where the ocean temperature kept us out of the waves for all but the briefest icy dips. Parts of various warships rested at the edge of the water, immersed in the sand and covered with barnacles and other sea life. They were irresistible despite their obvious dangers, teeming as they were with sea life. We were real champs at collecting baskets of grass shrimp, which we captured with a big flat net. Lifting up the net to discover our take was the greatest thrill; trapped in its fine weave we discovered all kinds of unexpected treasure—sea shells, minnows, crab, baby eel, shrimp. Most we threw back to the sea, but we kept the shrimp in buckets of sea water. Back home, my mother would put a big pot of salty water on the stove. When it came to a boil she'd throw the live shrimp in the pot for a minute or two before scooping them out, just pink and incredibly tender. We all gathered round to peel the shrimp, which we would eat later as our hors d'oeuvre on buttery, crisp slices of my mother's toasted bread. As many outstanding fresh shrimp as I've been fortunate enough to eat since then, I've never managed to surpass my memory of the sweetness and purity of those shrimp.

When we were older my father bought a Zodiac, a small rubber boat. My older brother Jacques was just of age to get the piloting permit required to take the boat out to sea without an adult. Once we had the boat and our independence from the whims of the adults, we fished often, hauling in all kinds of fish, but mostly bass and mackerel. We even managed to enrage my mother with our enthusiasm and proficiency as fishermen when we arrived one memorable day with almost one hundred fish—all mackerel. We had no freezer, of course, and eating or preserving so many fish before they rotted was impossible. She turned us back to the beach with instructions to sell the fish or give them away—anything but allow all that valuable food to go to waste. Both of my parents had always foraged, hunted, and fished and taught us to do the same. The one unbending rule was never to collect, kill, or fish more than you can use. That day of lucky fishing was a lesson for us all. Excited as we were, my brothers and I had gone a little crazy, pulling in fish after fish without knowing when to stop. We never did that again!

I credit those summer vacations with my love of fish, mushrooming, and projects of all kinds. As anyone who has met me knows, when I'm on our property in Healdsburg or at Peyraut in Bordeaux, it's a rare moment when I stop moving to do nothing—unless I'm sitting down to a meal or going to bed. When I'm outdoors, as I often am, foraging, gardening, or working on some project or another, I'm reminded of the energy and enthusiasm I felt as a boy, the unfolding excitement of summer adventures before me, my every pursuit defined by the vagaries of the weather. Back then my non-stop activity was fueled by my mother's memorable cooking. Cooking is now my job—but one I enjoy.

—*Jean-Pierre*

CASSOULET SOUTHWEST STYLE
Cassoulet du Sud Ouest

My mother was a serious cook. She loved to eat and went to great lengths to prepare innovative meals. Intrepid and ambitious, she worked with modest but high-quality ingredients. Although it was over fifty years ago, she intuitively followed the "local and seasonal" rule that every other chef working today believes to have invented.

When I was growing up with my four brothers and sister, we spent winter vacations skiing in the Pyrenees. We were an avid gang of skiers and reluctant to leave the slopes. The mountain wasn't much developed, with few places to stop for a warm drink, much less for lunch. Instead of packing us a bag lunch, my mother would meet her voracious pack of teenagers at a prearranged hour in the parking lot at the foot of the mountain.

One day I remember best, after a fabulous, cold, sunny morning skiing the fresh powder that had fallen overnight, we arrived at the parking lot exhausted and hungry. My mother was there, as usual, but when she opened the trunk of the car, there was a surprise inside—a steaming pot of fragrant cassoulet! How wonderfully odd it was to smell and taste that rich stew as it emerged from, of all places, the trunk of the car. However incongruous, it was the perfect dish for a cold winter day.

The warmth of the stew was never so welcome as it was that day as we stood spooning it up amid the snowbanks defining the parking lot. The creamy richness of the beans, the smoky, fatty bacon, and the spiced sausage satisfied me in a way nothing else could. Of course my mother had not forgotten a good bottle of red wine. I won't soon forget us all, gathered around the family car, passing the wine and eating our stew—a typical French family sharing the perfect winter picnic. —JEAN-PIERRE

Serves 6 to 8

1/4 cup duck fat or olive oil

8 ounces garlic sausage or Italian sausage

4 confit duck legs (see page 144)

1 clove garlic, peeled

Bean Stew (recipe follows)

Lamb Stew (recipe follows)

2 cups unseasoned coarse bread crumbs, toasted

Chicken stock (see page 24) or duck stock, as needed

CASSOULET

Preheat the oven to 300°F. In a medium sauté pan over medium-high heat, heat half of the duck fat, and when it's hot, add the sausage to the pan and brown on all sides. When the sausage is cool enough to handle, cut it into six pieces. Cut the confit duck legs in half at the joint. Rub the garlic clove over the inside of a large earthenware casserole or two or three smaller casseroles (depending on their size).

Retrieve the pig's foot and pork belly from the bean stew. Pick the meat from the pig's foot and discard the bone. Cut the pork belly into 1/2-inch pieces, combine it with the meat from the foot, and reserve. Cut the pork rind into 1/2-inch pieces and scatter them over the bottom of the casserole. With a slotted spoon, transfer one-third of the beans to the dish. Do the same with half of the pork belly, all of the duck confit, half of the lamb stew, and all of the sausage. Cover the meats

—continued—

with another one-third of the beans and the remaining pork belly and lamb stew; finish with the remaining beans. Combine the bean juices with the lamb sauce left in the pot, taste for seasoning, and pour just enough over the dish to barely cover the beans.

Sprinkle the dish with the bread crumbs and drizzle the remaining duck fat over the bread crumbs. Bake for 2 1/2 hours, then raise the heat to 350°F and bake until the crust is a rich golden brown and the cassoulet is bubbling over the edges, about another 30 minutes. Check the cassoulet during baking: if it's getting too dry, add more stock; if the crust is browning too quickly, cover it with foil. Let the cassoulet rest for at least 30 minutes before serving. Bring the entire casserole to the table, taking care to serve each guest some crust, beans, and pieces of the different meats.

BEAN STEW

1 pound dried white beans, cannellini or great Northern

1 pig's foot (optional)

12 ounces pork belly or pancetta

8 ounces pork rind (uncured skin)

1 carrot, peeled and halved

1/2 large onion, halved

1 tomato, cored and halved

Cloves from 1/2 head garlic, peeled

Bouquet garni: 1 leek, green part only, 6 to 8 parsley stems, 1 (4-inch) celery stalk, 2 bay leaves, 3 sprigs thyme (see page 21)

Salt and black pepper

Soak the beans overnight in enough cold water to cover. The next day, drain, rinse, and pick through for stones or damaged beans. In a large saucepan, cover the pig's foot, pork belly, and pork rind with cold water. Bring to a boil over high heat, reduce the heat, and simmer for 3 minutes, drain, and rinse in cold water. Drain again and reserve.

In a large saucepan, cover the beans with lukewarm water and bring to a boil over high heat. Drain and return to the pan. Cover with boiling water and add the carrot, onion, tomato, garlic, and bouquet garni. Bring to a boil and add the reserved pig's foot, pork belly, and pork rind. Reduce the heat and simmer, covered, for 1 hour, until the beans are tender (don't add any salt yet). Transfer to a large pan to cool, reserving the beans and meats in their cooking liquid; remove and discard the carrot, onion, and bouquet garni. Taste and season with salt and pepper as needed. Reserve the beans until it's time to assemble the cassoulet.

LAMB STEW

1 pound boneless lamb shoulder, neck, or shank meat, cut into 1-inch chunks

Salt and black pepper

$1/4$ cup duck fat or olive oil

1 carrot, peeled and coarsely chopped

1 onion, coarsely chopped

$3/4$ cup dry white wine

2 tomatoes, peeled and seeded

Bouquet garni: 1 leek, green part only, 6 to 8 parsley stems, 1 (4-inch) celery stalk, 2 bay leaves, 3 sprigs thyme (see page 21)

2 cloves garlic, peeled

2 cups chicken stock (see page 24) or duck stock

Season the lamb generously with salt and pepper. In a large, heavy sauté pan over medium-high heat, melt the duck fat and sear the lamb pieces until well browned. Work in batches if needed. Remove the meat with a slotted spoon and reserve. Add the carrot and onion, lower the heat to medium, and cover the pan. Sweat the vegetables until tender but not browned, about 6 minutes. Raise the heat, add the white wine, and boil, scraping up any brown bits with a wooden spoon, until the liquid is reduced by half. Add the reserved lamb and any juices, the tomatoes, bouquet garni, garlic, and stock. Bring to a boil and reduce the heat to simmer, covered, until the lamb is tender, about 1 hour, skimming off the fat and froth as needed. Discard the bouquet garni and reserve the stew until you're ready to assemble the cassoulet.

Note

If you don't have time for this extensive, complete cassoulet, you can omit the lamb stew altogether and simplify the recipe further by buying the duck confit, using bacon in place of the pork rind and belly in the beans. When your beans are cooked, assemble and bake the dish according to the instructions but without the layer of lamb stew.

WILD PHEASANT TERRINE
Galantine de Faisan Façon Mère Moullé

On Sundays during winter hunting season, my father brought home two, three, sometimes even four brace of pheasants, presenting them to my mother to prepare as if they were a colorful gift. As many of the delightful birds as my family could consume in one sitting, bones in piles mounting higher on the table, there were often still pheasants left over that had to be used before they spoiled. My mother did not believe in freezing her food—ever—so she devised this outstanding terrine to put the extra birds to use. Her secret, which gives the dish a particularly rich, gamey flavor, was leaving the gutted but still feathered birds in the refrigerator for nearly a week. I make this terrine when I have fresh game and the time to age it. I've added green pistachios and bright red cranberries to enhance the color, texture, and acidity of the terrine. These ingredients would have been exotic to my mother, but I think she would approve the liberty. Most of the pheasants and other game birds sold in the United States are fully dressed. If frozen, thaw the birds thoroughly in the refrigerator and then allow them to rest for a day; if purchased fresh, rest them for a day or two; birds you shoot yourself should be seasoned for 3 days in the refrigerator. If you can't find pheasant, you can make this terrine with any sort of game including grouse, goose, quail, partridge, woodcock, or even rabbit or venison. You can grind the meat in a food processor if you don't have a meat grinder—just be careful not to overwork it into a paste. It should be relatively coarse. Serve this terrine with a simple, lightly dressed garden salad, a few cornichons, and some toasted bread. —JEAN-PIERRE

Makes about 20 thin slices

2 young pheasants, dressed
    and aged, depending on
    freshness, for 1 to 3 days
    in the refrigerator

1 pound ground pork, or half
    veal and half pork

2 eggs

6 juniper berries, crushed

2 sprigs thyme, minced

1/4 cup Armagnac

1/4 cup sweet white wine or
    Madeira

2 teaspoons dried cranberries,
    soaked in water

1/2 cup shelled pistachios

Salt and black pepper

4 to 5 thin slices pork fatback

2 bay leaves

Preheat the oven to 375°F. Skin and bone the birds if you've shot them yourself; if not, they're likely packaged fully dressed. If not, get your butcher to do it. Reserve half the breast from each bird, grind the remainder of the breast with the leg meat. In a large mixing bowl, combine the ground pheasant, pork, eggs, juniper berries, thyme, 2 tablespoons of the Armagnac, 2 tablespoons of the sweet wine, cranberries, and pistachios; season with salt and pepper. Mix well with a wooden spatula. Cook up a little piece and taste for seasoning, adjusting with salt and pepper as needed. Cut the reserved pheasant breast meat into long strips and place in a shallow dish; add the remaining 2 tablespoons of Armagnac and 2 tablespoons of sweet wine. Season with a pinch of salt and black pepper and marinate for at least 30 minutes and up to 2 hours.

Line the bottom and sides of a 12 by 4-inch pâté mold with three slices of the fatback or as many as you need to cover the bottom of the dish. The slices should overlap slightly. Spoon half of the pheasant mixture into the mold and then place the marinated pheasant breast strips on top. Cover the breast strips with the remaining pheasant mixture. Finish with the remaining slice of fatback on top, and then the bay leaves. Finally, cover the surface with parchment paper and then with aluminum foil before closing with the lid of the terrine.

Place a roasting pan in the oven, fill with about 2 inches of boiling water, place the pâté in this bain-marie, and bake for 1 to 1^1/$_2$ hours. Use a thermometer to test the internal temperature; it is done at 160°F. Alternatively, use a wooden skewer to test the doneness; the juices should run clear.

Lift the mold from the bain-marie, then cover the terrine with a small board that fits inside the mold. Place a pound weight on the top of the board to press the terrine, and set to cool for 1 hour at room temperature. Remove the board and the weight, replace the lid, and wrap the whole mold, including the lid, in plastic wrap and refrigerate for 3 to 4 days or up to a week.

To serve, remove the pâté from the mold. Place the mold in a bath of hot water to loosen the terrine; run a paring knife around the edges to loosen it. Remove and discard the fatback and bay leaves and cut the terrine into slices.

DANDELION SALAD WITH LARDONS AND SOFT-BOILED EGGS
Salade de Pissenlits

In my family, foraging was not simply a way to save money and eat well, it was a passion—even a religion. Each season in the Jura had its bounty. Spring meant collecting wild lettuces and greens, morels, and flowers like daffodils, violets, and lily of the valley. The picking was women's and children's work—my father would have no part of it. More often than not, my brothers and sister and I would go out without my mother. We enjoyed the freedom of having the run of the woods and fields around our farmhouse.

Foraging wasn't all fun. There were rules, and more often than not most of what we eagerly offered did not please my mother. She had high standards—dandelions already bloomed were rejected, as were any dark green, overly mature leaves. As I discovered, the very best dandelion specimens could be found growing out of the piles of dirt left behind by the gophers. The dirt protected the plant, resulting in perfect, naturally blanched leaves. Back home, even if the salad was bitter and not particularly child-friendly, nothing was left in the big bowl at the end of the meal; the combination of creamy eggs, bacon, and vinaigrette was so delicious, we hungrily gobbled it. —JEAN-PIERRE

Serves 4

4 bunches dandelion greens (about 8 ounces), stemmed

8 ounces slab bacon, cut into lardons

4 soft-boiled eggs, cooked for 9 minutes

1 tablespoon red wine vinegar

1 tablespoon Dijon mustard

3 tablespoons olive oil

1/2 cup freshly made croutons (recipes follows)

Salt and black pepper

Put the greens in a large bowl. In a sauté pan set over medium-low heat, cook the lardons until crisp and lightly browned, 10 to 12 minutes. Set aside to drain on a paper towel. Once the eggs are cool, peel them but leave them whole. Make the vinaigrette by whisking together vinegar, mustard, and olive oil in a small bowl. Toss the dressing with the dandelion greens, lardons, and croutons and divide the salad among four plates. Top each with a soft-boiled egg cut into quarters and finish with a pinch of salt and black pepper.

FRESH CROUTONS

I use levain, pain de mie, baguette, whole-grain bread or brioche to make croutons—really whatever I have on hand that's beginning to get a little more stale than I like for the table. Of course, I also make croutons with fresh bread when I need them—it just takes longer to dry the bread. Olive oil is my first choice when I make croutons but I sometimes use butter or duck fat. You can dry croutons in the oven, on the grill, or on the stove in a pan. I won't tell you how long to cook your croutons just as I won't give quantities of either bread or oil here, because the amount you make and the amount of oil you use depends on the bread you have leftover, just as the cooking time depends on the kind of bread you use and how stale—or not—it is. One more thing I'll leave up to you is the size of the croutons—I like tiny, perfectly square croutons to garnish refined soups or delicate salads and larger, rough-cut or torn croutons for most other purposes. If you plan to grill your croutons, slice the bread but don't cube it until after the bread is cooked. —JEAN-PIERRE

Levain bread, baguette, pain de mie, or brioche, sliced and cubed

Olive oil or melted butter (you could also use duck fat, chicken fat, or pork fat)

Salt

Preheat the oven at 375°F. Toss the bread cubes in a large bowl with a splash of olive oil and a pinch of salt. The cubes should not be fully saturated with oil but they should each have a little gloss of oil. Spread the bread cubes on a baking sheet in a single layer and bake until they are fully dried out and crisp all the way to the center and have turned a toasty, light brown on the outside. (If you've use butter they'll get more color.) Cool right on the baking sheet and tightly seal to store any leftover croutons. They last about a week—not much more.

CREAM OF CHESTNUT SOUP
Velouté de Châtaignes

When I was a boy growing up in the Jura, my walk home from school brought me past a chestnut vendor. In winter, he stood there alone on the street next to his cart, the frigid wind dispersing the inky smoke billowing from his fire. When I had a few francs in my pocket, I bought the roasted chestnuts he sold cupped in a *L'Est Republicain* newspaper cone, greedily peeling away the steaming shells with my winter gloves on. It was a wonderful sensation to hold the hot chestnuts as their heat penetrated my thick wool gloves andtheir rich, lightly sweet flesh was delicious. At home, for special dinners, my mother often served a simple but memorable chestnut puree with a rack of roasted venison, rabbit, or other game. I kept this tradition after I married Denise and we moved to Bordeaux, collecting quantities of the nuts from the massive trees that grow on the Lurton family property. We pile them into a battered perforated sauté pan we found in an old shed on the property and roast them in our massive fireplace. We then eat them out of hand, just as I did as a boy. They are improved with a glass of *vin nouveau* out of the great vat in the cellar beneath Denise's family winery. Today, thanks to my thick chef's calluses, I no longer need to wear winter gloves for the job, but chestnuts should be peeled hot, as the skins toughen and stick once cool. —JEAN-PIERRE

Serves 4 to 6

1¼ pounds whole chestnuts in the shell

½ cup whole milk

1 tablespoon butter

3 shallots, diced

3 cups chicken stock (see page 24)

Salt

2 tablespoons crème fraîche

Bring a pot of water to a boil over high heat. Score the chestnuts top to bottom using a very sharp knife; blanch them in the boiling water for 6 to 8 minutes. Remove the pot from the heat but keep the chestnuts in the water. Pour the milk into a mixing bowl and peel away the outer shells and inner skins of the chestnuts, putting the peeled chestnuts in the milk as you work.

Heat the butter in a large saucepan over medium heat, add the shallots and chestnuts (reserve the milk), and cook for 2 to 3 minutes. Add the chicken stock, bring to a boil, and simmer for 25 to 30 minutes, until the chestnuts are tender. Working in batches, puree the chestnuts along with their cooking liquid in a food processor or blender. Strain the mixture through a fine-mesh sieve into a saucepan. Add some of the milk the chestnuts soaked in to thin the chestnut mixture and season with a pinch of salt. The soup should be thin enough to pour but rich and flavorful. In a small pan set over medium-low heat, dry-roast the remaining chestnuts until lightly browned and toasted, 5 to 6 minutes. Ladle the soup into warm bowls or soup plates. Garnish with the roasted chestnuts and a dollop of crème fraîche.

STEAK TARTARE

However it began, making and eating steak tartare became a familiar spring ritual at our house on Sundays. I remember it as a group process we all enjoyed together. Even my father helped, cutting the meat into a fine mince—a most unusual occurrence, as he rarely set foot in the kitchen. With four teenage boys to feed, my mother must have known how the carnality of eating raw, highly seasoned meat sated our monster appetites. Steak tartare disappeared from my life when I left home, not to reappear until much later—and then, good as it was, it was not the same tartare I remembered from those years. This recipe comes as close to the original as I 've ever gotten in the absence of my mother—you'll capture the real spirit of the meal if you pull everyone into the kitchen to involve them in chopping the meat and herbs, mixing in condiments, and toasting plenty of good bread. —JEAN-PIERRE

Serves 4

1 pound beef tenderloin, well chilled

3 anchovy fillets, chopped

1 clove garlic, pounded (optional)

1 tablespoon small capers

1 tablespoon chopped cornichons

1 egg yolk

1 tablespoon olive oil

2 shallots, diced

1 tablespoon Dijon mustard

Salt and black pepper

1 tablespoon chopped parsley

1 tablespoon chopped chives

3 drops of Tabasco sauce

4 dashes of Worcestershire sauce

Toasted levain bread, for serving

Watercress, parsley, or arugula for serving

Cut the beef tenderloin into thin slices, then into strips, and finally into very small cubes. Chop the whole pile of meat for 1 minute to give it a consistent texture. Cover and place the meat in the refrigerator.

In a small bowl, combine the anchovies, garlic, capers, and cornichons. In another small bowl, whisk together the egg yolk, olive oil, shallots, and mustard. Stir well and season with salt and pepper.

When you're ready to serve (not ahead of time), remove the meat from the refrigerator and combine it with the anchovy mixture, egg mixture, parsley, chives, Tabasco, and Worcestershire. Do not overmix. Serve with the toasted bread and watercress.

BAKED BELGIAN ENDIVES WITH HAM
Endives au Jambon

When I was growing up among the Bordeaux vineyards in the 1950s, money was scarce. In those difficult postwar years, the fields and vineyards were in disarray—the men who worked the land had been away at war for years. The women left behind on the property had tended the land and kept up the vines as best they could, but the grapes suffered and our wines were not selling. In those sad, lean years, few had the money for the luxury of a good bottle of wine.

We lived simply in the grand but by then shabby Château Bonnet. We ate what we grew. In winter, eating what we had on hand meant hearty, cold-loving endives two or three times a week during the winter months. Our endives grew in the shade under the overhanging eaves of two low sheds that stood next to our poultry yard. The tender, white bulbs grew completely buried in the sand; when the heads popped through to the surface, we knew the bulbs were ready to pick. My mother, ever resourceful, had many ways to cook endives, keeping us quite happy, however much we might have dreamed of bright green sweet peas or the snap of a midsummer green bean. I still love endives and often prepare them the way my mother did, in a simple gratin. —DENISE

Serves 4

4 Belgian endives

Salt and black pepper

4 thin slices boiled ham or
    pancetta

2 tablespoons butter

1/2 cup chicken stock (see
    page 24), water, or cream

1/4 cup grated Gruyère

Trim off the stem ends of the endives and remove any tough outer leaves. Boil the whole endives in lightly salted water for 15 minutes, or until tender. Drain and squeeze in a dry towel to remove most of the water. Season each endive with salt and pepper and wrap in a slice of ham. Use the butter to generously butter a 10 by 6-inch baking dish. Place the endives in the dish and pour in the stock; sprinkle with grated cheese, cover tightly with foil, and bake for 15 to 20 minutes, until the cheese is melted. Uncover and bake for another 10 to 12 minutes, until the cheese is golden brown. Serve one endive per person, with the juices spooned on top.

STEW WITH MARROWBONES
Pot au Feu Os à Moelle

Mondays were, without fail, laundry day. Every week of the year, in the heat of summer and the cold of winter, my mother reserved the day to wash all the soiled table linen, kitchen towels, bedding, and family clothing. This was an all-day job, as washers were primitive machines back then and dryers nonexistent—at least at our house. As a result, Mondays were for simple meals my mother could put together with little effort. Beef stew made frequent appearances on our Monday supper table for this reason—she simply combined big pieces of meat, bones, and vegetables in a cauldron, covered it with water, and set it to gently simmer for hours on our lovely, hardworking La Cornue gas range while she busied herself scrubbing, rinsing, wringing, and hanging her wash on the clothesline. (That two-oven, four-burner unit is still hard at work at our family house in Normandy, where my sister uses it every day.)

The Monday stew was different every time, depending on the season and the vegetables and herbs she had on hand, but no matter what the time of year, the stew invariably contained marrowbone, which my brothers and I fought each other to fish out of the stew (with five of us there were never enough to go around). Anyone who managed to capture a bone got the unsurpassed treat of warm, slow-cooked marrow smeared on my mother's excellent toasted bread, finished with just a hint of crunchy salt on top. This is my version of my mother's washday stew, complete with enough marrowbones for everyone at the table. Be sure to have some good bread on hand for toast. This dish is usually served with mustard and cornichons, but I also enjoy it with horseradish cream or salsa verde. —JEAN-PIERRE

2 pounds beef shanks, preferably grass fed

Salt and black pepper

1 pound marrowbones (see Note)

2 pounds short ribs or beef shoulder, preferably grass fed

Water

Bouquet garni: 1 leek, green part only, 6 to 8 parsley stems, 1 (4-inch) celery stalk, 2 bay leaves, 3 sprigs thyme (see page 21)

3 onions, quartered

4 leeks, trimmed and washed, green tops and white bases separated

1 stalk celery, cut into 2-inch lengths

6 to 8 carrots, peeled and cut into 2-inch lengths

1 small savoy cabbage, sliced (optional)

Dijon mustard, for serving

Cornichons, for serving

Crusty bread, for serving

If possible, season the beef shanks with salt and pepper 1 day in advance. Place the marrowbones, beef shanks, and short ribs in a large pot, cover with cold water, and bring to a boil over high heat. Reduce the heat to bring the liquid to a low simmer and skim all impurities from the surface. Lightly season with salt and cook for 35 to 40 minutes before adding the bouquet garni, onions, leek tops, and celery. Cook at a low simmer for another 1 1/2 hours, frequently skimming the surface. Discard the onions, leek tops, celery, and bouquet garni. Add the carrots and the tender parts of the leeks to the pot and simmer gently for another 1 1/2 hours, covered. The meat should be tender and moist, and the vegetables cooked through.

Meanwhile, cook the cabbage separately in a pot of boiling salted water for 15 minutes; drain. Line 6 to 8 shallow serving bowls with pieces of cabbage. Distribute the meat, a marrowbone or two, and the vegetables among the plates on top of the cabbage and ladle the hot broth over the top to finish. Serve with mustard, cornichons, and crusty bread.

Note

To protect the marrow and prevent it from falling out into the stew over the long cooking time, I like to wrap the marrowbones, covering each end with a carrot slice or a piece of leek tied in place with cooking twine. Sometimes I simply wrap the marrowbones in cheesecloth. You can choose your method or skip this step altogether.

VEAL RAGOÛT IN A CREAMY SAUCE
Blanquette de Veau

Today, I keep three grades of olive oil in my kitchen and use them all the time when I cook, but as a boy I never saw a bottle of olive oil in the house. Butter reigned supreme. My father was an agronomist who specialized in the milk industry. Cream, butter, milk, and cheese were the family business, and we were loyal to that heritage at table. In Normandy, where I was born and where we spent summers, I vividly remember the raw milk from our neighbor's cows. Once it settled, the cream rose to the tops of the jars where it stood out in a thick, silky layer. My father's work brought us to the Jura, most famous for Comté cheese, which we ate and cooked with at every stage of its development from soft, fresh, and mild to the much sharper, well-aged cheeses that are so difficult to find in this country. Finally, we followed his work to the Charentes Maritimes, where we indulged in the region's famously rich, flavorful butters. You might suspect, given the family's dairy-rich diet and our general preoccupation with all good things to eat, that we might all have been quite fat, but to this day we are all fit, slim, and healthy.

This recipe was one that the whole family looked forward to. The rich, creamy sauce with the tender, mild meat, soft pearl onions, and sautéed mushrooms is simple to make and ideal after a day spent outdoors skiing, hunting, or putting the garden to bed after the first frost. Note that the veal, mushrooms, onions, and sauce are combined at the last minute, just heated through, and served, which allows each of the ingredients to assert its own flavor while contributing to the rich pleasures of the dish. We would drink a young Burgundy wine with this, or a Beaujolais like Moulin-à-Vent. Serve this ragoût with plain steamed rice or steamed potatoes. —JEAN-PIERRE

Serves 4 to 6

2¹/₂ pounds veal shanks and shoulder

Water

2 onions

2 carrots

1 leek, white and light green part

Bouquet garni: 1 leek, green part only, 6 to 8 parsley stems, 1 (4-inch) celery stalk, 2 bay leaves, 3 sprigs thyme (see page 21)

Salt and black pepper

¹/₂ cup crème fraîche or heavy cream

2 egg yolks

1 teaspoon cayenne pepper

1 pound white mushrooms, quartered

1 tablespoon butter

1 cup pearl onions, blanched, drained, and peeled

2 tablespoons chopped parsley

Cut the veal into large pieces and place it in a large pot; cover with cold water and bring to a boil over high heat. Reduce the heat to low and skim the impurities from the surface. Add the onions, carrots, leek, and bouquet garni. Season with a pinch or two of salt and simmer for 50 to 55 minutes, until the meat is tender.

Remove the meat and vegetables from the pot and drain well, reserving the cooking liquid. Discard the leek, onions, and bouquet garni. Cover the meat and vegetables and keep them warm in a very low oven. Strain the cooking liquid into a saucepan and reduce by half.

In a medium bowl, beat together the crème fraîche, egg yolks, and cayenne pepper and whisk into the reduced veal juice. Simmer over low heat, stirring with a wooden spoon, until it thickens enough to coat the back of the spoon.

In a sauté pan set over high heat, cook the mushrooms in the butter for 10 to 12 minutes, until their liquid has released and evaporated. Season with salt and pepper and set aside.

Combine the creamy sauce, mushrooms, pearl onions, veal, and vegetables in a pot and set over medium heat. Bring barely to a simmer, stirring, and heat just until the ingredients are warmed through. Do not boil. Check the seasoning and serve in large bowls garnished with chopped parsley.

DUCK CONFIT WITH FRIED POTATOES
Confit de Canard aux Pommes de Terre

This dish is typical of southwestern French cuisine. When I make duck confit, I cook a large batch at once (twelve legs). They keep for over a month in the refrigerator, and they're useful in salads or rillettes (see page 145) or for a quick meal on their own. Denise and I regularly use our stash of confit legs as an emergency resource when unannounced guests show up—which they frequently do, whether we're in Bordeaux or Sonoma. It takes no time to turn the duck legs into a meal with a simple sauté and a simply dressed green salad on the side. —JEAN-PIERRE

Serves 6

Salt

2 bay leaves, crushed

1 tablespoon dried thyme

6 duck legs, skin intact and with excess fat trimmed away

4 quarts plus 1/2 cup rendered duck fat

1 1/2 pounds Yellow Finn potatoes, peeled and cut into 1/4-inch cubes

2 tablespoons minced garlic

Combine 6 tablespoons of salt with the bay leaves and thyme in a bowl. Season the legs heavily with the mix, using it all. Place the legs on a plate, cover, and refrigerate overnight.

The following day, melt the 4 quarts of duck fat in a large saucepan over low heat. Remove any excess salt from the duck and pat the legs dry. When the fat starts to simmer, gently add the legs and cook uncovered over very low heat for 2 hours. The legs should be submerged the whole time and the fat should never boil. Test for doneness with a skewer; it should slide through the meat easily. Gently remove the duck legs and place them in a glass or ceramic casserole dish. Allow the fat to cool a little before pouring it through a fine sieve over the legs, taking care not to add the juices that will have settled at the bottom of the pan. Cover and refrigerate. The legs will keep for a month or even longer so long as they remain cool and encased in the fat. Before reheating, be sure to bring them to room temperature.

To make the potatoes, bring a pot of salted water and potatoes to a boil over high heat and cook until they are tender but not falling apart, 10 to 15 minutes. Drain and allow them to sit briefly to dry and cool. Put the remaining 1/2 cup of duck fat in a large cast-iron pan set over medium heat. When the fat is hot, add the potatoes and cook, stirring and tossing regularly, until golden brown, about 20 minutes. Season with salt and the minced garlic.

Set a steamer basket over a pot of boiling water, set the duck legs in the basket, cover, and steam for 6 to 8 minutes, until heated through. Heat a sauté pan over medium heat with 1 tablespoon of duck fat and add the steamed duck legs, skin side down, and cook over medium heat until the skin is very crisp and brown, 8 to 10 minutes. Turn the heat off, flip the legs over and let them sit for 2 minutes in the hot fat.

BAKED MUSSELS WITH SAFFRON AND CREAM

Mouclade Charentaise

The flavors in this recipe were entirely novel to me and to my innocent palate when my family moved from the Jura to Charentes on the Atlantic Ocean in 1961. That was the year I was introduced not just to the exotic pleasures of saffron but to the other foreign-grown spices that had been brought to the region via the thriving Atlantic spice trade since the twelfth century. La Rochelle, not far from our home, was a crucial port of exchange from the New World to the old, as well as to India and China. Although I never grew to love heavily spiced foods, I can't deny the appeal of saffron, mussels, and cream. Mussels are at their plump, sweet best in the summer months. Scrub them carefully under cool water, discarding any that aren't tightly closed. Use the highest quality, freshest saffron you can find. It loses potency as it ages. —JEAN-PIERRE

Serves 4

2 pounds mussels (bouchot, if you can find them)

1 tablespoon olive oil

1 onion, finely diced

1 bay leaf

1 sprig thyme

1 cup dry white wine, plus more if needed

1/2 cup heavy cream

1 egg yolk

Pinch of cayenne pepper (enough to cover the tip of a paring knife)

Pinch of saffron threads or Madras curry powder

1/2 lemon

1 tablespoon chopped parsley

Scrub the mussels and pull the beards out. Rinse them in cold water and reserve in the refrigerator in a bowl covered with a damp towel. Once the mussels are bearded, they should be used right away.

Set a large skillet over medium heat. Add the olive oil and then the onion, bay leaf, and thyme. Cook for 4 to 5 minutes, until the onion is soft. Turn the heat to high, add the mussels and the wine, cover, and cook for 3 to 4 minutes, until the mussels begin to open. Remove the pan from the heat and transfer the mussels to a bowl to cool. While the mussels cool, strain the cooking juices, discarding the solids. Transfer the strained liquid to a sauté pan set over medium heat and reduce by half, tasting it frequently so it does not get too salty. Add an additional splash of wine or water to dilute the salt, if needed.

When the mussels have cooled enough to handle, remove the top shells and layer them flat in a gratin dish with the mussel facing up; make a couple of layers if needed. Keep them warm by placing them on top of the stove or in another warm spot while you make the sauce. In a saucepan, mix the cream, egg yolk, cayenne, and saffron. Whisk in the reduced mussel juices and place the pan over low heat, whisking all the while, until the sauce thickens enough to coat a spoon. Add a squeeze of lemon and then taste the sauce for seasoning. Remove from the heat, strain over the mussels, and finish with a sprinkle of parsley.

POACHED HALIBUT WITH
HOLLANDAISE SAUCE
Flétan Poché Sauce Hollandaise

This recipe—made with turbot not halibut, as here—was part of my mother's repertoire for friends and special guests. She always poached the whole fish in her *turbotière*, a special vessel shaped like the fish, beautiful, huge, and made of copper, with a special rack at the bottom to lift the fish when cooked. Today, that copper pot stands on a table in our living room. It's no longer used to poach fish for the good reason that today it's almost impossible to find a turbot or any flat fish that size. I put my sunglasses, wallet, and keys in it, and I hope my mother will forgive me this sacrilege! —JEAN-PIERRE

Serves 6 to 8

3 pounds halibut fillet, cut
    into 12 (4-ounce) pieces

Salt

6 cups water

1 carrot, peeled and sliced

1 onion, sliced

1 shallot, sliced

2 bay leaves

3 sprigs thyme

5 parsley stems

8 black peppercorns

1 cup dry white wine

2 tablespoons white wine
    vinegar

Hollandaise sauce (recipe
    follows)

Season the fish with salt and set aside.

In a large, heavy pot, make a court bouillon: Combine the water, carrot, onion, shallot, bay leaves, thyme, parsley, and peppercorns and bring to a boil over high heat. Reduce the heat and simmer for 15 minutes, then add the wine, a pinch of salt, and vinegar (the vegetables will not cook properly if you add the wine right away). Simmer over medium-low heat for 30 minutes more.

Turn the heat to low and slide the halibut into the hot court bouillon. Poach the fish gently for 20 to 25 minutes, until a paring knife inserted into the thickest piece meets little resistance. Use a slotted spoon to transfer the fish to a warm dish, pour the hollandaise sauce over the top, and serve.

HOLLANDAISE SAUCE

Hollandaise is a classic French sauce that has been revised and used in America for the famous eggs Benedict. It has been excluded from a lot of menus (for diet or health reasons, I presume), and this is too bad—it goes so well with fish, and also with asparagus and eggs, of course. It can be intimidating to make, but is in fact as easy as a mayonnaise. —JEAN-PIERRE

Makes 1/2 cup

4 tablespoons white wine vinegar

2 egg yolks

8 tablespoons butter, melted

Salt

Cayenne pepper

In a small pot set over medium heat, reduce the vinegar to 1 tablespoon. Transfer it to a bowl set over (not touching) a pot of barely simmering water. As you work, you'll want to keep the temperature of the bowl and its contents constant; the bowl should be warm, but not hot. You may want to turn the heat under the pot off entirely and work over water that is extremely hot but not boiling. Once you've adjusted the heat, add the egg yolks and whisk for 2 minutes, or until the yolks thicken. With a small ladle, start adding the melted butter slowly, whisking constantly, leaving behind the white liquid, or whey, at the bottom. If the bowl cools too much and the sauce is not thickening, bring the water back to a simmer. If, on the other hand, the sauce gets too thick, add some whey to thin it out. Taste the sauce and season with salt and a pinch of cayenne pepper.

MONKFISH IN SPICY TOMATO SAUCE
Lotte à l'Américaine

I never understood why my mother called this dish "à l'Américaine." Perhaps it was because she used whiskey instead of Cognac? She often made lobster and langoustines the same way, never varying the name. When I was a boy, this dish was a treat because it fell outside of her usual, fairly traditional, range. Here you'll find I've changed the ingredients to reflect my adult tastes, replacing the whiskey with white wine and lightening the dish as a whole by simply baking the fish. (My mother used to sauté the fish and then flambé the pan with whiskey before baking the fish in the spicy tomato sauce.) I suppose it's now more Provençal than American—if it ever was American to begin with. I've stuck with the name in her honor all the same. I like this dish best with warm toast and aioli or with a few boiled potatoes. —JEAN-PIERRE

Serves 4 to 6

2 pounds monkfish or Atlantic cod fillet

Salt

Cayenne pepper

1 pound tomatoes

Olive oil

2 onions, sliced

1 fennel bulb, sliced

4 cloves garlic, sliced

2 bay leaves

3 sprigs thyme

1/2 cup dry white wine

1 tablespoon chopped parsley

1 tablespoon chopped tarragon

Preheat the oven to 400°F. Cut the fish into four or six portions and season with salt and cayenne pepper; set aside.

Peel and seed the tomatoes: Plunge them into boiling water for 10 seconds, then cool them in ice water. Remove the skins and cut the tomatoes in half horizontally, squeeze the seeds out, and then coarsely dice the flesh; set aside.

Pour 2 tablespoons of olive oil into a sauté pan over medium heat and cook the onions and fennel until soft but not colored, 5 to 8 minutes. Add the garlic, diced tomatoes, bay leaves, and thyme and cook for another 5 to 7 minutes before transferring the mixture to a 10 by 12-inch baking dish. Place the portions of fish atop the tomato mixture, pour the white wine over the fish, drizzle on some olive oil, and bake, uncovered, for 25 to 30 minutes. When it's done, the fish should be just firm and flake apart at the thickest point. Sprinkle with the parsley and tarragon and serve in the same dish.

MEUNIÈRE-STYLE TROUT WITH BROWN BUTTER
Truite Meunière

I'll always have an image of my mother in shorts (!) cooking a huge trout by the side of the river on a beautiful spring day in the Jura. With only a camping stove, a rusty cast-iron pan, a spatula, and a lot of butter, she prepared lunch for the whole family. I also remember my father (who caught the trout) complaining that the fish was too tough because it was *too fresh*. The fish did curl up tight in the pan, making it impossible for my mother to properly brown both sides. During that time of year, the hills were full of flowers and morels. While exploring and gathering morels, my brothers and I would pick bunches of wild daffodils, narcissus, and lily of the valley for my mother. The morels we ate for dinner alongside other fish, these cooked with a little garlic and a great deal of cream; the flowers were affectionately admired. —JEAN-PIERRE

Serves 4

4 small trout, about
    6 ounces each

Salt and black pepper

2 tablespoons flour

1/2 cup butter

Juice of 1/2 lemon

1 tablespoon chopped parsley

2 tablespoons sliced almonds,
    toasted (optional)

1/2 lemon, cut into wedges,
    for garnish

Season the inside and outside of the trout with salt and pepper. Mix a little salt and pepper into the flour in a flat bowl or large plate and roll the trout in the flour mixture.

In a sauté pan or cast-iron skillet over medium heat, melt 1/4 cup of the butter until hot and bubbling. Lay the trout in the pan and sauté for 6 to 8 minutes on each side. Transfer the fish from the pan to a hot platter and discard the burnt butter. Melt the remaining 1/4 cup of butter in the same pan until golden brown. Add the lemon juice, parsley, and almonds to the butter and pour it over the fish. Serve hot with lemon wedges.

ASPARAGUS WITH SALSA VERDE

Asperges en Sauce Verte

My mother often served asparagus, either warm with hollandaise sauce or cold with mayonnaise. What I like about this dish is that it's easily either an elegant first course for a formal dinner or a refreshing side dish, ideal for a picnic or a casual lunch. We grow asparagus in our gardens in Bordeaux and Sonoma and cook them minutes after they are picked. They're so fresh they take no time to cook. Keep in mind that white asparagus must be peeled; the thin skin on delicate green asparagus can be left alone. In France during the spring months, you mostly find fat, white asparagus, which are much more popular there than they are in the United States. The best white asparagus are tender even though they are quite large—you can tell that they're fresh if they snap easily without bending when you "snap" them to remove the rough bottom. —DENISE

Serves 2 to 4

Salt

1 pound asparagus, peeled with bottom ends snapped off

2 shallots, diced

1 tablespoon chopped capers

2 tablespoons chopped green onions, white and light green parts only

2 tablespoons chopped parsley

2 tablespoons chopped chives

1 tablespoon chopped tarragon

2 soft-boiled eggs, coarsely chopped

1/2 cup olive oil

Salt and black pepper

1 tablespoon Dijon mustard

1 tablespoon red wine vinegar

Bring a large pot of salted water to a boil over high heat. Add the asparagus and cook until just tender, 4 to 5 minutes for medium spears, 2 to 3 minutes for very fresh, thin spears. Lift the asparagus out of the boiling water with tongs and cool on a clean kitchen towel.

To make the salse verde, in a small bowl, combine the shallots, capers, green onions, parsley, chives, tarragon, eggs, and olive oil and then season with salt and pepper. Let the mixture sit for at least 15 minutes, whisking in the mustard and red wine vinegar just before serving. Taste the sauce for seasoning.

Serve the asparagus on a platter at room temperature with a spoonful or two of the salsa verde drizzled over the top. Store the remaining sauce in the refrigerator for another use. It's excellent on chicken and steak.

STUFFED SAVOY CABBAGE WITH CHESTNUTS AND PORK SAUSAGE

Chou Farçi avec Châtaignes

This classic winter combination of sausage, chestnuts, and cabbage would have been deeply familiar to my grandfather. Not surprisingly, the first time I had this dish, it was cooked in a cauldron over the heat in the fireplace precisely as it would have been cooked one hundred years ago. During December or January, try adding black truffles to the stuffing, and perhaps even small pieces of fresh foie gras. The incredible combination of flavors are retained within the cabbage and yet the broth cannot but take on the potent aroma of the truffles. —JEAN-PIERRE

Serves 6 to 8

1 savoy cabbage

1/2 cup milk

12 chestnuts, peeled (see page 38)

2 tablespoons olive oil

1 small onion, diced

2 shallots, diced

3 cloves garlic, chopped

2 sprigs thyme

8 ounces wild mushrooms, sliced

Salt and black pepper

1 pound ground pork or 4 Italian sausages

1 tablespoon chopped parsley

4 cups chicken stock (see page 24) or water

Remove any discolored or rough outer leaves from the cabbage. Cut out the core of the cabbage and remove the leaves, one by one. If the center leaves are too hard to peel, throw the head of cabbage in boiling water for 2 or 3 minutes to soften it, then separate the leaves when they're cool enough to handle. Blanch the uncooked leaves in plenty of salted boiling water; drain and lay flat on a towel-lined tray, and reserve.

In a medium saucepan over low heat, warm the milk and cook the peeled chestnuts until they are soft enough to break into chunks, 6 to 8 minutes. They should be soft but not mushy. Once they're cooked break them into small pieces, none larger than a marble, and set aside.

In a sauté pan over low heat, heat 1 tablespoon of the olive oil and cook the onion, shallots, garlic, and thyme until soft but not colored. Transfer to a bowl and set aside to cool. Add the remaining 1 tablespoon of oil to the same pan (no need to wash it), turn the heat to high, and sauté the wild mushrooms until they render most of their liquid. When the pan begins to go dry, season them with salt and black pepper and set aside to cool. When the mushrooms are cool enough to handle, chop coarsely and set aside.

In a large bowl, mix together the pork, onion mixture, parsley, mushrooms, and chestnuts. Make a bite-size patty and fry it in a small skillet; taste and correct the mixture's seasoning with salt and pepper, if needed.

Place the largest cooked cabbage leaf on a sheet of cheesecloth. The cheesecloth should extend at least 2 inches beyond the cabbage leaf on all sides; if your cabbage leaves are very large you may overlap the cheesecloth if needed by laying another sheet across the first in the opposite direction to form a sort of cross. Spoon out a 1/2-inch thick layer of stuffing over the leaf, covering it but leaving a 1/2-inch margin around the edge. Place another layer of cabbage leaves on top of the sausage, then add another layer of meat and so on until you run out of stuffing.

Grab the four corners of the cheesecloth and form the assemblage into a large ball, squeezing it together as tightly as you can. Tie two opposite ends of the cheesecloth corners together, then the remaining two. Refrigerate for 1 hour or until you are ready to poach the cabbage.

To cook, bring the chicken stock to a simmer in a large pot over medium heat. Place the cabbage in the hot liquid and simmer gently for 30 to 35 minutes. With a large slotted spoon, remove the cabbage ball, allowing the liquid to drain away. Place on a platter and and remove the cheesecloth. Cut into thick wedges or slices and portion out into soup bowls. Cover with hot chicken broth and serve.

ROASTED PHEASANT WITH CREAM AND ENDIVES

Faisan Rôti à la Crème et aux Endives

I was fifteen years old the first time I was given the long-awaited privilege of carrying my own gun. My family was then living not far from the forests and foothills of the Jura Mountains and the irresistible opportunities for hunting and foraging they offered. I'd been out with my father countless times before, trailing along as he shot and killed rabbit and deer, as well as pheasant, grouse, and other game birds. That day we were, as usual, accompanied by our three dogs. Despite their best efforts, nothing much was flying. We walked and walked, scanning the brush and skyline for movement. I was eager to shoot, tired, and a little frustrated, when a crow flew close overhead. I raised my gun, took aim, and shot, knowing through each motion that I was forbidden to shoot crows. My father watched but didn't say a word. He simply picked up the bird and calmly put it in the large back pocket of his jacket. Back home at dinner my mother brought to the table a pot filled with a steaming stew, much like a coq au vin. My father, still calm and serious, looked at me and said, "You eat what you kill." He ladled the stew onto my plate. The crow was incredibly bitter, the flavor of the meat so powerful that I can practically taste it just thinking about it.

It was an excellent lesson. I hunt as often as I can, but I've followed my father's rule without fail ever since. This recipe for pheasant, a bird I love, is one my mother devised to use the thick cream the Jura region is so famous for. She paired it with the only greens, endives, still available after the hard frost during the last months of the hunting season. —JEAN-PIERRE

Serves 4

1 hen pheasant, dressed

Salt and black pepper

4 slices pork fatback or bacon

5 tablespoons butter

2 cloves garlic

1 onion, diced

1 carrot, peeled and diced

1 sprig thyme

1/2 cup dry white wine

1 cup chicken stock (see page 24) or water

1 pound Belgian endives, trimmed, cored, and sliced lengthwise into ribbons

1 cup heavy cream

Preheat the oven to 450°F. Season the pheasant inside and out with salt and pepper, and truss, securing the fatback over the breast with kitchen string.

Melt 2 tablespoons of the butter in a large ovenproof sauté pan and brown the bird on all sides. Discard the cooking fat and replace with 1 tablespoon of fresh butter. Add the garlic cloves, onion, carrot, and thyme and return the bird to the pan. Roast for 20 to 25 minutes, basting frequently with the cooking juices. The pheasant is done when the juices run clear from the thickest point of the thigh when pierced with a knife. Game is tough when overcooked so be sure not to leave it in the oven longer than you must. Remove the string and fatback and place the bird on a platter, breast side down; let it rest in a warm spot for 10 minutes.

Pour off the excess fat from the roasting pan and set over medium heat. Deglaze with the wine while scraping the browned bits from the bottom of the pan. Bring to a boil and add the stock; lower the heat to an easy simmer and reduce the sauce by half. Strain out the vegetables and reduce the sauce again to 4 tablespoons.

Melt the remaining 2 tablespoons of butter in a skillet over medium heat and add the endives; cook, tossing, for 3 to 4 minutes. Season the leaves with salt and pepper, add the cream, and simmer for 4 minutes more. Set aside and keep warm.

To serve, carve the pheasant, cutting the legs in half and slicing the breast meat. Arrange the meat on a hot platter, ladle the sauce over the bird, and serve with the creamy endive.

COMTÉ CHEESE SOUFFLÉ

Soufflé au Comté

We lived in Franche-Comté for ten years when I was a child, years that have been extremely valuable to me as a chef. The quality of the ingredients there at the time was unreal—surpassed perhaps only by their diversity. Jura, in the south of the region, is the epicenter of the world for Comté cheese. We ate a great deal of cheese—on bread, in gratins and quiches, and, of course, in soufflés. My mother's soufflé mixed three different types of Comté that had been *affiné*, or aged and tended, for various lengths of time: soft and creamy Comté, aged less than six months; a young, one-year-old cheese that was firmer with a stronger flavor; and finally a fairly dry, older Comté, or *comté fort*, aged to sharp maturity for more than two-and-a-half years. If my mother had a signature dish, this cheese soufflé might just have been it. —JEAN-PIERRE

Serves 4

1¼ cups whole milk

3 tablespoons butter

3 tablespoons all-purpose flour, plus more for dusting

Salt and black pepper

Nutmeg

3 eggs, separated

6 ounces Comté cheese, grated

Preheat the oven to 425°F.

Scald the milk in a small saucepan over medium heat and set it aside.

In a sauté pan over medium heat, melt 2 tablespoons of the butter. When it's hot, whisk in the flour and cook for 4 to 5 minutes, stirring frequently with a rubber spatula. Add the warm milk to the flour mixture slowly, whisking steadily as you pour. Season the batter with a pinch of salt, black pepper, and a few shreds of grated nutmeg. Cook over low heat for 15 minutes, stirring occasionally. Transfer to a mixing bowl and let the batter cool for 10 to 15 minutes before whisking in the egg yolks and cheese.

Use the remaining 1 tablespoon of butter to coat the insides of 4 individual (6 ounce) ramekins and then dust them with flour.

Beat the egg whites until soft peaks form and fold them gently into the mixture. Fill the ramekins about two-thirds full with the soufflé mixture. Bake for 12 to 15 minutes, until the soufflés are well browned on top. You may also bake the soufflé in one large, 5-cup soufflé dish. Cook the soufflé longer, 18 to 20 minutes, until it rises measurably above the rim of the baking dish and is nicely browned on top. Serve immediately.

BORDEAUX CANNELÉS
Cannelés de Bordeaux

These delicious little cakes are a Bordeaux specialty dating back to the fifteenth century. They are now famous all over the world, but it's difficult to find an authentic, properly made version, particularly in the United States. Preparing the batter the day before you bake will help to make these somewhat tricky, delicate cakes a success. Your reward for all that planning and patience will be a perfect cannelé with a crusty, caramelized exterior and, when you bite into it, a tender rum- and vanilla-scented center. The original copper molds, if you can find them, are quite beautiful (and expensive!). The set I use were passed down to me from my mother. Today, most of the molds you find in stores are either stainless steel or silicone. If you're working with a new set of copper molds, carefully cure them with a fine coating of warm beeswax mixed with oil. You don't want any wax left in the molds—it will end up on your cannelé.

As instructed, let the batter rest for at least twenty-four hours (if not forty-eight hours) before baking the cakes. Turn them out of the molds when they're still warm. Be sure to indulge in the baker's reward by popping one into your mouth while they're fresh and crisp right out of the oven. —DENISE

Makes about 15 cannelés

4 cups whole milk

4 eggs

2 egg yolks

1/2 cup all-purpose flour, sifted

1/2 cup plus 1 tablespoon sugar

3 tablespoons butter, melted

1 teaspoon pure vanilla extract

1 teaspoon rum

Scald the milk in a small saucepan over medium heat. Beat the eggs and egg yolks together in a bowl, then slowly whisk in the warm milk. Add the flour, 1/2 cup of sugar, 2 tablespoons of the butter, the vanilla, and rum. Strain the mixture through a fine sieve into a bowl or storage container, cover, and refrigerate for at least 24 hours, and up to 48 hours.

Remove the batter from the refrigerator for at least 1 hour before baking. Preheat the oven to 400°F. Brush the cannelé molds with the remaining 1 tablespoon of butter and dust with the remaining 1 tablespoon of sugar.

Fill the molds three-quarters of the way up with the batter. Bake for 40 to 50 minutes, until the surface is dark brown. Unmold the cannelés while they're still hot by turning the molds upside down and tapping the bottoms. If the cakes won't release, use a paring knife to loosen them from the sides and try again by holding the mold over a plate and knocking them on the side of the counter. Serve on a platter to finish a meal or with a cup of milky coffee for breakfast.

BAKED PINK LADY APPLES
WITH JELLIED RED CURRANTS
Pommes au Four aux Groseilles

Each fall we prepare to be overwhelmed with fresh apples of every variety from the vast range of apple trees that overrun the orchard at our property in France. Our usual answer to this lovely problem is to make a lot of apple butter and apple compote because we can store these items, eating them slowly over the winter months as we did as children. We store as many of the remaining apples as we can fit on flat trays in the coolest room in the house. They keep for months this way, filling the house with their sweet, distinctive aroma as they ripen and begin to dry. We cook these stored, slightly desiccated apples. There are many ways to put them to work in the kitchen—in savory stuffings and tarts, and with yogurt for breakfast—but this recipe is the one I turn to most often. Simple to make and not overly sweet, these baked apples make a perfect side dish for *boudin noir* (blood sausage) or for any pork or fowl. On their own, of course, they make an easy, light dessert that can be served with a scoop of ice cream or a dollop of crème fraîche. —DENISE

Serves 6

6 large tart apples, such as
    Pink Lady, Rome, or Granny
    Smith
2 tablespoons red jam, such
    as cherry, raspberry, or
    currant

Preheat the oven to 350°F. Cut the top off each apple and then hollow out the center using a melon baller or a sharp-edged spoon. Set the apples upright in a baking dish, not touching, and place 1 teaspoon of any red berry jam on top of each apple. Bake for 35 to 40 minutes, until the apples are very soft and beginning to brown in spots. Serve warm or at room temperature with a savory main dish or as dessert.

CREAMY RICE PUDDING
WITH COGNAC
Riz au Lait au Cognac

Rice pudding is one of the most common desserts in French homes. Living in Berkeley, I made it for my girls often. Sometimes I add a little candied orange peel (page 175) or flavor it with cocoa (or simply use chocolate milk). You can buy rice pudding, of course, but I don't know why anyone would buy something that's so simple to make at home. If you have leftover rice, there's no better use for it than this pudding. In place of porridge in the morning, it makes an excellent breakfast, particularly in winter when you want something hearty to begin the day. —DENISE

Serves 4 to 6

4 cups whole milk

3/4 cup white rice uncooked

1 cup packed dark brown sugar

**1 split vanilla bean or
    1 teaspoon pure vanilla
    extract**

1 tablespoon Cognac

Combine the milk, rice, brown sugar, and vanilla bean in a saucepan. Set over low heat and cook, stirring frequently, for 40 to 45 minutes. The pudding is done when the rice is soft and the milk is mostly absorbed. Remove the vanilla bean and use a paring knife to scrape any remaining pulp into the pudding. Stir in the Cognac, and then pour the pudding into small dessert dishes or into a large bowl and set to cool outdoors or in a cool spot inside. Serve cool or warm, but don't refrigerate before serving, as it changes the taste of the milk and gives the pudding a less pleasing, slightly gluey texture. Of course, you should store any leftover pudding in the refrigerator, and you should not let the pudding sit out at room temperature for more than 3 hours.

SYBILLE'S TUILES
Les Tuiles de Sybille

These elegant cookies get their name from the traditional terra-cotta roof tiles, or *tuiles*, characteristic of southwestern France. Growing up, I never could get enough of them—they were a delicacy my mother reserved for special occasions, and when she made them, it always seemed the guests or my siblings ate them before I discovered them.

Today, tuiles are a staple in French pâtisseries—they are so common that you can buy them boxed up in the supermarket! Never mind these lesser incarnations. Made at home, these cookies are fragile and ephemeral—best eaten still crisp the day they are made. This recipe is from my friend Sybille de Brosses. If you don't have a rolling pin to mold the cookies, use a wine bottle instead. (If your kitchen is anything like mine, there's always one of those to be found.)

If you like, ground praline or sliced almonds make excellent additions to this basic recipe. You may also add a glaze once the cookies are settled on their drying rack. I like dark chocolate melted with a little butter to give them a pretty gloss. A coffee glaze made by combining a shot of espresso with a little confectioners' sugar is also excellent. —DENISE

Makes about 2 dozen cookies

2 egg whites
¹/₂ cup sugar
¹/₄ cup butter, melted
¹/₂ cup all-purpose flour

Preheat the oven to 350°F.

In a bowl, beat together the egg whites and sugar with a fork. Add the flour and melted butter and mix until the flour is just incorporated. Liberally butter a baking sheet and use a tablespoon to make even little piles of the semiliquid dough. (They will spread and cool all the same whatever size you make them.) Bake for 8 to 10 minutes, until the surface turns a light golden brown. While the cookies are still hot, use a spatula to place them over a rolling pin to cool and curl into their characteristic curl. Serve as a garnish for another dessert or on their own with tea or coffee.

sunday lunch

IN FRANCE, a lot of activity revolves around the big affair known as Sunday lunch. It's a time for family to gather at home with extended family and special, honored guests. The lunch lasts several hours; it is a place to exchange news about the week, to catch up on whatever is important, and to kid around with each other. Food is the centerpiece. We ate delicious food at my parents' house. The lunch was always a treat, as we were in boarding school and it was really the only meal of the week we spent with our family. The centerpiece of the meal was always a chicken from our poultry yard and French fries made with potatoes from our vegetable garden; there were also hors d'oeuvres, cheeses, and desserts. All that was served with many different wines that we tasted even as kids—it was just a drop, but if you were in the Lurton family you had to develop a taste for wine. (We hated having to try these wines until we got a little older.)

My mother-in-law's Sunday meal was in a totally different league. The first time I went to her house, I was not particularly afraid of meeting the family, but I was more than impressed by the food. At home, we ate simple food in a glorious dining room. At my in-laws', we ate glorious food in a very middle-class dining room. Elisabeth, Jean-Pierre's mother, started preparing her Sunday lunch on Friday. She made the puff pastry for the first course, wrote up her list of ingredients for the market, and marinated the game. She always served one hors d'oeuvre, one fish dish, one poultry dish, one red meat, vegetables, cheeses, and two desserts. It meant working Friday, Saturday, and also Sunday morning to feed twelve people.

The first time I attended the lunch with Jean-Pierre, I was astonished by the work she put into each dish. Each one was elaborate! The sauces were so rich, and there were many of them. I can still recall the menu: puff pastry stuffed with mussels and scallops in a cream sauce, pheasant pâté, venison, cheese, tarte tatin, and floating island to finish. I am not a big eater, but that first lunch I ate so much to please her that I got sick on the way back home. All that mattered was that I passed the test of the Moullé Sunday lunch! —DENISE

recipes

LIFE IN BERKELEY
IN THE SEVENTIES

La vie à Berkeley dans les Années Soixante-Dix

Jean-Pierre and I both arrived in Berkeley in the mid-seventies. We met for the first time on busy Shattuck Avenue, on the gritty sidewalk in front of Chez Panisse. California was in turmoil in those days, with political, cultural, and social changes as palpable as the brilliant sunshine.

Neither Jean-Pierre nor I was unfamiliar with the kind of radical change that swept Berkeley in those years. We had each in our own way taken part in the student protests that rattled France from 1968 to 1970. In May 1968, mobs of disaffected students demanding reductions in fees and improvement in the educational system flooded the city, barricading the quaint streets, unearthing the ancient cobblestones to hurl at the police, blocking traffic and generally creating havoc amid clouds of tear gas. Although I never threw any bricks or rocks, I did hide several revolutionaries, secreting them away in the massive cupboards—large as small rooms—tucked away throughout my parents' château. Who would think to look for radicals in an eighteenth-century château? For his part, Jean-Pierre was caught distributing pamphlets at his school and was thrown out by the headmaster.

I remember that moment in both France and California as a time to question the bourgeois values we'd ingested since birth. The sense of unfathomable possibilities and unexpected outcomes in France gave us each, in our own ways, the courage and vision to set off for the United States with nothing more than a heavy backpack and a few hundred francs in cash. We weren't yet together, but we were ready to see the world at right around the same time, ready to leave behind the traditions and formalities of our upbringings for the heady freedom of Berkeley in the seventies. There, the spirited insistence on change easily overwhelmed our stuffy French sensibilities.

Radical student movements were one thing—we had some familiarity there. Another matter was the shocking informality of American culture and the flurry of foreign foods. Japanese, Chinese, Mexican: All of these cuisines, and their unfamiliar spices and bizarre combinations were entirely novel. The very concept—never mind the taste—of a taco; the combination of tequila, lime, and salt in a deliciously icy margarita; the mind-bending experience of eating raw, unseasoned fish as sashimi and sushi; the rich, spicy pork of Chinese dumplings; the rich, milky flavor of ricotta in an Italian pasta dish—all of it was revelatory, a true *voyage* to a world we'd had no idea existed. Our thirst for upheaval was complete. Whether it was food or clothes or open manners, California fueled our rebellion, giving us the impetus to settle in and move forward as a part of this surprising new reality.

I came to Berkeley because I was ready for adventure. Jean-Pierre arrived in the United States via Washington, DC. He came from a background of formal, traditional French cooking, with a degree in restaurant management in addition to his chef's training. He knew the business in its classical form from top to bottom—how to make elaborate sauces; how to break down the carcass of virtually any bird, fish, or animal; how to bake bread and pastry; how to make a proper stock—everything, in short, that the best formal French training provides.

When Jean-Pierre accepted a job at Chez Panisse, this sort of knowledge and experience was useful, but not in the way one might expect. As the first professional chef to work in the kitchen there, he brought with him many of the basic kitchen techniques they lacked; but at the same time, confronted with a loose kitchen style, unfamiliar ingredients, and a new menu each day, he was challenged to shed much of the constraint and formality that had defined his cooking up until that point. The learning curve for everyone was steep. He loved it.

Today, it's hard to believe just how undeveloped American food was at the time and how charmingly amateur the kitchen and dining room at Chez Panisse was. The food revolution was certainly underway, but it was new. There was no decent bread to be had, very little decent cheese, and few California wines worth drinking, but glimmers of an increasing interest in food and wine, and the sophistication that went with it, were popping up everywhere in the Bay Area. The Cheese Board, across the street from Chez Panisse, opened in 1967 and began importing French cheeses. (Never mind that they didn't at first know exactly when a cheese was ripe—they learned.) Cocolat, a sophisticated French-inspired pâtisserie, was one of the first to make and sell elaborate, not too sweet desserts of the kind rarely if ever found at that time in the United States. Another early innovative store was Pig by the Tail, which sold pâté, rillettes, French-style sausage, and other prepared French dishes. We loved all of these places, with their familiar tastes, and became friends with many of the owners.

In those early days, we looked forward to eating better every time we returned to France—an authentic *saucisson*; rich, creamy butter; a crusty baguette; raw milk from the dairy down the road from our house; perfectly ripe French cheese of all kinds; and, not to forget, outstanding wine. This hunger for our native food and wine has now practically disappeared because virtually anything once only in available in France can now be found in the United States including cheese, charcuterie, specialty meats, wine, and the best vegetables and fruit. Today the Bay Area has numerous bakeries producing some of the best bread in the world. (Sorry, France. It's true.) Of course, we still enjoy the variety and depth of cheeses we can buy in France, as well as the charcuterie and offal most Americans don't care for, including pig's feet, proper *tête de veau*, and sweetbreads. The taste of food is still different in France because the *terroir* is different—it's good to be reminded of that. Vegetables grow in a different soil, animals eat different grasses, and the most common breeds of animal and poultry are not the same. The subtle differences that make French food what it is have not disappeared.

The trade-off for all the good food and general sophistication we take for granted today is that the Berkeley we found when we arrived doesn't exist anymore. It's still a place I admire for its remaining pockets of creativity and energy, but it is now a far wealthier community, exclusive and essentially bourgeois in many ways. The attachment to security, predictability, and comfort that defines Berkeley today was in no small part what the rebels of the seventies, me and Jean-Pierre included, were intent on disrupting. Risk, freedom from routine, and a spirit of wild independence has in time yielded unexpected results—and not just in the food world. Arriving, as we did, steeped in traditional French social and cultural mores, many of them vestiges of the eighteenth century, the community of cooks, winemakers, and the rebels of all stripes that we discovered in Berkeley have left us with a legacy we never quite imagined for ourselves. The food in this chapter reflects that legacy, which is a complex mix of who we were and who we've become as a result of transplanting ourselves into a community that was, as we can now see in retrospect, one of the most radical moments in American social history. The recipes in this chapter are of a time that is identified by the discovery of ingredients and techniques that, by the French standards we were raised on, are deeply unorthodox. From a perspective of more than thirty years later, we have gained distance and even a nostalgia for what then seemed so fresh and new. Both Jean-Pierre and I have great affection for these early recipes—fig with goat cheese, beef with marrow and garlic, skate with vinaigrette— none of which would have been imaginable in the mid-seventies when they were first served at Chez Panisse as the classic they've become. Perhaps the best part about them is their enduring appeal based on their bright, fresh simplicity.

—*Denise*

FRESH FIG SALAD WITH THYME, HONEY, AND GOAT CHEESE

Salade de Figues au Miel et Fromage de Chèvre

The simplest recipes require the best ingredients. Without flavorful ripe figs and balanced, fresh goat cheese, this salad will be uninteresting. Even the honey must be of the best quality—I keep my own bees, which feed on the blooms from the vineyards and fruit trees that surround our house. The honey they produce is the best on this earth. (Yes, I'm a bit biased in favor of my own hives, but it really is outstanding honey.) This is a good example of what I mean when I say "the best" ingredients. The subtle and not so subtle flavors of every element that goes into this almost childishly simple recipe will determine the end result. With mediocre ingredients you will indeed have nothing better than what a child could put together. But if the figs come from your own or a neighbor's tree and the lettuce is newly picked from the vegetable garden, and the goat cheese is from the neighbor who has a few goats and made the cheese that day, then, and only then, will you have a magnificent salad worthy of your efforts.

Not everyone can keep a fig tree, vegetable garden, or hive, just as few people know a farmer who makes goat cheese on a daily basis. But the point holds: Really stretch yourself to gather the very best ingredients, and set the standard of what is "the best" as high as your imagination allows. —JEAN-PIERRE

Serves 4

8 ounces fresh goat cheese

5 tablespoons olive oil

Salt

Leaves from 2 sprigs thyme, chopped

2 tablespoons balsamic vinegar

8 ounces garden lettuces

8 ripe figs, halved top to bottom

1 tablespoon honey, warm

Cut the goat cheese into thick wedges if you have a disc or into slices if you have a log. Season the pieces with 2 tablespoons of the olive oil, salt, and thyme and set it aside for a few minutes.

Combine 1 tablespoon of the balsamic vinegar with a pinch of salt in a mixing bowl and then whisk in the remaining 3 tablespoons of olive oil. Toss the lettuces with the vinaigrette and arrange on plates or a platter. Place the goat cheese and the figs around the greens. To serve, drizzle the remaining tablespoon of balsamic vinegar over the goat cheese and figs, and finish with the honey.

honey

WE PUT IN OUR FIRST HIVE at Peyraut about fifteen years ago. Jean-Pierre liked the work of caring for the bees right from the start. It's delicate work. The hives must be cleaned once a year and, of course, the honey must be collected as well and then set to drip through a filter, very slowly, into the storage jars. We never heat the honey, preferring it raw on yogurt, in tea, on ice cream, and for dressings and other savory applications.

We all enjoy admiring the precise, intricate work of the bees. The combs they construct are almost like art with their fine, perfectly symmetrical rows. We loved showing the girls when they were growing up just how incredibly orderly nature could be.

Many beekeepers collect all the honey from their bees in the fall and leave them sugar to survive the winter. Jean-Pierre doesn't believe in this practice and always leaves them with plenty of their own honey to weather the cold. Bees all over the world are stressed and dying off in great numbers. Jean-Pierre has lost some of his bees as well but has replenished them recently, and the new hives seem to be thriving. It seems clear that we must stop poisoning the flowers and other plants the bees feed from with pesticides and herbicides. Although it may not be the direct cause of the die-off, it makes the bees vulnerable, slowly weakening the hives. —DENISE

WARM ENDIVE SALAD WITH
LARDONS AND WALNUT OIL
Salade d'Endives aux Lardons

A warm salad has a particular appeal, especially during the winter months when it's difficult to find fresh summer greens. I like the possibilities warm lettuce offers when combined with other ingredients. Dandelion or chicories like Belgian endive, frisée, or radicchio are ideal because they stand up to a little heat; rather than wilting or turning slimy, they retain their crisp texture even when hot. Adding croutons, poached or hard-boiled egg, nuts, or mushrooms will make an entirely new salad when the method here is followed. Replacing the bacon with duck gizzards or warm duck confit will bring a rustic accent and could transform this salad from a first course or lunch into the main meal. —DENISE

Serves 4

4 Belgian endives

Leaves of 1 head frisée

4 slices pancetta or smoked bacon

1 tablespoon Dijon mustard

1 tablespoon sherry vinegar

Salt and black pepper

1/4 cup olive oil

1 tablespoon walnut oil

2 tablespoons coarsely chopped walnuts, toasted

Cut the endives in half and then into strips lengthwise and combine with the frisée in a bowl that will fit over a large pot to form a double-boiler. Fill the pot with water and set over high heat. Meanwhile, cut the bacon into 1/2-inch lardons and render them slowly in a cast-iron skillet over low heat until light brown. Drain the lardons and reserve the melted fat.

Make a vinaigrette in a small bowl by whisking the mustard, vinegar, and salt and black pepper together with the olive oil and walnut oil. Place the bowl of greens over the boiling water and pour over the vinaigrette. Gently toss the greens with the vinaigrette, then add a teaspoon of bacon fat and continue mixing until the greens are lightly warmed. Divide the greens among the plates, sprinkle with the toasted walnuts, and scatter the warm lardons over the top.

GRILLED BEEF FILET WITH MARROW AND GARLIC

Filet de Boeuf Grillé à la Moelle

The beef is accompanied by a version of the classic shallot and parsley butter. It enriches the meat juices of the beef with additional fat to produce an irrisistble, unctuous effect. This is particularly important if you use, as you should, grass-fed beef, which can be on the lean side. It needs the prodding of a rich sauce to be at its best. I like to serve this rich beef with greens, such as sautéed spinach or a braised chicory such as endive. —JEAN-PIERRE

Serves 4

2 marrowbones

1 pound beef tenderloin, cut into 4 filets, preferably grassfed

Salt and black pepper

1 tablespoon olive oil

2 whole heads garlic, separated into unpeeled cloves

½ cup chicken stock (see page 24) or water

Preheat the oven to 325°F. Remove the marrow from the bones and soak it in ice water for 2 to 3 hours (save the bones for another use). Season the beef filets with salt and black pepper and a drizzle of olive oil and set them out on the counter to temper.

Drain the marrow and force it through a sieve into a small bowl; set aside. In a small roasting pan, combine the garlic and chicken stock with a pinch of salt. Bake until the garlic is lightly brown and tender, 15 to 20 minutes. Puree the garlic with the marrow in a food mill or spice grinder or by hand using a mortar and pestle, until you have a smooth, butterlike spread.

Prepare a fire with medium-hot coals or set a gas grill on medium heat (see Grilling, pages 27–28). On a cleaned, well-oiled grate, grill the tenderloin filets for 4 to 5 minutes on each side, until just colored on the exterior but still quite rare at the center. Arrange the meat on a platter, spread a spoonful of marrow butter on each one and let the meat rest in a warm place (perhaps, in the oven with the door open) for 2 to 3 minutes, until the juices and marrow combine.

STUFFED PORK LOIN WITH
PRUNES AND ROASTED APPLES
Filet de Porc Farçi aux Prunes et Sautés de Pommes

When I was growing up, we killed a pig or two every fall following an old French tradition that's still practiced today in many rural areas. Back then, friends and family gathered, and for two or three days we worked together, first killing the pig, then using every part to make sausage, boudin, and cured ham. I'll never forget the potent broth made with the lungs of the animal. Surprising stuff! It was a great deal of work but done joyously. I looked forward to it each year as it was an excuse to gather, eat, drink, and even sing. (Some of the men, perhaps having had a few glasses of wine, sang operas together as they diced the meat to make sausages and *saucissons*.) Often, the pork loin was kept fresh and stuffed with the last of the fall fruit. This is a typical dish in Southwestern France, a region famous for its dried plums. Combining prunes and fresh apples results in a sweet and sour dish that's fairly unusual in French cooking. —DENISE

Serves 10 to 12

10 prunes

1 (5- to 6-pound) pork loin roast

Salt and black pepper

2 bay leaves

3 sprigs thyme

1 sprig rosemary

Fennel fronds

8 to 10 cloves garlic, unpeeled

2 tablespoons olive oil

4 tart apples, such as Golden, Pink Lady, or Granny Smith, peeled, cored, and sliced into eighths

2 tablespoons butter

Soak the prunes in a bowl of hot water for 30 minutes or so and season the meat generously with salt and black pepper. With a round metal rod (a sharpening steel is ideal) or a knife, make a hole in the center of the loin from one end to the other, taking care to work the steel down the center of the loin without puncturing through the sides. Drain the prunes and stuff them as well as you can into the hole from one end to the other. Tie the roast with kitchen string to help it keep its shape and to hold the stuffing in before setting it in a roasting pan. Mix the bay, thyme, rosemary, fennel, and garlic cloves together with the olive oil and pour the mixture over the roast. Leave it at room temperature for 1 hour.

Preheat the oven to 425°F. Roast the loin for 40 to 45 minutes, basting frequently. The center should reach a temperature of 135°F to 140°F. Let the meat rest, covered, for 15 minutes before carving.

While the meat cooks, combine the apples and butter in a sauté pan set over medium-low heat. Sauté the apples for 10 to 15 minutes, or until they're soft and golden but still intact; set aside. To serve, slice the loin into generous rounds, placing the meat on a platter with the roasted garlic cloves and the juices from the pan. Finish by fanning the apples around the meat.

POACHED EASTERN SKATE
WITH SHALLOT VINAIGRETTE
Raie Pochée à la Vinaigrette d'Echalotes

Poaching fish is a disappearing art. This is a shame, because the flavors produced in the exchange between the fish and the aromatic court bouillon simply can't occur when you grill or sauté. Cooking virtually any fish whole or on the bone, as the skate is cooked here, results in richer, fuller flavor. I think of it the way I think of the difference between roasting a whole chicken versus cooking a breast. When it's cooked, a whole bird renders rich juices from the bones and skin. This juice permeates the meat, giving it a succulence you can't achieve any other way. The same is true of fish. If you're nervous about poaching fish, an easy method is to add the vegetables, herbs, aromatics, and fish to a pan of cold water all at the same time. Place the pan on the stove and as soon as the water boils, turn off the heat, cover, and let the fish sit in its poaching liquid until cool. I think you'll find the fish perfectly cooked. —JEAN-PIERRE

Serves 4

1 carrot, peeled and cut
    into rounds

1 onion, coarsely diced

Fennel fronds

Parsley stems

1 sprig thyme

1 bay leaf

1 teaspoon black peppercorns

Salt

1/4 cup white wine

1 tablespoon white wine
    vinegar

1 to 2 skate wings or about
    6 ounces per person

2 shallots, finely diced

1 tablespoon red wine vinegar

1/4 cup olive oil

2 tablespoons capers, coarsely
    chopped

2 tablespoons chopped parsley

Black pepper

1 tablespoon minced chives

Make a court bouillon by combining the carrot, onion, fennel, parsley stems, thyme, bay leaf, and peppercorns in a large pot set over high heat. Cover with cold water and bring to a boil before adding a pinch of salt. Turn the heat to medium and simmer for 10 minutes before adding the white wine and the white wine vinegar. Simmer for another 5 minutes before adding the fish. Cook the fish for 8 to 10 minutes, then remove it gently from the pot and set aside to drain and cool on a platter lined with paper towels or on a rack. Once the fish is cool, remove the skin on both sides and separate the wings from the tough cartilage.

To make the vinaigrette, combine the shallots, red wine vinegar, and a pinch of salt in a small bowl. Whisk in the olive oil and then add the capers, chopped parsley, and black pepper. Place the skate wings on a platter and spoon the vinaigrette over the fish. Finish by sprinkling chives all over the fish.

ROASTED SOLE FILLET WITH MUSHROOMS AND BREAD CRUMBS

Filet de Sole Rôtie aux Champignons

This dish was one of the sixty preparations we had to learn for the final examination at the hotel school in Toulouse that I attended before moving to the United States. It is a pure exercise in mastering the repertoire of classical French cuisine. To pass the exam, we had to quickly and expertly fillet the fish under the watchful eye of the examiners. Today, I might prefer to prepare a whole Dover sole on the grill—but it still doesn't hurt to know how to fillet a fish. At the least you'll need to do it at the table. There will be no examining chef watching your every move but you will have the eager eyes of the diners on you all the same. —JEAN-PIERRE

Serves 4 to 6

1½ pounds Dover sole fillets or
    2 to 3 per person

Salt

Piment d'Espelette (see page 18)

1 pound white button
    mushrooms

4 tablespoons butter

2 shallots, minced

2 tablespoons chopped parsley

¼ cup white wine

Preheat the oven to 375°F. Season the fillets with salt and piment d'Espelette. Trim the stem ends and cut the mushrooms into quarters. Rinse briefly under cold running water, drain, and dry thoroughly. Melt about half the butter in a sauté pan. When it's hot, add the mushrooms and a sprinkle of salt and sauté for 3 to 4 minutes before adding the minced shallots. Cook until the mushrooms are brown and tender, about 4 more minutes. Place the mixture on a cutting surface, finely chop, and set to cool before adding half of the chopped parsley.

In a small buttered baking dish, roll each fillet around your finger to form a cylinder, fill the inside with the mushroom mixture, and place it in the dish. Repeat this operation for each fillet. Drizzle with the white wine and dab the remaining butter on top of the fish. Bake for 20 minutes, or until lightly golden.

To serve, drizzle the juices from the serving dish over the fish and sprinkle with the remaining parsley.

NEW POTATO SALAD WITH
TOMALES BAY MUSSELS

Salade de Pommes de Terre Nouvelles
avec Moules de Bouchot

We cook and eat a great many mussels in the summer months when they are at their peak. Tomales Bay mussels are as close as I've come to the incredible Atlantic mussels I grew up gathering as a kid. Small, juicy, and sweet, they are unsurpassed in flavor. Many times I've had guests arrive proclaiming they don't much like mussels. It gives me great pleasure to watch them change their minds as they discover the distinctive flavor and texture of these cold-water beauties. Many a day I've returned late from the market with a big bag of mussels, having dallied as I often do to chat with friends. The mussels always save me from the wrath of the hungry crowd—I can have them on the table in less than fifteen minutes. Best simply steamed in a big pot with a splash of white wine, herbs, and diced shallots and onions (and sometimes even a little garlic), mussels are one of the greatest pleasures of summer. This little salad is effortless and shows off the mussels in the best possible way, serve with a separate green salad or as is for a light first course or lunch. —JEAN-PIERRE

Serves 4

1½ pounds new fingerling
    potatoes

1 pound small mussels

½ onion, diced

1 bay leaf

1 sprig thyme

½ cup dry white wine

½ cup mayonnaise, preferably
    homemade (see page 86)

Lemon, for juice

Wash the potatoes (don't peel them) and cook in plenty of salted boiling water until tender, 10 to 12 minutes. Scrub and rinse the mussels in cold water, pull their beards out, and cover them with a damp cloth.

In a large pot, combine the onion, bay leaf, thyme and wine. Bring to a boil and cook for 3 minutes before adding the mussels. Cover and cook for 5 to 6 minutes, until the mussels have opened. Remove the pot from the heat and transfer the mussels to a shallow dish, reserving the liquid in a separate bowl. When the mussels are cool enough to handle, remove them from their shells and place them in their liquid.

Slice the potatoes and put them in a mixing bowl. Add half of the mayonnaise and gently toss to coat. Drain the mussels, put in a bowl, and coat them with the remaining mayonnaise. Taste a mussel for seasoning and add a squeeze or two of lemon juice, as needed. Arrange the potatoes and mussels together on a platter and serve at room temperature.

—continued—

MAYONNAISE

Makes 1/2 cup

1 egg yolk, at room temperature

1 tablespoon Dijon mustard

Salt

3/4 cup olive

1 teaspoon water or white wine vinegar

Juice of 1/2 lemon (optional)

To stabilize the bowl so that you have a free hand to add the oil, set a mixing bowl in a pot lined with a dishtowel. Whisk together the egg yolk, mustard, and a pinch of salt in the mixing bowl. Continue whisking, slowly adding just enough of the olive oil to thicken the mixture. (Adding the oil too quickly can cause the mayonnaise to collapse.) Add the water or vinegar, whisking continually, and then add any remaining olive oil. Taste and correct the seasoning with a squeeze of lemon juice. If the mayonnaise needs salt, dissolve it in a 1/4 teaspoon of water before whisking it into the sauce.

If the mayonnaise collapses, splits, or remains thin, reserve the mixture but start again with a clean bowl and a new egg yolk. Whisk olive oil into the yolk very slowly just until it thickens. Rather than adding water, vinegar, or more oil at this point, slowly whisk in the batch of collapsed mayonnaise and then adjust the seasoning.

To Make Aïoli

Omit the Dijon and add 1 tablespoon of pounded garlic as a final step.

To Make an Herb Mayonnaise

Add 1 tablespoon chopped mixed herbs including parsley, chives, tarragon, and chervil as your final step.

DEEP-FRIED PACIFIC OYSTERS WITH TARTAR SAUCE
Huîtres du Bassin Frites et Sauce Tartare

The most essential point for making a success of this dish is not overcooking the oysters. They should be very gently poached in their own juices, just to shape them, no more. If you prefer, the oysters can be dredged raw and then fried, but they will be slippery and difficult to manage. I never tire of the classic combination of the herb-heavy tartar sauce with hot fried oysters but you might also use salsa verde or herb chantilly for a more elegant meal. Allow the sauce to sit for at least 15 minutes to allow the flavors to come together. —JEAN-PIERRE

Serves 2

12 medium-size fresh oysters

¹⁄₄ cup all-purpose flour

2 eggs, beaten

¹⁄₂ cup bread crumbs

4 cups grapeseed oil

¹⁄₂ cup Tartar Sauce (recipe follows)

TARTAR SAUCE

1 egg yolk

Salt

¹⁄₂ tablespoon white wine vinegar

¹⁄₂ cup olive oil

1 tablespoon chopped cornichons

1 tablespoon chopped capers

1 tablespoon chopped parsley

1 tablespoon chopped chives

1 tablespoon chopped chervil

Open the oysters, taking care to reserve their juice. Strain the juice into a small saucepan set over medium heat. When the liquid simmers, add the oysters and poach for 30 seconds. Remove from the heat and set aside to cool.

Whisk the egg yolk, a generous pinch of salt, and vinegar together in a mixing bowl. Once the yolk has lightened in color, slowly pour the olive oil into the mixture, whisking all the while. If the sauce becomes too thick, add a few drops of water. Stir in the cornichons, capers, parsley, chives, and chervil. Taste for salt and acidity, adding a drop of vinegar or another pinch of salt, if necessary.

Set up three plates with the flour in one, the eggs in another, and the bread crumbs in the third. Drain the oysters and, one at a time, dredge them in the flour, then in the egg mixture, then in the bread crumbs.

Heat the oil to 375°F in a heavy saucepan over medium-high heat, reducing the heat if the oil smokes, but making sure the oil stays hot enough while you're frying. Fry the oysters in batches of three or four for 1 to 2 minutes, until golden brown. Drain on paper towels as you work. Arrange the fried oysters on a small platter and serve the tartar sauce on the side in a small bowl.

ASPARAGUS SOUP WITH HERB BUTTER AND ROASTED GARLIC

Soupe d'Asperges au Beurre d'Herbes et Ail Rôti

Asparagus, along with fava beans, are one of the first green vegetables to arrive at the market in spring. I'm always right there to seize my share of the first crop after a winter of root vegetables, cabbage, and hearty greens. At Chez Panisse, I was so excited to have them in the kitchen I'd put asparagus on the menu practically every night. In the beginning of the season, when asparagus are young and tender, I use them in warm or cold salads with other winter vegetables. I also briefly grill the tender spears and serve them cold with fresh salsa verde (page 59) or hot with rich hollandaise sauce. They are outstanding lightly cooked and composed on a white plate with a poached egg and pancetta. Tempting as these choices are, an unassuming asparagus soup has many virtues and as many variations. Simply by altering the garnish on this basic recipe, you can take the soup in a new direction. In addition to the toppings used here, a spoonful of crème fraîche, a scattering of minuscule croutons, and a julienne of prosciutto or fried pancetta are also delicious. —JEAN-PIERRE

Serves 6 to 8

2 pounds green asparagus

2 tablespoons olive oil

1 tablespoon butter

2 onions, chopped

2 leeks, tender white and light green parts, chopped

6 cups water

Salt

3 tablespoons Herb Butter (recipe follows)

2 tablespoons Roasted Garlic Puree (recipe follows)

Snap the ends off and peel the asparagus. Slice coarsely, setting aside half a dozen tips for garnish.

In a large soup pot, heat the olive oil and butter, add the chopped onions and leeks, and stir. Cover and cook for 6 to 8 minutes, until very soft. Add the water, bring to a boil, and season with a pinch or two of salt. Add the asparagus and cook at a simmer until the asparagus are tender, 4 to 6 minutes. Add a cup of ice cubes to the pot to stop the cooking and to preserve the vivid green color. Blend together with an immersion blender or working in batches in a jar blender. Pass the soup through a sieve and taste for seasoning, adding salt as needed.

Poach the asparagus tips in salted boiling water for 3 minutes, cool on a clean dishtowel after removing them from the pot. Cut in half lengthwise.

Serve the soup in warm bowls with a spoonful of herb butter and a dollop of the roasted garlic puree in the center flanked by asparagus tips.

HERB BUTTER

You could not go in a restaurant in the 1970s without having your grilled steak topped with the now-famous maitre d'hotel butter. In addition to topping steak, it is excellent on under the skin of a chicken, and as a way of finishing a simple soup, as here. My mother often applied her version to the fresh-out-the-water mackerel my brothers and I frequently caught and brought home in the summer. She grilled the fish over a very hot fire and served it covered with a simple mix of melted butter, fresh herbs, and mustard.

Be flexible when you make this butter. The combination of herbs you use should evolve through the season depending on which herbs are at their peak—basil in summer, a little sage in fall, savory in winter.

Makes about ⅓ cup

4 tablespoons butter, softened
1 tablespoon chopped parsley
1 tablespoon chopped chives
1 tablespoon chopped chervil
Salt

In a small bowl, use a fork to work together the butter, parsley, chives, chervil, and a pinch of salt.

ROASTED GARLIC PUREE

I'm particular about the garlic I use, but when it's in season and at its sweet, mild, flavorful peak I tend to get carried away. I buy hardneck varieties at the farmers' market when I don't grow my own. I particularly like the mellow, rich flavors that slow-roasted garlic develops when cooked in a little stock and olive oil—pureed and eaten as a condiment with bread, chicken, meat, or in soup, it brings with it an authority and interest that's never unwelcome—at least to my palate.

Makes about ½ cup

6 heads of garlic
½ cup chicken stock
   (see page 24)
1 tablespoon olive oil
Salt

Preheat the oven to 350°F. Remove the outer skin of the garlic heads but leave the head intact. Put the garlic, chicken stock, olive oil, and a pinch of salt in a small cast-iron pan or a roasting pan with a lid. Cover and roast for 35 to 40 minutes, until the garlic is tender all the way to the center. Process the garlic with the cooking liquid in a food mill, food processor with the blade attachment, or in a blender until smooth. Taste for salt and serve warm or at room temperature.

MARINATED KING SALMON WITH HERBS AND SAUVIGNON BLANC

Saumon Sauvage Mariné aux Herbes

This recipe was extraordinarily popular over the years at the restaurant and is featured in one of the Chez Panisse cookbooks, the *Café Cookbook*, which came out in 1999. Over the years, as the café chefs frequently put it on their menus, they came up with many adaptations. The recipe is excellent with all kinds of fish, but I particularly like the acidity of the wine and the power of the herbs when they go to work on oily, rich fish such as king salmon, mackerel, or sardines. Serve with *pain de mie* (fine, soft white bread) or add the fish to a lightly dressed salad of mixed greens. —JEAN-PIERRE

Serves 6 to 8

1 (2- to 3-pound) fillet of wild king salmon, skin on

1/2 pound kosher salt

2 cups Sauvignon Blanc

1/2 cup olive oil

2 shallots, diced

2 tablespoons coriander seeds

2 tablespoons fennel seeds

1 1/2 lemons, one whole lemon cut into eight wedges and the other half thinly sliced

Salt

4 stems parsley plus 1 tablespoon parsley, chopped

1 tablespoon chopped chives

1 tablespoon chopped chervil

Place the salmon in a shallow dish, skin side down, and cover with kosher salt. Refrigerate for at least 6 hours, or overnight. Rinse the fish well and pat it dry. Discard the salt, wipe out the dish, and return the fish to it.

In a small bowl, mix together the wine, olive oil, shallots, coriander, fennel seeds, lemon slices, and parsley stems and pour over the fish. Cover with plastic wrap and refrigerate overnight, or for up to 3 days. To serve, remove the salmon from the marinade (reserve the marinade), slice very thinly, and lay the fish out on a platter.

Strain the marinade through a fine-mesh sieve into a bowl and taste, correcting the seasoning with a pinch of salt as needed. Add the tablespoon of chopped parsley, chives, and chervil to the marinade and spoon over the sliced fish. If you wish, add a few coriander seeds from the marinade and garnish with freshly cut lemon wedges. Once the fish is salted and marinated it keeps, unsliced, for 2 to 3 days in the refrigerator.

hierarchy and service

IN FRANCE, your place in the social hierarchy is set from birth, determined by your parents' class status. Class in France is not fluid in the same way it is in the United States; though "equality" was a rallying cry of the French Revolution, two centuries later it has still not arrived in France. The explicit and implicit power of social and cultural hierarchy, and the fixity of one's position in that hierarchy, is not much changed. Many foreigners are offended by the condescension of French waiters, shopkeepers, and taxi drivers. Americans in particular feel entitled to service with a smile when spending money, and if they aren't treated well, they know they can take their business elsewhere. In France, the social hierarchy shapes a different set of expectations. Perhaps the French behave so brusquely, often holding themselves apart and putting those they serve in their place, because they feel they must assert the status of their profession and guard their social position. —DENISE

recipes

BACK TO BORDEAUX

De Retour à Bordeaux

The former stone barn that we've transformed into our home at Peyraut in Bordeaux is the nucleus of our lives. Its location, style, and history express our French roots and anchor our connection to the French countryside, with its traditions of foraging, gardening, hunting, and preserving. The house and grounds, with gardens, orchards, vineyards, and pebbled courtyard, allow us to share the French way of life with others. We created our travel company Two Bordelais in 1989 because we wanted Americans to experience the rhythm of life, the food, and the values of Bordeaux beyond the popular Médoc—after all, only 5 percent of the wine from Bordeaux comes from the first-growth cellars. We wanted people to see the real Bordeaux, as much as we wanted to sustain the disappearing traditions that make it so distinctive. So we wrote a brochure and sent it out to everyone on Denise's extensive mailing list developed over many years in the wine business. The first year, we did three tours with five or six people on each tour; after that, the tours were full and we often did six or seven a year, each with up to twelve guests. The experience our guests have hasn't changed much over the years. It remains centered around experiencing the refined but ultimately simple cooking that defines us, as well as learning the rewards of foraging (black truffles, wild mushrooms, greens), wine-making, hunting, fishing, and sourcing exceptional local ingredients.

Our tours have introduced hundreds of Americans to many of the tiny producers we value. Whether they make chocolate-covered Guinette cherries, cow bells, goat cheese, or oak barrels, artisans have an increasingly difficult time surviving in a global economy. When the price of goods is valued over quality, and when personal relationships and shared family histories based on regional identity erode, there's little hope artisans can continue to practice their trade as they have for generations. We try to do what we can to support them. We share a deep nostalgia for these rapidly disappearing traditions. Perhaps our years in California enabled us to recognize the value of what many French men and women take for granted or have left behind in their move toward a faster, more convenient way of life.

In the eighties, few wine tourists who came to Bordeaux visited the Médoc and even fewer ventured to Entre-Deux-Mers. Hilly and more lush than the dry, flat landscape of Bordeaux, Entre-Deux-Mers is referred to as the Tuscany of Bordeaux. The winegrowers of the region are more farmers than aristocrats, and the area is characterized by pretty countryside, a mix of classical eighteenth-century architecture in stone and brick, easy rolling pastures, and, of course, vineyards. Tiny roads wind in and out of the vines, snaking past medieval churches and graveyards, humble tasting rooms with dogs sleeping in the sunny gravel driveways, and admirable vegetable gardens secreted behind nearly every house.

Our guests see all of this as they find themselves immersed in the culture of Bordeaux. There are no tour buses or hotels as we move across the countryside, visiting and tasting in cellars not open to the public, admiring row upon row of barrels in the quiet majesty of ancient and modern cellars. The guests stay in a pretty little *gîte* not far from our house. They spend four busy days with us filled with shopping at the farmers' market in Libourne, cooking lessons in our kitchen, cheese tasting in the cellar of one of the best *affineurs* in France, a backstage tour of Saunion chocolate shop (which dates back to the eighteenth century), butchering at Daignac, and sitting down to eat with us.

The recipes here are all about the food we eat most when we're in Bordeaux. There, we use the outdoor bread oven to make crusty bread, *pissaladière*, whole chicken, leg of lamb—really whatever we can fit into this very hot oven. We make use of the fireplace in our kitchen to cook and roast meat, often hanging a leg of lamb or a row of game birds over the fire, using the metal spit and pulley that we discovered in the attic at Bonnet. Two Bordelais, and our time with our guests there, is work, of course. But we come to know and almost always enjoy our guests over the five days they're with us. For them, it's a way to live the French country life by becoming, however briefly, part of a French family. Most of our guests depart on the final day with great reluctance, as they end their stint at French family life, bags stuffed to bursting in their attempt to hold onto as much of it as they can by taking what they can away with them.

—*Denise*

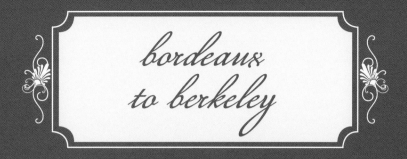

bordeaux to berkeley

BORDEAUX IS A TRADITIONAL PLACE, proud of its heritage and protective of its history, rituals, and hierarchy. It is true that a new energy is flowing through the region and in the city of Bordeaux, with its new mayor, the cleaning of the once gray and now bright white eighteenth-century brick buildings, a modern tramway, and a fresh population of entrepreneurs, artists, architects, lawyers, and winemakers. Still, the château owners—the *négociants* and other landed, wealthy families—remain a caste, more open to outsiders than they once were, but mostly an exclusive group who work, entertain, and marry together.

I grew up amidst a gray world of calculated family weekends, controlling religious schools, and the strict demands of parents. Discipline was the main rule in our set. It was difficult to escape the regularity of meals, school duties, family meetings. By design, nothing of any consequence was left to a last-minute decision. The only one who broke these rules—notably—was my father. He did what he wanted, when he wanted, and sometimes asked us to participate in his crazy hobbies—flying a small two-seater plane, going to watch race cars crashing into each other at the track, building a new car out of three broken ones, and going out sailing when the weather was forbidding. My father was the hero of many who chanced to meet him because he was such an aberration in rigid Bordeaux society. Women were crazy about him, and he adored them back with the same passion that made him and the empire of wine he built so extraordinary. He was not a father to listen and advise: He was on the go, eager for the next new thing. If you wanted to have a piece of him, you needed to play along with his incorrigible sense of adventure.

Perhaps having such a father prepared me for Berkeley; it was not a shock for me, for example, to be living in a house where people did drugs and slept around with abandon. Despite the social rigidity of my upbringing, I found it easy to accept this loose existence and not to judge it. Everyone I met—drifters and tradespeople and brilliant students on the path to professional success—had in common this easy tolerance that did not exist in Bordeaux. It was infectious and most refreshing. —DENISE

FARM-RAISED CHICKEN
ROASTED IN THE WOOD OVEN
Poulet Fermier Rôti au Four à Bois

Although it's difficult for me to choose favorites when it comes to recipes, this must be one. I've certainly served it often enough to friends and family who generally find it as irresistible as I do. Perhaps it's the roasted garlic cooked in the fatty juices—they're always eaten quickly, disappearing before the chicken. Perhaps it's the cavity filled with herbs, which makes the bird smell of the garden. Whatever the magic, selecting the right bird, preferably from a farmer you know and trust, is crucial. If this isn't an option, buy the freshest USDA certified organic chicken you can find. A wood fire adds another dimension to this dish that may be difficult for many to duplicate. The oven will do fine, even if the chicken will be missing that distinctive smoky flavor imparted by cooking with wood. You can either serve the roasted chicken on its own with a big garden salad or, for a heartier winter option, add some small potatoes and any other root vegetables you might have on hand, to the pan midway in the roasting process and let them cook in the lovely juices. —JEAN-PIERRE

Serves 2 to 4

1 (3- to 4-pound) chicken

1 large bunch mixed herbs, such as parsley, thyme, savory, marjoram, fennel, and bay

2 tablespoons butter, olive oil, or duck fat

Salt and black pepper

10 to 15 cloves garlic, unpeeled

White wine, chicken stock (see page 24) or water, for deglazing (optional)

Preheat the oven to 425°F (500°F for a wood-fired oven). Remove the chicken from the refrigerator at least 1 hour before cooking to let it to temper. Stuff the cavity of the bird with the herbs, then rub the skin all over with the butter and season generously with salt and pepper. Place the bird in a roasting pan or terra-cotta dish just large enough to hold it along with any vegetables you may want to tuck along the edges.

Roast the bird for 15 minutes breast side up, 15 minutes on one side, 15 minutes on the other, and finally 15 minutes breast side down. Add the garlic after the first 30 minutes, tucking the cloves around the bird in the pan juices. Finish cooking with breast side up for 10 minutes, if needed. (If using a wood oven, you may need to cover the bird for the final 20 minutes or so to avoid blackening the skin. It depends on the intensity of your fire.)

Let the bird rest for 10 minutes breast side down and loosely covered with foil. This will moisten the breast meat while keeping the chicken hot. For a quick sauce, deglaze the roasting pan with white wine over medium heat, scraping the pan as it reduces. Taste the sauce for seasoning and serve on the side or pour it over the carved meat before serving.

LEG OF VEAL GRILLED WITH PORCINI MUSHROOMS
Quasi de Veau aux Cèpes Grillé

We are fortunate to have an excellent butcher shop, Les Eleveurs Girondins, not far from our house in Bordeaux. I make good use of it by frequently serving this dish to guests and family over the summer months we spend at Peyraut. Les Eleveurs Girondins is not your typical butcher shop: All the men who work in there are semiretired butchers, and the meat that they offer is exclusively grass-fed and sourced from farms not more than fifteen miles away. They sell some of the very best meat I've tasted as well as the incredible Blonde d'Aquitaine which they refer to as "their" beef. A cross of the Garonnaise, the Quercy, and the Blonde des Pyrenees, the butchers don't believe in slaughtering the animal until it's at least three years old.

In the United States the USDA requires ranchers to slaughter their animals before the age of three to prevent the development of mad cow disease. I've been trying to convince Bill Niman to butcher his grass-fed cattle later, exceeding the usual two-year limit he now adheres to. When he was finally able to try beef from an animal slaughtered at four years old, he agreed that the extra age made a significant difference and that the meat had better flavor and marbling. Grass-fed cattle simply need longer to mature and fatten than animals fed with corn and other grains. In addition, females should be allowed to calve once before slaughter, as the pregnancy causes them to put on additional fat.

Sometimes during my stay in Bordeaux I go early in the morning to help the men at Les Eleveurs Girondins butcher. We breakfast together on a substantial steak and a glass of local red wine. After eating we set to work, continuing steadily until noon. Even after working for forty years in a professional kitchen, breaking down whole sides of beef, I find myself learning new things from these masters. Sadly, the butcher shop is run by a group of older men; very few men or women from the younger generations show interest in waking at five to take on the messy, highly skilled work required to turn a two hundred kilo (450 pound) animal into clean, beautifully cut beef.

When it comes to veal, the butchers at Les Eleveurs Girondins only use *veau sous la mère*, or real milk-fed veal. This is a state-regulated AC label in France, making it easy to identify. The calf suckles milk directly from the mother while grazing on a little grass. The meat is darker in color than most veal and has an excellent flavor. A similar product can found in the United States and is often called "rose veal." It's available from a number of producers, most of them organic. —JEAN-PIERRE

—continued—

Serves 6 to 8

3 pounds veal loin, cut into
   1¹/₂ inch slices

Salt and black pepper

3 tablespoons olive oil

2 bay leaves

1 bunch thyme

1 bunch parsley, stems only

¹/₄ cup dry white wine

2 pounds fresh porcini, cleaned,
   trimmed, and sliced, or
   1 pound soaked dried
   porcini and 2 pounds brown
   button mushrooms

2 cloves garlic, finely chopped

8 tablespoons butter, softened

2 shallots, finely diced

2 tablespoons chopped parsley
   leaves

2 pounds spinach leaves, rinsed
   but not dried

Season the slice of veal with salt and pepper and place in a deep gratin dish. Mix 2 tablespoons of the olive oil, bay leaves, thyme, parsley stems, and white wine together in a small bowl and pour over the veal. Cover with plastic wrap and set aside at room temperature.

Heat the remaining 1 tablespoon of olive oil in a sauté pan set over medium heat, add the mushrooms, and cook, stirring frequently, until golden brown. When nearly cooked, add the chopped garlic and toss for 2 minutes to prevent the garlic from burning; remove from the heat and set aside.

In a small bowl, use a fork to mix together 6 tablespoons of the butter with the shallots and chopped parsley leaves, a pinch of salt, and a grind of black pepper.

Heat the remaining 2 tablespoons of butter in a sauté pan set over high heat and add some of the spinach; use tongs to turn the greens, adding more spinach as the leaves wilt. When all the spinach has wilted, add a pinch of salt, toss well, remove from the heat, and set aside.

Prepare a fire and allow it to burn down to medium, or set a gas grill to medium-high (see Grilling, pages 27–28). When the fire is ready, place the veal on the grill, and cook for 8 to 10 minutes on each side, until the meat is just cooked through. It should be pink but not bloody. Place the meat on a large serving dish, spread it with the shallot butter, and set it aside to rest for 5 or 6 minutes before serving. Briefly reheat the mushrooms and spinach, serving them either on the side or right on the platter with the veal.

A Note on "Quasi de Veau" or Veal Leg Steak

You will not find this cut in America so I would recommend using either a rack or a loin cut into 1¹/₂ inch thick slices. Ask the butcher to do this for you. In France, the cut is from the upper part of the leg. The leg is sliced crosswise right through the bone into thick, bone-in steaks. If your butcher has filleted a leg of veal by separating the muscles, as is often the case, you can ask him to slice them into a couple of steaks.

the pace of french life

WITH A MINIMUM OF FIVE WEEKS of paid vacation on top of generous sick leave and maternity and paternity leave, the focus in French life is less on work than on time spent at home or at leisure. The French can't quite grasp the American obsession with work and success, nor are they, in general, nearly so ambitious. Lunch is an hour at the table, not fifteen minutes at a desk. The work week is thirty-five hours, not sixty, as it is for so many Americans. Even leisure isn't pursued with quite the same aggression—sports are a pleasure, not a preoccupation. In turn, meals are more elaborate, with long Sunday lunches a regular, almost sacred occurrence. It's this world and its pace we introduce to our guests on our tours. As much as a tour with Two Bordelais is focused on food, it's equally a means of sharing this recognizably French lifestyle—indeed, the two can't be separated. —DENISE

GRILLED DUCK BREAST WITH BLACK CURRANTS AND CASSIS

Magret de Canard Grillé aux Baies de Cassis

Cooking duck breasts on a grill or in a fireplace can be tricky but it's worth the trouble—there's nothing quite like the lightly smoky flavor you get from the fire. As anyone who has ever grilled duck knows, the ample fat under the skin drips on the fire as it melts, causing flare-ups that char the duck. To avoid this, place a pan in front of your fire and angle your grill toward it so that the rendered fat runs down the grates rather than dripping down on the fire.

This sauce, with its potent fruitiness, contrasts nicely with the fatty duck. I've added fresh currants to the cassis to give it an extra bit of acidity (you may use frozen). At its best, cassis is redolent of berries and imparts a concentrated essence of fruit with a subtle sweetness that benefits from the earthiness of red wine. Crème de cassis, like anything else, varies significantly in quality according to how it's made and where the fruit is grown. The best brands are made in Dijon, where two of the most fragrant currant varieties find their ideal growing conditions on sunny hillsides deeply rooted in the renowned chalky clay of Burgundy. The best currant varieties, Noir de Bourgogne and Royale de Nacre, make the most distinguished cassis. I like the cassis made by Edmond Briottet, but as long as the brand you buy is labeled crème de cassis de Dijon, you can be certain it was made from berries grown in the commune of Dijon and regulated by the strict rules that govern the production of the liqueur in France. —JEAN-PIERRE

Serves 4 to 6

3 whole duck breasts

Salt and black pepper

1/4 cup black currants

2 tablespoons crème de cassis

1/2 cup red wine

1 cup chicken stock (see page 24)

1 tablespoon butter (optional)

Trim away and set aside the tenderloins from the duck breasts before removing any extra fat or silverskin from the breast. Use a very sharp knife to score the skin in a cross pattern and season the meat all over with salt and black pepper. Set aside to temper before cooking.

Combine the black currants, crème de cassis, and red wine in a small saucepan and reduce by half over medium heat. Add the chicken stock and the reserved tenderloins and simmer for 30 minutes or until the liquid is reduced to 1/4 cup.

Prepare a fire and allow it to burn down to medium or, set a gas grill to medium-high (see Grilling, pages 27–28). Grill the breasts, skin side down, for 10 to 15 minutes, until the skin is nicely browned and slightly crispy. Turn the breasts over and cook for another 5 minutes before transferring to a plate. The breasts should be medium-rare, or still quite pink, at the center. Let the meat rest for 2 or 3 minutes before placing the breasts skin side down and slicing each into 6 to 8 pieces. Add the butter to the sauce and reheat until the butter is melted and the sauce just comes to a mellow simmer. Arrange the sliced breast meat on a platter and finish by pouring the hot sauce over it.

GRAPEVINE-GRILLED RIB-EYE STEAKS

Entrecôte Bordelaise aux Sarments

When it comes to grilling in Bordeaux, the choice of wood is invariably the same: grape vine cuttings or stalks. The cuttings are saved and bundled up in winter when the vineyards are pruned. The cuttings are thin and don't burn quite as hot as the more precious stalks, the gnarled wood that is only available when an old vineyard is removed. You don't need a grill or a fireplace to cook over wood—in Bordeaux many people dig a fire pit in the dirt, place the wood in the pit, and set the grill right on top once the wood has burned down to hot coals. This French version of a campfire-cooked steak is not to be missed. Serve with potatoes cooked in duck fat (page 51) and a simple green salad. —DENISE

Serves 4 to 6

1½ pounds rib-eye steak
Salt and black pepper
2 shallots, minced
½ cup butter, softened
2 tablespoons chopped parsley

Season the steaks with salt and pepper and set out at room temperature for an hour or so to temper. Prepare a large fire and allow it to burn down to hot coals (see Grilling, pages 27–28). If you have a gas grill, set it to the highest heat.

To make the butter, combine the shallots, butter, parsley, a pinch of salt, and some black pepper.

Before cooking the steak, place a generous bunch of vine cuttings over the hot coals and let them burn completely. (If you don't have vine cuttings, use hardwood chips instead—my favorites are fig, almond, and apple.) Grill the steaks for 3 to 4 minutes on each side, depending on the intensity of your fire. Remove to a platter and, with a spoon, spread the butter over the steaks. Set the meat aside to rest for 5 minutes as the butter melts, mixing with the meat juices.

BAKED SEA BASS IN THE OVEN WITH SALT CRUST

Bar au Four en Croûte de Sel

The purity of cooking in a salt crust is irresistible. And the simplest way to allow the full, delicate flavor of the fish to shine when you do cook this way is with a squeeze of lemon and a drizzle of superior olive oil. Of course, sea bass goes beautifully with a simple butter sauce or a cold salsa verde (page 59), depending on your menu and the season.

I think you'll find this simple to prepare, but perhaps somewhat complicated to execute. The most difficult part is determining when the fish is cooked. I have two tricks I use: The first is to insert a bamboo skewer through the salt crust into the thickest part of the fish. If the skewer slides right in without meeting resistance, the fish is done; the second is to use your nose—when the fish is cooked it will begin to smell fragrant and tempting, as good, freshly cooked fish will. Whatever you do, cooking in a salt crust leaves plenty of room for error. Even an overcooked fish will remain moist and delicious. Alternatively, if you remove the salt crust and find the fish undercooked, simply return the whole fish to the dish and place it in the oven to finish cooking.

You'll need 3 to 4 pounds of rock salt to mix with the egg white. The egg whites form a hard crust when mixed with the salt which makes the unmolding of the fish easy. Wrapping the fish in cheese-cloth, as I suggest, prevents it from falling apart when you remove the crust. If you're feeling brave, the cheesecloth and egg whites may be omitted, but it will be more challenging to remove the fish from the baking dish. —JEAN-PIERRE

Serves 5 to 6

1 (3- to 4-pound) whole sea bass or striped bass, cleaned, with scales on

3 sprigs parsley

2 fennel branches

2 sprigs thyme

2 bay leaves

6 egg whites

1 lemon

2 tablespoons excellent olive oil

Preheat the oven to 450°F. Fill the cavity of the fish with parsley, fennel, thyme, and bay leaves. Do not salt. Wrap the fish in a double layer of cheesecloth. In a large bowl, beat together the salt and egg whites until thoroughly blended. Using a ladle, place a 2-inch layer of the salt mixture at the bottom of a heavy baking dish. Add the wrapped fish and cover with the remaining salt mixture, taking care to seal the fish inside by thoroughly covering it with the egg mixture.

Bake for 30 minutes, then turn the oven down to 400°F and cook for another 40 minutes. Test by inserting a wooden skewer into the thickest part of the fish to test for doneness; if it meets no resistance, it's done. Pay attention to the smell of the fish as it cooks as well. To serve, remove the fish from the salt crust and cut away the cheesecloth. Remove the skin and place the fillets on a platter, leaving behind the bones as much as possible (some bones are likely to remain). Squeeze some lemon juice over the fillets along with a drizzle of olive oil before serving.

GRILLED SPRING SHAD
WITH SORREL SAUCE
Alose Grillée à l'Oseille

Shad season only lasts for a few precious weeks in spring. In Bordeaux, fishermen catch them with nets and sell them to directly to vendors at the farmers' markets in the immediate region. There is no middleman, which means the fish go from the boat to the market, the morning catch arriving still stiff, their silver skin sparkling. The locals are not fools—they know when a delicacy with such a short season is available. Having waited a year for another taste of the famous *alose*, or shad, you need to be at the market early if you plan on bringing some home for yourself.

I like to grill the fish whole in the fireplace, seasoned and stuffed with herbs and sorrel and served as the locals have done for ages with a French version of salsa verde that includes mixed herbs (predominantly tarragon), along with capers and soft-boiled eggs. The main drawback of this delicate, most delicious fish is the numerous, somewhat distracting bones. I simply take my time eating the fish, savoring each bite with care, never allowing the inconvenience to interfere with my pleasure. Over the years, my friends in Bordeaux have tried to assure me that stuffing the fish with sorrel causes the bones to dissolve. This must be rural myth or simply wishful thinking; I have yet to experience this particular magic when it comes to navigating a bony piece of shad. —JEAN-PIERRE

Serves 8 to 10

1 large shad, 5 to 6 pounds, cleaned and scaled

Salt and black pepper

4 ounces sorrel leaves, large stems removed

2 tablespoons olive oil

3/4 cups Salsa Verde (see page 59)

Season the fish with salt and pepper and stuff the cavity with sorrel. Drizzle olive oil over the fish, coating it thoroughly.

Build a fire and and allow it to burn down to medium-hot coals, or set a gas grill to medium heat (see Gilling, pages 27–28). Be sure the grate is clean and well-oiled. Grill the fish for 15 to 20 minutes on one side and another 15 minutes on the other side. (If you have one, a fish grill is good to use. By flipping the grill, the fish is turned as well.) The skin should be crispy and the fish should have no trace of blood inside. Arrange the fish on a large platter and serve with salsa verde.

Note

When grilling a large fish, you may want to leave the scales on to prevent it from sticking to the grill. If you do, cook the fish until the skin is dark brown or almost black. The skin will protect the flesh of the fish, keeping it moist. Just peel the skin off before serving.

WARM FOIE GRAS WITH
ONION CONFIT AND ORANGE

Foie Gras Chaud au Confit d'Ognion à l'Orange

In the old days, especially in the southwest of France, foie gras was simply part of daily life, even for the most modest farmers. Denise's Aunt Anne and her husband Marius lived for years on a farm not far from Toulouse. They lived simply on very little, with most of what they ate coming from their small plot of land. This land consisted of a few cherry trees, some raspberry bushes, sunflowers, a patch of corn, a few chickens, a pig, ducks, and a handful of geese that they fed by *gavage*, force-feeding them grain.

One year, we were invited to help slaughter the ducks and geese. It was hard work. We were roused at 5 o'clock each morning to sit down to the ritual breakfast of soup, pâté, and, of course, a glass of red wine. This breakfast does not hold a fond place in my memories. It was hard on my stomach and very far from my usual "city guy" breakfast of a buttery croissant and café au lait. There was no question of complaining; we were up to our eyes in fat, innards, feathers, and the smell of blood.

On the first day, we killed the ducks and geese, then hung their carcasses in a cool place so they would be ready to process the next morning. There was no refrigerator or freezer. A huge fireplace, a big copper caldron, knives, and canning jars were all we had—and all we needed—to spend the next day transforming those birds into confit, pâté, stuffed necks, and foie gras.

After the birds were plucked, the heads and feet were removed. Next, the precious liver was extracted. Peering in to have a first look at its liver was a little bit like playing the lottery; you never knew what size the liver would be. We held our breath and hoped for the prize—an overgrown, creamy yellow liver—foie gras. Once the liver was removed, it was rinsed and seasoned with salt, pepper, and a splash of sweet wine. Next, the bird was carved and the legs, breast, and wings were seasoned with salt, bay leaves, and thyme. I was grateful we saved a few of the breasts to eat fresh for our dinner. We set them to grill over vine cuttings in the fireplace, sprinkled only with shallots, parsley, and salt: a perfect reward for a day of hard work. —JEAN-PIERRE

Serves 4

4 (1/2-inch-thick) slices grade A
  foie gras (about 16 ounces)
Salt and black pepper
3/4 cup olive oil
1 pound onions, thinly sliced
2 teaspoons sugar
Zest of 2 oranges
1 carrot, peeled and julienned
2 tablespoons sherry vinegar
2 tablespoons red wine vinegar

Season the foie gras with salt and pepper and reserve in the refrigerator covered with plastic wrap. Heat a sauté pan over medium heat with the olive oil and onions. Cook, stirring frequently, until the onions are soft and lightly golden in color. Add the sugar and the orange zest and cook for another 2 minutes before deglazing the pan with the two vinegars. Transfer the onions and their liquid to a bowl and set aside. In a medium skillet over medium-high heat, add the liver and sauté for just 1 minute on each side. Transfer the liver carefully to a plate lined with paper towels to absorb any excess fat. Arrange on warm plates with the onion confit and serve.

true farming

ON ONE OF OUR TOURS, we hosted a successful peanut farmer from Georgia. This lovely man owned a massive farm made up of acre upon acre of peanut plants. He cultivated the fields and harvested his crop by sitting in an air-conditioned cab in a massive tiller high above the land. Several times over the growing season, he sprayed the fields from the air, flying over in small crop duster to spread pesticides and herbicides. As we walked the vineyard at Château Bonnet, I talked about the influence of the weather, how we pruned the vines by hand each spring and harvested a portion of the crop in midsummer to produce the best wine. I explained the different *terroirs* throughout my father's properties and why we might grow Merlot on one and Sauvignon Blanc on another. I went on at length to explain the effects of too much rain, heavy winds, a late spring frost, an exceptionally cold winter, a dry autumn—all the vagaries of weather that would ultimately determine the quality of the vintage. What surprised him was how connected we were to nature, walking the land, tasting the grapes, and worrying over every change in the weather. From his perspective, farming was a rather impersonal business that had very little to do with uncertain weather or the vagaries of the soil. Each year, his peanut crop was about the same as it had been the year before. But our conversation opened his mind to the possibility that his crop, which had been the livelihood of his family for generations, was personal, and that his manipulation of it as much as his remove from it robbed him of the experience of being connected to his life's work. —DENISE

GREEN BEAN SALAD
WITH SMOKED DUCK BREAST
Salade d'Haricots Verts au Magret de Canard Fumé

Green beans, or haricots verts, as they have come to be known even in English, are one of the most rewarding vegetables to grow. Picked young and thin, they take just minutes from the plant to the pot to the table—harvest, snap, and into a pot of boiling water they go. Ready to drain five minutes later, they need no more adornment than a pinch of salt.

When the beans are not minutes, but hours or days old, as they often are when bought at the farmers' market, they need more time to cook, somewhere between eight and ten minutes. Supermarket beans, on the other hand, invariably having been in transit or sitting in the cooler case for days before you take them home, need much longer. I give these older, frequently more mature beans almost fifteen minutes to cook. When I teach, I tell my students that achieving a perfectly cooked bean requires tasting one every two to three minutes. A bean attains its optimum flavor when fully cooked and is neither mushy nor snappy. That raw, slightly grassy flavor marks an undercooked bean no matter how fresh, young, and tender it might be. —JEAN PIERRE

Serves 4 to 6

2 pounds green beans, trimmed

2 shallots, finely diced

2 tablespoons balsamic vinegar

2 tablespoons sherry vinegar

Salt and black pepper

1/2 cup olive oil

1 head frisée

8 thin slices, Duck Breast Prosciutto (see page 145), or prosciutto

1/4 cup coarsely chopped walnuts, lightly toasted

Cook the beans in plenty of salted, boiling water for 8 to 10 minutes (depending on how large and fresh your beans are). They should be tender but not soft. Drain and spread out on a towel or platter to cool. Do not refrigerate.

Combine the shallots with the balsamic and sherry vinegars, a pinch of salt, and a grind of black pepper. Leave to marinate for 3 minutes before whisking in the olive oil. Set aside for 10 minutes to integrate the flavors.

In a large mixing bowl, gently toss the green beans and frisée together with the vinaigrette. Taste for seasoning and then arrange the beans and frisée on a large platter, leaving space around the edges. Sprinkle the walnuts on top of the beans and frisée before arranging the sliced duck breast around the salad. Serve at room temperature.

OYSTERS ON THE HALF SHELL
WITH HANDMADE SAUSAGE
Huîtres et Crépinettes Grillées

Some of the best oysters in France originate in the rich tidal waters of the Bassin d'Arcachon, a beautiful bay and beach resort just one hour's drive from our house in Bordeaux. The conditions are optimal for cultivating oysters, with rich tidal waters providing nutrients to the beds tended by hundreds of independent farmers. In summer, when the water temperature rises, the farmers put out tiles to collect newborn larvae, and then plant the tiny seedlings or spats in the fertile bay. The combination of the lightly metallic, clean, and briny oysters with the richness and warmth of these mild sausages is like nothing else. A glass of the local Entre-Deux-Mers Sauvignon Blanc, like my family's Château Bonnet, which is blended with a touch of Sémillon for fullness, transforms the simple combination into a truly extraordinary treat. —DENISE

Serves 4

2 to 3 dozen Pacific oysters, scrubbed under running water and shucked

2 shallots, diced

Dry white wine

1 tablespoon white wine vinegar

1 teaspoon cracked black pepper

8 ounces ground pork

1 tablespoon chopped thyme

Salt and black pepper

6 slices rye bread

Butter

1 lemon, quartered, for serving

If you have access to fresh seaweed, use it as a bed for the shucked oysters; use crushed ice if you don't have seaweed. Place the oysters in a cool place until ready to serve.

To make the mignonette, combine the shallots, 1/4 cup white wine, vinegar, and cracked pepper in a small serving bowl. Set aside.

Using your hands, thoroughly mix the pork, thyme, a pinch of salt and a grind of pepper, and a splash of white wine in a mixing bowl and shape into small round patties, about 1/2 inch thick. In a small cast-iron pan, cook the patties until golden brown on both sides and cooked through or no longer pink at the center, 10 to 12 minutes.

Toast and butter the bread. Serve the chilled oysters with the hot sausage patties, mignonette, and toast. I like to bring the four elements to the table separately. Add a squeeze of lemon, if desired.

GRILLED EEL SKEWERS
WITH PANCETTA
Brochette d'Anguilles Grillées dans la Cheminée

Eel are deliciously fatty, which is why I like them grilled over a hot fire. The locals around our house at Peyraut sauté them with the skin on and eat them sliced with loads of fresh garlic and parsley. This recipe is a tribute to their elemental approach.

Today, it's a rare treat to find eel in the local market in Branne where we do most of our shopping. Eel are rapidly disappearing from the rivers in France. A few fishermen, busy with shad and lamprey the rest of the year, still catch a few of the eel that make their way up the Dordogne River not far from our house. Years ago, eel large and small were sold live, slithering gracefully in circles through the water in big buckets at the fish stand, a mesmerizing display of vigor, and the ultimate proof of freshness (baby eel, called *piballes*, are now protected). Many of the older generation won't even consider buying eel if they aren't still fighting in the market bucket.

Finding eel at your fish market may be difficult, but this recipe can be made using any firm fish or shellfish. I'd suggest tuna, swordfish, scallops, or large shrimp. —DENISE

Serves 4

1 pound eel (a single section of a larger eel or two or more smaller eels, cleaned, and skinned or four 4-ounce eels, cleaned and skinned)

8 ounces pancetta, sliced into 3-inch lardons

Salt and black pepper

1 tablespoon olive oil

4 cloves garlic, minced

2 tablespoons chopped parsley

Slice the eel into 1-inch sections; you should have about 20 pieces. Using wood skewers that have been soaked in cold water, make brochettes alternating pieces of pancetta and eel, using 4 or 5 pieces of fish per skewer. Season with salt and black pepper.

Prepare a large fire and allow it to burn down to hot coals or set a gas grill on high (see Grilling, pages 27–28). Clean and oil your grill before placing the skewers on the hot grate. Grill for 5 to 6 minutes on each side, or until the fish has a nice brown color. Arrange the skewers on a plate, drizzle a little very good olive oil over the top, and finish with sprinkles of garlic and parsley. Let the brochettes sit for a minute or two to cool slightly before serving.

CREAM OF CELERY ROOT SOUP
WITH BLACK TRUFFLES
Crème de Celeri aux Truffes

This is a soup I make often during truffle season, from December to early March, depending on the year. A trick I learned from the Peyberes, a fourth generation truffle *négociant* in Cahors is to add a touch of garlic in the truffle butter to maximize the earthy flavor of the celery root. If you cannot find fresh black truffles, don't substitute truffle oil. Instead, use truffle butter, adding the garlic to the premade butter. —JEAN-PIERRE

Serves 4 to 6

4 ounces Jerusalem artichokes

2 onions, coarsely chopped

4 leeks, white and light green
  parts, chopped

6 tablespoons butter, softened

Salt

1 bay leaf

1 sprig thyme

4 celery roots, peeled and diced

1 ounce black truffles, finely
  chopped (save a few slices
  cut into a julienne for
  garnish)

1 clove garlic, minced

Grapeseed oil for frying

Black pepper

Peel the Jerusalem artichokes. Cut a dozen or so very thin slices from one of the artichokes using a mandoline; reserve the slices in cold water. Set the remaining peeled artichokes aside.

In a heavy saucepan over medium heat, sweat the onions and leeks with 2 tablespoons of the butter, a pinch of salt, bay leaf, and thyme. Cook, covered, until soft, 8 to 10 minutes. Add 4 to 6 cups of cold water, or enough to cover the leek mixture, and turn the heat to high. When it comes to a boil, add the celery root and the Jerusalem artichoke, reduce the heat, and simmer for 20 minutes, or until the celery root is tender. Remove the pot from the heat remove the bay leaf and thyme, and puree the vegetables with their liquid in a blender. Pass the puree through a strainer and taste for salt.

Place the remaining 4 tablespoons of butter in a small bowl and mix in the chopped truffle, garlic, and a pinch of salt. Keep at room temperature, covered, until needed (do not refrigerate).

Heat 2 cups of oil in a large saucepan to 375°F. Strain and dry the reserved artichokes on a paper towel and deep-fry the slices in small batches until golden brown. Reserve on a paper towel in a warm spot.

Return the soup to the pot and bring it to a simmer before ladling it into warm soup plates. Use a fork to stir in a dollop of soft black truffle butter, add the crispy Jerusalem artichoke chips in the center, and finish with the reserved julienne of black truffle scattered on the surrounding surface.

PARSNIP SOUP
Soupe de Panais

In winter when the air is chilly but humid, it goes right through to my bones, particularly in an old, drafty stone house like ours at Peyraut. When I feel the chill, nothing tastes better or warms me up like a bowl of soup. This is one I make often, since parsnips hold up in the cellar when many of the fall vegetables have either been eaten or grown soft and spotted with age. Ingredients are always scarce in winter, and cooking creative, varied meals each day can be challenging. I particularly like the pure flavor of parsnip that comes through here—at once sweet, rich, and earthy. Because parsnips are naturally creamy when cooked, there's no need to add heavy cream. With a slice of hearty bread and plenty of sweet butter, this humble soup is a comforting meal on any cold, wet day. —DENISE

Serves 4 to 6

3 tablespoons olive oil

1 onion, diced

1 large leek, all but the rough top green part, sliced

5 large parsnips, peeled and sliced 1¹/₂ inches thick

Bouquet garni, 1 leek, green part only, 6 to 8 parsley stems, 1 (4-inch) celery rib, 2 bay leaves, 3 sprigs thyme (see page 21)

1¹/₂ teaspoons salt

Black pepper

3 cups water

In a large stockpot set over medium heat, combine the olive oil, onion, and leek. Cook until translucent but not brown, stirring often. Add the parsnips, bouquet garni, salt, a grind or two of black pepper, and water. Cover and cook over medium heat for 30 to 35 minutes, until the parsnips are tender. Remove the bouquet garni from the pot and blend the scoop in a jar blender in batches or with an immersion blender right in the pot. Taste for seasoning and serve hot.

SUMMER VEGETABLES
IN TERRA-COTTA
Tians de Légumes d'Été

This dish produces a beautiful, dramatic effect with its tightly layered, orderly variation in color. Be sure to bring it to the table undisturbed, leaving it in the gratin dish it was baked in. As simple as the recipe is, it's important to slice the vegetables the same shape and size. If one vegetable is much larger than the others, cut it to fit. The more precisely the slices fit together, the better the effect. Our daughter Elsa is the master of this dish and demonstrates how to make it all fit together neatly during our cooking classes in Bordeaux. —DENISE

Serves 4 to 6

2 tablespoons olive oil

2 onions, sliced

2 sprigs thyme

2 bay leaves

5 or 6 basil leaves

Salt

2 zucchini, sliced into 1/4-inch-thick rounds

2 long eggplants, sliced into 1/4-inch-thick rounds

4 ripe tomatoes, sliced into 1/4-inch-thick rounds

Black pepper

Preheat the oven to 350°F.

In a large sauté pan over medium heat, combine 1 tablespoon of the olive oil with the onions, thyme, bay leaves, and basil. Cook, stirring frequently, until soft, and season with a pinch of salt. Remove the thyme and bay leaves from the onion mixture and arrange a layer of the cooked onions in a medium-size gratin dish. Be sure the sliced vegetables are roughly the same diameter—if they're not, cut them in half so that they will make fairly orderly layers. Densely shingle the sliced tomato, eggplant, and zucchini on top of the onion. Alternate the vegetables as you work, overlapping them in a tight line or circle (depending on the shape of the gratin dish) so that they are almost standing up in the dish. Once finished, the sliced vegetables should resemble shingles on a roof. Sprinkle with a pinch of salt and a grind of black pepper and drizzle the surface with the remaining 1 tablespoon olive oil.

Bake for 1 hour, or until the liquid bubbling up around the edges has evaporated. Halfway through the baking, press the vegetables with a spatula to keep them moist.

NATASHA'S RUSSIAN MORNING CHEESE

Le Fromage du Matin de Natasha

Growing up, we had two cows, just for milk. Milk was a main staple, as we ate a lot of dishes made with milk, like soufflé, béchamel, lots of rice pudding, polenta cake, and crème anglaise. Our milk arrived at our doorstep every morning, still warm from the cows. Once it cooled, a thick layer of cream formed on the surface; my mother scooped this out and kept it in a separate jar in the refrigerator. We had more milk than we could use, so my mother often made this fresh cheese. I was reminded of it recently when my friend Natasha made it for me while we were at Peyraut. The taste of the light, milky cheese brought back fond memories. I like it on bread or scattered with fresh herbs, but it's also delicious drizzled with honey. The cheese should be made with raw milk—if you can't find any, use regular pasteurized milk. Almost all the milk at the grocery store today is ultrapasteurized. This will not work as all the enzymes and friendly bacteria—not to mention the grassy flavors—have been killed at high temperature. —DENISE

Makes a round cheese for 6 to 8 servings

1 gallon whole milk, preferably raw and not ultrapasteurized

4 cups buttermilk with live cultures

Pinch of salt

2 teaspoons Caraway seeds or herbes de Provence (optional)

Combine the milk and buttermilk in a large pot. Cover and set out at room temperature for 24 hours, until the milk has soured and turned to the consistency of soft pudding. Add a pinch of salt and place the pot over low heat; add the caraway. Watch the milk carefully; once it curdles, it's ready to come off the heat. You can tell it's curdled when you see the texture of the liquid change: The solids in the milk will come together, separating from the liquid, which you'll see in the pot. Strain the curds by lining a colander with a double layer of cheese-cloth. Transfer the curds to a bowl and let let them sit for 2 hours or so to solidify before serving. The cheese is most delicious when it's still slightly warm and very freshly made, but it's good cold as well. Seal any cheese you don't use right away in a container and refrigerate for up to a week.

WARM APPLE FEUILLETÉ
Feuilleté Chaud aux Pommes

I am not a big fan of sweet cakes, candy, and heavy desserts. I prefer tarts or crumbles with fresh fruit or simple, not-too-sweet custards. These lighter desserts are enough to satisfy my desire for a taste of something sweet after a meal without leaving me feeling unpleasantly full. This simple apple tart made with puff pastry suits me perfectly—it's fresh tasting and only as sweet as your apples if you choose to omit the sugar. To make a more decadent dessert, serve with crème fraîche, Prune and Armagnac Ice Cream (page 127), crème anglaise (page 179), or heavy cream whipped with a pinch of sugar and a splash of vanilla. —DENISE

Serves 6 to 8

1 to 2 sheets puff pastry, chilled

4 Gravenstein apples, peeled, cored, and cut into 1/4-inch-thick slices

2 tablespoons sugar

1 tablespoon butter, melted

Preheat the oven to 425°F. Cut the puff pastry into eight rounds of 5 inches in diameter (they should be about 1/8 inch thick), lay on a baking sheet, and refrigerate. Toss the apples with the sugar. Prick the bottoms of the puff pastry rounds all over with a fork before arranging the sliced apples in a spiral, overlapping them as much as possible. Brush the apples with the melted butter.

Bake the tartlets for 10 minutes at 425°F, then turn down the heat to 350°F and continue to bake for 15 to 20 minutes more, until the pastry is a toasty brown and fully cooked through on the bottom. Serve warm.

DENISE'S CHOCOLATE POT DE CRÈME

Les Pots de Crème au Chocolat de Denise

When I need a not-too-sweet dessert to serve to a guest who adores the intensity of chocolate, this is my choice. Without flour or cream, it's light and delicious, with a rich flavor that comes solely from egg yolks and dark chocolate. Outstanding chocolate is everywhere these days. Look for one with high cocoa content—between 65 and 95. The more cocoa solids chocolate contains, the richer it will be, with that distinctive bitterness unspoiled by too much sugar. Don't skip the water bath—it keeps the air in the oven moist and prevents the custard from cooking too quickly. Serve without refrigerating if at all possible; once refrigerated the custard will lose much of its flavor, becoming slightly one-dimensional. —DENISE

Serves 6

2 cups milk

3 ounces dark (70 percent cacao) chocolate, cut into 1/2-inch pieces

6 egg yolks

1/2 cup packed brown sugar

Preheat the oven to 375°F.

Scald the milk in a saucepan over medium heat, bringing it *almost* to a boil. Turn off the heat and put the chocolate into the hot milk. Set aside to cool a bit, stirring now and then as the chocolate melts.

In a mixing bowl, beat the yolks with the brown sugar until lightened in color and texture. Whisking all the while, pour the warm chocolate milk slowly into the bowl with the egg mixture (you don't want the eggs to cook in the hot milk).

Pour the mixture into six small ramekins and place them in an ovenproof dish filled with 1/4 inch of hot water. Bake for 35 minutes, or until there is a thin golden border visible at the edge of the ramekins. Serve warm or at room temperature.

Ice Creams
LES CRÈMES GLACÉES

There's nothing particularly difficult about making ice cream if you have a decent machine. Getting it right is not just a question of using the best ingredients, it's a question of balance. Yes, non-ultrapasturized milk and cream, super fresh eggs from free-range hens, and fresh, truly flavorful fruit, nuts, and spices all make an immense difference in determining the quality of your ice cream. Good chocolate with a high proportion of cocoa solids is also essential, as are freshly picked herbs. But it's the balance between flavor, richness, and texture that's most challenging to get right. Ice cream can be too rich, and when it is the fat obscures the flavor of the other ingredients even as it lends the ice cream a smooth, silky texture. If I'm using a recipe with a custard base (containing egg yolks), I prefer a mix of half milk and half heavy cream.

One of my favorite ice creams is Meyer lemon. When it's made with pure cream, the acidity and brightness of the citrus is obscured as the pure richness of all that butterfat takes over the more subtle notes of the lemon. The texture with half milk and half cream is slightly more granular than it might be if made with a higher ratio of cream, but I don't mind the icy texture if what I'm eating is super flavorful. Good chocolate ice cream isn't all that different. Outstanding chocolate, with its toasty notes, acidity, and fruit, can be overwhelmed by sugar and heavy cream. —DENISE

PRUNE AND ARMAGNAC ICE CREAM

Glace aux Pruneaux et Armagnac

Every summer Denise and I spend a few weeks in Arcachon, a town on the Atlantic Ocean near Bordeaux. There we frequent an ice cream parlor with an extraordinary selection, from praline ice cream to black currant sorbet.

The husband and wife who make the ice cream and serve it remember us from our visits over the years. I nonetheless marvel each time I enter only to find a *cornet* of prune and Armagnac ice cream in my hand before I've said a word beyond, *"Bonjour, Madame."*

The recipe here is an old creation of a great chef from Gascony, André Daguin. I've made it many times over the years—no matter how many other flavors and combinations I try, this one remains my favorite. Over time I've altered the recipe from its original enough that I suppose I should call this version my own. I can attest to its excellence eaten with nothing but a dish to hold it and a spoon to deliver it to the mouth, but it does make a remarkably brilliant combination when it begins melting on the plate next to Denise's Warm Apple Feuilleté (page 124). —JEAN-PIERRE

Makes about 5 cups

4 cups whole milk

1 vanilla bean, cut lengthwise in half

8 egg yolks

³/₄ cup sugar

³/₄ cup coarsely chopped prunes in Armagnac (see page 245)

Pour the milk into a saucepan with the vanilla bean and bring to a simmer slowly over low heat. Let sit, covered, for 5 minutes so the vanilla can infuse its flavor into the milk. Combine the egg yolks and sugar in a mixing bowl and whisk until thick and bright yellow. Gradually add the hot milk to the yolk mixture, whisking vigorously all the while, then pour all of it back into the saucepan. Set the pot over medium-low heat and cook, stirring continually with a silicone spatula or wooden spoon until it thickens slightly. When it's ready, the custard should coat the back of the spatula or spoon. Strain the custard through a fine-mesh sieve into a bowl set over ice and continue stirring for another minute or two. When the mixture is chilled, add the prunes to the custard and pour into an ice cream machine. Freeze according to manufacturer's directions and serve.

LEMON VERBENA ICE CREAM
Glace à la Verveine du Jardin

Two large lemon verbena plants flourish in our Bordeaux garden, spreading their lemony scent about each time anyone brushes up against one of them. For years, Jean-Pierre and I have followed a ritual of concocting a light tisane before bed. It's a simple infused tea made with a handful of fresh leaves. It's a lovely digestive and helps us sleep.

In summer, when the nights are hot and the cherry trees are groaning with ripe fruit, we make a batch of this fragrant ice cream instead of a tisane. After dinner, we put a scoop in a bowl with a handful of cherries cooked lightly with a little water and sugar. The combination is wonderful with any sweet cherry—Bing, Lambert, or Rainier—but it's even better made with sour cherries, such as Montmorency or Grillotes. —DENISE

Makes about 3 cups

2 cups whole milk

1/2 vanilla bean, cut lengthwise

12 lemon verbena leaves

6 egg yolks

1/2 cup sugar

1/2 cup crème fraîche

In a saucepan set over medium-low heat, scald the milk with the vanilla bean. Add the lemon verbena leaves, cover, and then set aside to steep. In a separate bowl, whisk together the egg yolks and sugar until thickened and light yellow. Pour some of the warm milk over the egg mixture, whisking vigorously all the while. Whisk the tempered yolks into the remaining milk in the saucepan and cook over medium-low heat, stirring constantly with a silicone spatula or a wooden spoon until the mixture thickens enough to coat the back of the spatula or spoon. Strain the custard through a fine-mesh sieve into a mixing bowl and whisk in the crème fraîche. Cover and refrigerate. When the custard is cold, freeze in an ice cream machine according to manufacturer's directions and put aside in an airtight container in the freezer until ready to serve.

BACK TO BORDEAUX

129

ELSA'S CHOCOLATE CAKE WITH GANACHE

Le Gâteau au Chocolat d'Elsa avec Ganache

This recipe for flourless chocolate cake or soufflé cake belongs to our daughter Elsa. She's an excellent baker and cook—I trained her myself since she was a girl, finishing her education over the two years she worked with me in the kitchen at Chez Panisse. Elsa blames her sweet tooth on Denise's side of the family, particularly on her grandfather, André Lurton. He adores chocolate and will eat anything sweet. I've never seen him too full to finish his dessert even after a six-course meal. Her paternal grandmother, my mother, was an excellent cook but never a dessert, person, preferring a glass of wine and cheese to finish her meal. When Elsa was a girl she spent almost every weekend baking with her sister, Maud. They baked cakes, tarts, cookies, and whatever else they could dream up—in the process making a remarkably thorough mess of the kitchen. The results were mostly edible and much was exceptionally delicious. Before long, Elsa was a talented baker with an even more pronounced lust for sweets. Serve this cake on its own or with a little crème fraîche or very lightly sweetened whipped cream. —JEAN-PIERRE

Serves 8 to 10

9 1/2 ounces dark chocolate, chopped

1 1/2 cups butter

9 egg yolks

1 cup sugar

5 egg whites

Salt

About 1 1/4 cup Chocolate Ganache (recipe follows)

Preheat the oven to 325°F. Butter and flour a 9-inch round springform or regular cake pan, shaking out any excess flour.

Combine the chocolate and butter in a double boiler set over medium heat. If you don't have a double boiler, use a bowl set over a pot of boiling water (the bowl should not touch the boiling water beneath it). Whisk together the egg yolks and sugar in a mixing bowl until thickened and lighter in color. Whisk the melted chocolate into the egg mixture. In a separate bowl, whisk the egg whites with a pinch of salt until fluffy and stiff enough to hold soft peaks. Fold the whites into the chocolate mixture in three parts until there are no visible streaks of white.

Pour the batter into the prepared pan and bake for 20 to 30 minutes. Let the cake cool for 10 to 15 minutes before inverting onto a wire rack.

When the cake is thoroughly cool, use a very sharp serrated knife to cut the cake into three even layers. Carefully place the bottom layer of the cake on a cake stand or plate and spread with one-quarter of the chocolate ganache. Place the second layer of the cake on top and repeat the process. Place the third layer of the cake on top and spread the remaining chocolate ganache over the top and sides of the cake. Set the cake to cool for 2 hours at room temperature. Dust with confectioners' sugar before serving.

—continued—

CHOCOLATE GANACHE
Ganache au Chocolat

Our friend Thierry Lallet has a shop and a chocolate workshop in Bordeaux; it's not open to the public, but we take our tour guests for a fairly incredible hour immersed in the world of chocolate. He buys his cocoa beans from a range of sources around the globe, some of which have supplied his chocolate-making family for decades. As we stand in his workshop above the store, we are surrounded by workers covering cherries with fondant and cooking various fillings on the big gas stove that will become the centers of his chocolates. He explains, as we taste, about percentages of cocoa solids and how they affect the acidity, sweetness, and mouth feel of the chocolate; about the art of proper tempering (he has a special machine that maintains the chocolate at the perfect temperature); and how his fine, intricate chocolates are made, each one by hand. At the end of the visit we descend to the shop and taste Thierry's creations. Among the many treats I can't leave the shop without, I always buy some plain chocolate to make our desserts at home. —DENISE

Serves 8 to 10

1 cup heavy cream

5 ounces dark (70 percent) chocolate, chopped

Gently heat the cream over medium-low heat until very hot but not boiling. Remove the pot from the burner and add the chocolate. Allow the cream and chocolate to sit for 10 minutes or so, then stir until smooth. Store tightly sealed in the refrigerator for up to a month and reheat very gently to use on ice cream or to glaze cakes and fill cookies.

PEYRAUT HAZELNUT CAKE
Gâteau aux Noisettes de Peyraut

When we acquired our house in the Southwest of France, I planted hazelnut trees to create a nice tight hedge around the house for privacy. I was also hoping to grow my own truffles. My first mission was more successful than my second—at least thus far. The trees have grown up large and bushy, creating a beautiful natural hedge. I'm still waiting for the magic of my second idea to develop. Until then, I console myself with an abundance of hazelnuts in the fall. I spend days collecting and storing the sweet, flavorful nuts to eat over the winter and through the summer until the next crop is ready. (A very sweet family of red squirrels lives in my woods, and I leave nuts for them as well.) When I return to France after a winter in California, I'm greeted by cartons and cartons of the hazelnuts collected the previous fall. At this point it isn't long until the next crop arrives so I try and use them in as many ways as I can dream up. I warm them up in the oven, and then sprinkle them with a little salt and a drizzle of olive oil to serve with our aperitifs. I often make a *praline*, which I then fold into ice cream. But my favorite use for theses hazelnuts is this classic *gateau aux noisettes*. It is light and extremely nutty but not too sweet. I like a slice for breakfast with a big milky coffee or as an after-dinner sweet. —JEAN-PIERRE

Serves 6

4 eggs, separated

1/2 cup sugar

1 teaspoon pure vanilla extract

1 cup hazelnuts, finely ground

1/2 cup almond flour or blanched almonds, finely ground

1/3 cup plus 2 tablespoons all-purpose flour

Salt

1/4 cup butter, melted and cooled

Preheat the oven to 350°F. Butter and flour a 9-inch round cake pan.

Whisk together the egg yolks, sugar, vanilla, ground hazelnuts, almond flour, and flour.

In a separate bowl or in the bowl of a stand mixer with the whisk attachment, beat the egg whites into stiff peaks with pinch of salt and gently fold them into the nut-sugar mixture. Mix in the butter and pour the batter into the prepared pan.

Bake for 20 to 25 minutes, until a toothpick inserted into the center of the cake comes out clean, and the cake has slightly pulled away from the edge of the pan.

Serve at room temperature with whipped or poured heavy cream.

FIG TART
Tarte aux Figues

The massive fig tree on our property in France produces hundreds of figs each year. Year after year, I watch the fig tree bloom, the fruit form, and then ripen. When I can smell the sweet, earthiness of the figs, I begin to dream of new ways to put this subtle, lovely fruit to work in the kitchen. I have improvised every possible use for a fig. I make jam, put them on flat bread, eat them raw with prosciutto, and cook with duck. I have even tried drying them in my cellar for Denise, who loves dried figs. By the time I've done it all, and the figs are at their peak of juicy, sweet ripeness, I make my fig tart. Its simplicity brings out the flavor of the figs. There's not much sugar here, and no cream—it's all about the fruit. —JEAN-PIERRE

Serves 6 to 8

1/2 cup almond flour or very finely ground blanched almonds

7 tablespoons sugar

3 tablespoons butter

25 Mission figs, trimmed

1/4 cup water

Sweet Tart Dough (recipe follows)

Preheat the oven to 400°F. In a bowl, use a fork to work together the almond flour, 3 tablespoons of the sugar, and butter to make a paste. Set aside.

Cut 5 of the figs into quarters and combine with the water and remaining 4 tablespoons of sugar in a small saucepan set over low heat. Cover, stirring occasionally, until the fruit breaks down into a chunky glaze, 10 to 15 minutes.

Roll the dough into a rough 1/2-inch thick circle and place on a baking sheet (don't worry about making a perfect circle). Spread the almond paste over the tart dough, covering as much of the surface as possible. Keep the dough cool.

Cut the remaining 20 figs in quarters. Leaving a 11/2-inch border, arrange fig quarters in a tightly packed circle around the circumference of the dough, and then create a smaller circle within the circle, overlapping the fig quarters. Fold the dough border over the figs and bake for 25 to 30 minutes, until the figs are beginning to color and the crust is a deep, golden brown. Remove from the oven and use a brush to spread the fig glaze over the cooked fruit. Serve hot or at room temperature.

—continued—

SWEET TART DOUGH
Pâte Sucrée

When you make tart dough at home, make a double batch and freeze the extra tightly sealed in plastic wrap. This dough can be used for simple, buttery cookies or for any tart, including a tarte tatin. Today, of course, we have access to decent store-bought dough, and that certainly saves time but it will never replace your own homemade dough. —JEAN-PIERRE

Makes pastry for one 9-inch round tart

1/2 cup butter, very cold and cut into small pieces

1/3 cup sugar

1/4 teaspoon salt

1 teaspoon vanilla extract

1 egg yolk

1 1/4 cups all-purpose flour

In a food processor with the blade attachment, work the butter, sugar, and salt together until the butter is the size of a garden pea. Add the vanilla and egg yolk and then, little but little, the flour. Pulse until all the ingredients are incorporated without overworking; the dough should be loose and crumbly. Place a large sheet of plastic wrap on your work surface, dump the dough onto the plastic wrap and enclose it to form a tight ball. Press the ball down to bring the dough together and form it into a disc (this is much easier to do while the dough is wrapped in plastic). Refrigerate for at least 4 hours, or overnight, before using, allowing the dough to warm up for 15 or 20 minutes before rolling it out.

Mini-Recipes Around the Duck

LA CUISINE DU CANARD GRAS

Duck in Southwestern France is as integral to the region as beef is to Texas or crayfish to New Orleans. That means it's so central to the local culture and heritage that if you fail to grasp its meaning, you're missing more than just a key ingredient or set of recipes: You're missing out on what makes the people in the region who they are and how they got that way. This is a corn-growing region filled with small farms. There are no large cash crops here and little mechanization. It's a fairly poor area, where people live close to the land. Growing animals for food is a crucial part of these farmers' lives because it's really the only way to add protein to a diet based almost exclusively on vegetables, potatoes, and bread.

Every rural property dweller in Gascony has long kept ducks, along with a few geese. Ducks can be consumed head to tail—or feet. (Traditionally, even the feathers are reserved and used as filler for featherbeds or pillows.) Waste is antithetical to *paysan* culture, and the duck is very much grounded in that culture; the preparations that follow demonstrate how to use every part of the bird. When the time comes for the annual *cuisine du canard gras*, a three-day celebratory work party with neighbors and friends, the birds are killed and the preservation, and immediate consumption of the various parts, begins. —JEAN-PIERRE

FOIE GRAS

To begin, cut the bird's throat and then hang it to bleed for a couple of hours. Then pluck and clean the bird, reserving most of the organs for use in forcemeat or pâté.

When you cut open a duck to clean it, you hope the liver will be enlarged—a *foie gras*—by all the heavy feeding, but some are and some aren't. Every time I gut a duck, I feel like I'm scratching the coating off my lottery ticket: Will the liver be blond and engorged or just a regular, deep crimson liver? Of course, the liver is delicious all the same.

The livers must rest overnight or, ideally, for twenty-four hours to chill and set. To clean the liver, remove all the blood vessels. Season with salt and pepper and marinate by just covering in either sweet wine or Armagnac. Pack the liver in a clean glass jar, cover tightly with a lid and rubber seal, and sterilize by submerging in boiling water for $1^1/_2$ hours. The wine and alcohol is absorbed into the liver during this process. It can then be kept several years in the pantry before being opened for a special occasion. You can also cook it for 20 to 30 minutes, this is called mi-cuit. It will keep for several months refrigerated.

After you've taken care of the liver, the rest of the bird can be cut up. Save the feet and head and any bones for soup, reserving the tongue separately (it's a delicacy in the South of France). The tongues are either put on skewers and grilled or used in soups. The neck is set aside to make *cou farçi*.

DUCK FOIE GRAS TERRINE
WITH SAUTERNES
Terrine de Foie Gras au Sauternes

I would take great pleasure in writing a book about foie gras. I could extol its astonishing versatility in the kitchen, the subtle and not so subtle differences between duck and goose foie gras, and many other pleasures of this extraordinary ingredient. The flavor and texture of foie gras is one of the great privileges of an excellent table.

Sadly, the practice of force-feeding geese and ducks necessary to producing the distinctive, engorged liver is now under great scrutiny, particularly in the United States. Of course, ducks and geese have been raised this way and treasured for their livers for hundreds of years. I suspect a visit to the duck farm of my good friend Sylvie in Gascony (*la ferme blanche*) would enlighten all but the harshest critic. She raises her birds with great affection and care, just as she has for decades. And yes, in the end they are food for the table, not unlike any animal raised for slaughter.

This recipe is a classic French preparation. I think you'll find it relatively simple to make. The most difficult part may be finding a fresh liver. Once prepared, this classic recipe can be put to use in many ways.

For a birthday, Christmas, or very special guests, you might serve this foie gras with a glass of the highly respected Barsac or Sauternes white wines from Château Climens or Château Yquem. That combination of the velvet fattiness of the rich foie gras with the gently sweet, powerfully fragrant wine is not to be missed. —JEAN-PIERRE

Serves 6 to 10

1 fattened duck liver, about 1¹/4 pounds

Black pepper

2 teaspoons salt

¹/4 cup Sauternes or another Bordeaux sweet wine

1 teaspoon Cognac

Take the liver out of the refrigerator 1 hour before using it. Carefully separate the two lobes and remove blood vessels and skin without damaging the liver. You will have one small and one large lobe and possibly a few smaller pieces.

Place the clean liver on a small platter or tray, season with pepper and half of each the salt, wine, and Cognac. Turn the liver over and repeat on the other side, using the remaining half of the ingredients. Cover with plastic wrap and place in the refrigerator to marinate overnight.

Take the liver out of the refrigerator to temper for 1 hour before starting the second step. Preheat the oven to 200°F. Place the large lobe in a terrine (8 by 4 by 3 inches deep) first, then the small broken pieces, and finally the small lobe. Pour over any remaining juices from the tray and press with your fingers. Place a deep pan for a bain-marie in the oven and pour in enough water to come halfway up the side of the

—continued—

terrine. Cover the terrine with its lid and place it in the bain-marie. Bake for 40 to 45 minutes, until the internal temperature reaches 120°F.

Remove the terrine from the water bath and set it on the counter to cool for 15 minutes. Prepare a piece of thin wood or cardboard wrapped in tin foil that will fit in the terrine flat on top of the liver. Lay the foil-covered piece over the liver and invert the terrine, holding back the solids while pouring off the fat into a separate container. Discard the juices. Leaving the improvised foil cover in place, pressing it down very gently into place against the liver before placing a 1-pound can on top of it. Set aside with the weight on top for 20 minutes before removing the weight and the foil cover. Pour the reserved fat back into the terrine, cover with the regular lid and wrap the whole, lid and all, tightly in plastic wrap. Refrigerate for at least 3 days and for up to 10 days before serving.

Unmold the finished terrine by dipping the whole container, still tightly sealed in plastic wrap, in hot water. Release the terrine to a clean cutting surface and slice using a hot knife. Serve with toasted country bread as a hors d'oeuvre or with a lightly dressed green salad as a first course.

The terrine will keep for up to 10 days unopened, but once you have started to use it, finish it within a few days.

DUCK FAT
Graisse de Canard

To render all the fat you can from the skin and carcass of the duck, cut the fat into little cubes and simmer with a little water over very low heat for 2 to 3 hours, taking care not to burn it. The fat should be clear and fragrant without any burnt smell. Properly drained of all residual liquid, the pure fat will keep for months in the refrigerator, where you can use it in cassoulet (page 35) or duck confit (below), or simply as an excellent, flavorful fat in place of butter or oil in many recipes.

DUCK CONFIT
Confit de Canard

Season the legs with coarse salt, dried thyme, and bay leaves and refrigerate or place in a cool cellar for 24 hours. The wings and the neck can be added to the legs and used for a *garbure* (cabbage and bean soup) or added to a cassoulet. Pat the legs dry and cook in rendered duck fat at a steady, easy simmer over low heat for about 3 hours, or until tender. Pack in a terra-cotta or glass jar covered with the cooking fat (or use them to make rillettes; see below). The confit will last several months in your refrigerator.

DUCK RILLETTES
Rillettes de Canard

While the duck legs are cooked (see above) and still warm, remove the skin and shred the meat. Place the shredded meat in mixing bowl and combine it with a little duck fat, a lot of black pepper, and some pounded garlic. Pack the meat in canning jars and cover with additional duck fat. Preserved in this way, the meat will keep for several months refrigerated. It is irresistible served on warm toast as an hors d'oeuvre or with a green salad for lunch.

DUCK BREAST
Magret de Canard

Duck breasts are generally grilled over vine cuttings and cooked rare to medium-rare, like steak. Before freezers became common in south-western France, the breasts would be preserved *en confit*, but I find the meat dry prepared this way. Today, locals freeze the fresh breasts and use them as needed. They can also be made into prosciutto (see below).

In Gascony, the tenders from the breast are not used so casually; they are left attached to the breastbone and grilled whole in the fireplace. This is delicious, but extremely messy to eat because silverware is useless: the only way to get the tender meat off the bone is with your hands. Two or three carcasses are served to each person, which makes an interesting spectacle—greasy chins and fingers all around. It's certainly not something to serve to your most elegant guests!

DUCK BREAST PROSCIUTTO
Prosciutto Magret de Canard

Turning a duck breast into prosciutto is quite simple. Generously coat the breast with a mixture of coarse salt, thyme, and bay leaf. Then wrap and refrigerate. After 2 days of salt-curing in the refrigerator, brush off any excess salt, pat dry, and wrap each breast in a cheesecloth. Tie the ends tightly with string and hang vertically for a week in a cool and dry place. Turn and hang from the other end for another week. Once the meat is quite firm, remove the cheesecloth and rub the breast with ground black pepper. Wrap in plastic film and keep in refrigerator; it will keep for at least 2 weeks. Slice and serve like prosciutto.

STUFFED NECK
Cou Farçi

Cou farçi makes excellent use of a part of the duck that is too often just thrown unceremoniously into the stockpot. It's also a good way to make use of all the tiny scraps that are produced in the course of the *cuisine du canard gras*. Peel the skin off the neck and fill the hollow center with pieces of duck meat, liver, and fat. Tie up the smaller end of the neck skin with string, and sew up the other end with a needle and thread. Poach in simmering water or, better yet, in duck fat. To preserve, use the same method as for the duck liver.

recipes

DENISE IN THE KITCHEN

Denise dans la Cuisine

As the first-born of seven, I started helping my mother in the kitchen early on. There was a great deal to do with so many children, workers, and guests to feed. Shopping at the farmers' market in Branne on Thursdays was a rare treat. Most of the time, we ate what we grew in the vegetable garden and gathered from the fruit trees planted in the vineyards. Chickens, pigeons, ducks, geese, and pigs were slaughtered for meat and preserved. Eggs from our chickens and milk from our cow kept us well fed most months. Nobody had a freezer in those days. We preserved food for winter in glass jars and stored what we could in the damp cool air of the root cellar—cabbage, cauliflower, leeks, onions, and apples. Meats were preserved by smoking, curing, jarring, or as sausage or confit. There was no shortage of meat and poultry, and on occasion we had fresh game at the table when my father hunted.

Our family made nine at the table, but more often than not my father invited assistants, clients, visiting winemakers, *négotiants*, and neighbors to join us. My family was known for its table. The abundant food was expertly prepared under my mother's careful eye, and the reputation of the house didn't suffer from my father's generosity in pouring his wines. I learned early on to help my resourceful, hardworking mother in the kitchen. Although she grew used to it over the years, my father never gave her much more than a couple of hours' notice that she'd need to set six extra places for the family's one o'clock lunch. I don't quite know how she did it so gracefully.

I can best describe the food I grew up on as classic French country food—what today might be thought of by many Americans as bistro food. We always had three or four courses, beginning with a salad, maybe shredded carrots with oil and vinegar dressing, followed by a main course, perhaps roasted chicken or rabbit in mustard sauce with the vegetables that were then in season—peas in June, green beans in July, tomatoes and eggplant in August, wild mushrooms in September, cauliflower in October. We'd then have a plate of cheese and finish with a simple dessert—crème anglaise with berries from the garden, rice pudding, polenta pudding, or simply sliced fresh fruit eaten with a dollop of crème fraîche. Cakes were kept for Sunday lunch and for special occasions, as were elaborate sauces and complicated dishes. My mother always had confit of duck, pâté, and rillettes on hand to supplement for the frequent appearance of extra guests.

My mother was intelligent, elegant, and beautiful; she was also a peasant woman—a *paysanne*—a term that doesn't have quite the same connotation in French as it does in English. Let's just say she knew country food—how to put very limited ingredients together to make an excellent meal. Nothing was wasted, and we wanted for nothing. I'd like to think I cook as my mother cooked, using what I have in the garden or in the refrigerator, whether it's leftover cheeses for a soufflé or ratatouille from a mix of vegetables in summer.

I rarely read recipes. Instead, I follow the instincts and knowledge I've gained over the years. Aside from my training at my mother's side in the kitchen at Château Bonnet, thirty-five years living with Jean-Pierre has taught me a great deal about food—how could it not? But my cooking remains my own. I never aspire to cook the way Jean-Pierre cooks or to attempt the elaborate meals he puts together. I enjoy cooking for him, my way. The last thing most chefs want to do when they finish in the kitchen is come home and stand behind their own stove. Jean-Pierre is no exception. Ever since our first date, I've cooked for him on his days off and late at night, when he used to arrive home from Chez Panisse, hungry after a night filled with a great deal of tasting but very little real eating.

Many people are afraid to cook for chefs. This is silly, I promise you. Most chefs are not critical of the meal when someone is generous enough to cook for them. To be cooked for, at home or at someone else's house, to sit at the table eating, drinking, and talking, is what matters. My advice: keep the food fresh, simple, and honest.

The older I get, the simpler I like my food and the more sensual I find the experience of sitting down to the table. Now more than ever, I am fed by the color of a squash soup, the red of a tomato from the garden, the green of gently cooked leeks. From the linen to the glasses to the plates, I don't feel satisfied by food if there is no aesthetic pleasure in the eating of it. I take small portions and rarely help myself twice. It's not that I don't like food—I love food of all kinds—but I don't need to consume large quantities to appreciate its pleasures. On the contrary, a small plate with just a few bites is more appealing than vast quantities of rich food heaped on my plate.

Despite my love of familiar, simple foods, when we travel I am the one who searches for new tastes and special restaurants to explore. Jean-Pierre is often less interested than I am in adventures involving food, but once he's there he's never sorry. Recently we traveled to Tennessee where we ate grits for the first time. The corn had just been ground, and once cooked the result was like baby food in the best possible sense—nurturing, comforting, and elemental. I appreciated experiencing the novelty of this iconic food I'd never eaten before and that I was fortunate enough to try it in its purest form. The experience reminds me of other moments when I tasted something new and so perfect that it imprinted itself on my mind: the intensely concentrated misolike soup I tried from a street vendor in China; potato puree at Joël Robuchon's Jamin in Paris—one spoonful was enough, but I've never forgotten it.

Many people think that an outstanding meal must be complicated, demanding a lot of time spent in an expensive kitchen with every tool and gadget. This notion couldn't be more wrong. When you visit a peasant kitchen in France or Italy, the space is often tiny. You'll find very few pots and pans; often a quirky, older stove; just a couple of knives, their blades thin from repeated sharpening; and serving plates and dishes passed down from parents and before them from grandparents, more often than not worn and chipped but still substantial and beautiful. A great deal can be done in such a space. Our kitchen in Bordeaux is very basic. We have an excellent range, true, but there are no gadgets and very few knives, most of them old and worn with use. The refrigerator is in the next room, far from the stove and sink; cheeses and extra milk are stored there, but not much else.

Richard Olney was a truly great cook. Despite his ample girth and immense appetite, he cooked in the tiniest kitchen, mostly working out of the fireplace. Many Americans who visited him over the years were bewildered by the space and its lack of polish and sophistication. But the food was, as I like to say, beyond the beyond. Similarly, I remember years ago when I was visiting my friend David Tanis in Paris. I sat chatting and drinking a glass of wine as he effortlessly cooked a super fresh, memorably delicious meal in a minuscule kitchen—it can't have been more than nine by six! He was, as I say, cooking to the point: being careful with the space and the impeccable ingredients he had to work with at that moment. Nothing more was needed.

Cooking must be a pleasure, not a duty. When I cook out of duty, the food doesn't taste the same. It's always better to cook what you like, simply and honestly, than to cook a fancy meal to impress. It is better to make a delicious salad rather than an elaborate dish if you're not in the mood. I'm discriminating about whom I share food with because sitting down together at the table is about much more than eating. As the French say with their notorious brusqueness, why give pearls to pigs?

I hope you like the food you make using these recipes just as I hope you will make them in the spirit of generosity, as a way of sharing your resources and talents with people you care about as you slow down, sit at the table, reflect, rest, and enjoy the sensual pleasures of your meal.

—Denise

STUFFED TOMATOES WITH TUNA AND HERBS

Tomates Farçies au Thon et aux Herbes

Days when I must engage with the French bureaucracy in any form are days when I crave the simplest lunch. As you may know, the French are convinced life is unfair and ever so complicated. This is both good and bad. It has given us the AOC (*Appellation d'Origine Controllée*) system that regulates the origin, naming, processing, and final quality standards for wine and cheese, as well as chickens and oysters, among other things. This dark streak has also given us great skeptics like Michel de Montaigne. Less helpful is the French love of bureaucracy that all this skepticism seems to have spawned. When I bought cell phones for my daughters in the United States, I walked into the store, bought the phones, chose the family plan, and signed the contract. Done. When I did the same in France, the company demanded birth certificates, proof of address and residency, school certificates, and I can't remember what else. It took days, not minutes. Why? Because the French are certain someone is trying to game the system. Escaping this sort of tiresome charade is one of the reasons I love the openness and simplicity of life in the United States. My pleasure in my American-style freedom and optimism drives me to pare down my life, flout the rules, and trust everyone.

This ridiculously simple dish is my answer to the French affection for complication: flavorful, fresh, ripe tomatoes stuffed with tuna, a few herbs, and a dollop of mayonnaise. Simple as it is, it's wonderfully rewarding as a light summer meal. Feel free to use leftover raw or cooked tuna or a can of high-quality wild tuna packed in water (canned tuna in oil is too rich, at least for me, but do as you like!). With this slightly retro stuffed tomato on my plate and a glass of lightly chilled Château de Cruzeau, Pessac-Leognan white just within reach, I'm thoroughly at peace and utterly satisfied—in fact, *pas mal* doesn't begin to cover it. —DENISE

Serves 4

8 medium tomatoes, such as
    Early Girl

Salt

10 ounces canned tuna in water
    or fresh cooked tuna, flaked

4 to 6 tablespoons aïoli
    (see page 86)

1 tablespoon chopped parsley,
    plus 8 sprigs for garnish

1 teaspoon chopped tarragon

2 tablespoon chopped chives

Black pepper

1 head red leaf lettuce

Cut out the stems of the tomatoes and scoop out the top third of the flesh, leaving the skin intact. Salt the interiors of the tomatoes and set them upside down on a towel to allow some of the juices to run out.

In a mixing bowl, combine the tuna, aïoli, parsley, tarragon, chives, a pinch of salt and plenty of black pepper. Stuff each tomato with tuna, and finish by adding a leaf of parsley on top to make it pretty. Refrigerate to chill before serving atop a leaf or two of lettuce.

BRAISED RABBIT WITH MUSTARD AND ONIONS
Lapin à la Moutarde

Growing up at Bonnet I remember the butcher who came by the house faithfully once a week despite the fact that my mother almost never bought anything from him. I often wished we did—his truck was full of tempting meats, including prepared pâtés, sausages, rillettes, head cheese, blood sausages, and all the various cuts of pork, veal, horse, beef, and lamb you can imagine—and possibly some you can't. I would dream of these tastes as I sat down once again to eat the poultry and rabbits we raised on the property. Despite my yearning for variation, I grew to love this dish, made with Dijon mustard and caramelized onions. My mother taught me to make it at a young age, and it was one of the first dishes I cooked for Jean-Pierre when we began dating in Berkeley back in the seventies. He was working at Chez Panisse at the time and had nearly forgotten about this French classic, which he grew up eating as often as I did. It wasn't long before a version of it appeared on the menu at Chez Panisse. I still make it today, no longer yearning as I once did for what seemed so exotic on the butcher's truck and so out of reach. —DENISE

Serves 4 to 6

1 fresh rabbit, cut into 7 or
    8 pieces
Salt and black pepper
2 tablespoons olive oil
2 onions, sliced
6 tablespoons Dijon mustard
1 bay leaf
3 sprigs fresh thyme
2 cups dry white wine, such as
    Sauvignon Blanc
2 tablespoons chopped parsley

Season the rabbit pieces with salt and pepper. Heat the olive oil in a large skillet over medium heat. When the oil shimmers, add the rabbit and turn the pieces until they are well browned, 10 to 12 minutes. Remove the rabbit pieces, add the onions, and cook over low heat, stirring frequently, until lightly caramelized, 15 to 20 minutes. Brush both sides of the meat with mustard and add the pieces back to the pan with the onions. Add the bay leaf, thyme, wine, and enough water to just cover the rabbit. Simmer gently for 35 to 45 minutes, until the rabbit is tender and the sauce begins to thicken. Taste the sauce for seasoning and sprinkle on the parsley. To serve, bring the pot directly to the table or transfer the rabbit and sauce to a deep serving dish.

CAULIFLOWER SALAD
WITH EGGS AND ANCHOVIES
Salade de Chou-Fleur aux Anchois

When I was a girl growing up in Bordeaux, the winters were rigorous—long, cold, and dark. We ate hearty food to keep ourselves warm in the drafty, virtually uninsulated eighteenth-century château where I grew up. The food was traditional, with the same dishes reappearing often. We relied on late fall crops, with hearty vegetables that could take a little frost, like cauliflower, doing a great deal for our diet. Our chickens helped round out our diets with a reliable source of fresh eggs. This deserving salad, which I ate more often then I care to remember as a girl, makes me nostalgic for my mother's table. I make it often, thinking of her bustling presence, unfailingly to be found hard at work in the kitchen. —DENISE

Serves 4 to 6

1 head cauliflower, broken
    or cut into small florets

3 tablespoons olive oil

1 tablespoon balsamic vinegar

6 anchovy fillets, coarsely
    chopped (optional)

$1/2$ teaspoon salt

Black pepper

6 eggs, hard-boiled for
    12 minutes and peeled

1 tablespoon chopped chives

Parsley

Pinch of fleur de sel

Steam the cauliflower for 10 to 12 minutes, until just softened. In the salad bowl, whisk together the olive oil, vinegar, anchovies, salt, and pepper. Add the cauliflower and toss. Chop the eggs and add them to the salad. Sprinkle with chopped chives, parsley, and a pinch of fleur de sel.

RATATOUILLE TART

Tarte à la Ratatouille

This unassuming tart is essentially a quiche; but because it's made with fresh ratatouille, it's lighter and more colorful. I make it in the summer when the garden is producing more vegetables than we know what to do with. This tart is extraordinarily versatile—if you don't have ratatouille, you can make a tart by adding cured meat, lightly cooked sweet peppers, or caramelized onions. —DENISE

Serves 4 to 6

1 (10-inch) round tart
   (recipe follows)

1 cup ratatouille
   (recipe follows)

2 eggs, lightly beaten

1/2 cup grated Gruyère

1 teaspoon salt

Preheat the oven to 400°F. Roll a round of dough out about 1/8 inch thick and about 12 inches in diameter. Settle the dough in a tart tin, taking care to let it sit easily without stretching or pulling at it. Cool the dough right in the tin for 30 minutes to an hour before pricking the bottom of the crust with a fork to allow the steam to escape. Blindbake for 15 to 20 minutes, until the bottom is no longer doughy but the sides are not yet colored. Set aside to cool.

Thoroughly mix together the ratatouille, egg, cheese, and salt in a bowl. Pour the mixture into the cooked shell, spreading it out to cover the whole base. Return it to the oven and bake for 25 to 30 minutes, until the filling bubbles and appears to be set. Allow the tart to cool and set further for 15 to 20 minutes before serving. Do not refrigerate unless the tart will be out at room temperature for more than 2 hours. I like to bring it to the table uncut and serve it there.

Makes 3 to 4 cups

1 tablespoon salt, plus more
   if needed

2 globe eggplants, cut into
   large dice

4 tablespoons olive oil

2 onions, thinly sliced

4 cloves garlic, sliced

3 zucchini, cut into large dice

1 green or red pepper, diced

5 tomatoes, diced

6 leaves basil

Black pepper

2 sprigs thyme

RATATOUILLE

Salt the eggplant with 1/2 teaspoon of the salt and set aside for 30 minutes to 1 hour.

In a large saucepan or Dutch oven set over medium-low heat, heat 2 tablespoons of the olive oil and add the eggplant. Cook for 12 to 15 minutes, until soft and lightly browned. Transfer to a plate and set aside. Add the remaining 2 tablespoons of oil to the pan with the onions. Cook until soft and golden, 12 to 15 minutes, before adding the garlic, pepper, and zucchini. Sauté for another 10 minutes, or until the pan begins to dry out and the vegetables are sticking. Add the tomatoes last, along with the remaining 2 1/2 teaspoons of salt, a couple grinds of black pepper, basil, and thyme. Cook, covered, for 60 to 70 minutes over very low heat, stirring occasionally. The eggplant should be very soft and the tomatoes and zucchini should have rendered their juices. Taste, adding salt if needed.

TART DOUGH
Pâte Brisée

This basic dough can be used for virtually any recipe calling for pastry, including a sweet tart. Although we've included a recipe for sweet pastry, Pâte Sucrée (page 139) there are times when the added sweetness of sugar in a crust, even in a fruit tart, is not wanted. This dough is ideal for quiche, a savory tart or used in place of puff pastry for hors d'oeuvres. The egg yolk, if you choose to use it, gives the dough a richer color and a more tender texture.

Makes pastry for one 10-inch round tart

2 cups all purpose flour

1/4 teaspoon salt

3/4 cup (6 ounces) cold butter, cut into pieces

1/4 cup cold water

1 egg yolk (optional)

Combine the flour, butter, and salt in the bowl of a food processor with the blade attachment. Pulse or blend for 30 seconds or until the ingredients are barely mixed. If you're using the egg yolk, beat it into the water before adding it to the flour mixture. Process either the egg mixture or, if you're not using an egg, the water alone, for 10 to 15 seconds or until the dough forms a loose ball. Do not over mix. Divide the dough in half and wrap each one separately in plastic wrap. Press gently to form a disk and refrigerate for at least 30 minutes before rolling. The dough can be frozen for up to 3 months.

BUTTERNUT SQUASH SOUP WITH TOASTED SESAME SEEDS

Soupe de Potiron aux Graines de Sésame

Butternut squash is a winter vegetable with a rich, sweet flavor that can be transformed into a soup with very little trouble. For a richer soup, use chicken stock rather than water. Adding croutons covered with grated Comté and sliding the soup under the broiler makes a winter lunch. For a pretty touch without a great deal of fuss, sauté pumpkin seeds in olive oil with a pinch of salt and sprinkle them on top, or add a drizzle of your best olive oil before serving. —DENISE

Serves 4

1 medium butternut squash

2 tablespoons butter

1 onion, thinly sliced

Salt and black pepper

1 bay leaf

2 cups chicken stock (see
    page 24) or cold water

2 tablespoons sesame seeds,
    toasted

Crème fraîche (optional)

4 slices country bread, such as
    levain or pain complet

1 clove garlic

Preheat the oven to 400°F. Cut the squash in half, scoop out the seeds, and wrap the squash halves tightly in foil. Bake for 20 to 30 minutes, until soft.

While the squash cooks, melt the butter over medium-high heat in a large saucepan. Add the onion and sauté for 10 to 12 minutes, until soft. When the squash is done, allow it to cool for a moment before scooping out the flesh and adding it to the pot with the onion. Add a pinch of salt, a grind of black pepper, bay leaf, and stock. Set the pot over medium heat, cover, and cook for 30 minutes. Puree the hot liquid through a blender until smooth and spoon into individual bowls or a single tureen. Sprinkle the surface of the soup with sesame seeds and drizzle with crème fraîche, if you'd like. Serve the bread on the side, first toasting it and then rubbing it with the garlic clove.

SUMMER VEGETABLES STUFFED WITH PORK SAUSAGE
Petits Légumes Farcis du Jardin

This is mostly a summer dish that makes good use of all the beautiful vegetables that seem to just keep coming by midsummer. I use peppers, zucchini, small eggplants, and tomatoes. When I make it in winter, I use fingerling potatoes or onions. You can use prepared sausage bought at a good, reputable meat market, or make your own with Jean-Pierre's recipe (page 60). Chicken, pork, veal, beef, or a mixture is fine. Serve with a simple salad on the side. —DENISE

Serves 6

1 pound homemade sausage
    (see page 60) or prepared
    pork sausage

¹/₂ cup unseasoned bread
    crumbs

1 egg

1 teaspoon salt

Black pepper

4 to 6 small zucchini, halved
    lengthwise, or 3 to
    4 large tomatoes, halved,
    or 6 fingerling potatoes,
    peeled and parboiled, or
    6 small eggplant, halved,
    or 6 medium sweet onions,
    halved, or 6 small bell
    peppers, any color, halved
    and seeded

1 tablespoon olive oil

Preheat the oven to 400°F.

Combine the sausage, bread crumbs, egg, salt, and a grind of pepper in a mixing bowl.

Use a melon baller or a measuring spoon to hollow out a sizeable hole in the center of each vegetable. Fill the holes with the meat, allowing it to slightly overflow. Place the halves, stuffing side up, in a baking dish, drizzle with olive oil, and bake for 30 to 40 minutes, until the stuffing is nicely browned on top and has reached 160°F and the vegetable is cooked through. Tomatoes and zucchini are done when the sausage is browned. I like to parboil potatoes for 15 minutes or so before stuffing them to speed the oven cooking process. Eggplants should remain in the oven until very soft and thoroughly cooked. However long you cook the vegetables, be sure the meat reaches 160°F. Serve hot.

CAULIFLOWER WITH BÉCHAMEL SAUCE

Gratin de Chou-Fleur à la Sauce Béchamel

In rural France before freezers and refrigerators became commonplace, cooking was more about using what was on hand than about imagining a dish and then going out to shop for the ingredients. Cooking this way requires a great deal of creativity that's familiar to me from observing my mother in the kitchen. To this day, I enjoy the challenge of rooting around the refrigerator to see what might be left over from the last meal or trip to the market, peeking in the cabinet for stray dry goods, and walking through the garden to see what I can find to put together a meal. After years, my intuition and experience tell me what will come together successfully once I get in the kitchen. I find that improvising in this way gets my energy flowing, bringing a certain urgency and challenge to a task that can be fairly routine. No dish is ever the same when it's made up this way, which means each meal is something of a surprise. Cauliflower, as one of the last vegetables remaining in the root cellar after the summer harvest, makes frequent appearances at our table today, as it did when I was growing up. This is a simple, classic béchamel sauce to serve with this unassuming and sometimes underappreciated vegetable. In the spirit of its origins, make it with the cheese you have on hand, so long as it has a little bite to it, and serve with whatever protein you happen to have handy—even leftover chicken or beef. —DENISE

Serves 6

1 head cauliflower, trimmed
    and cut into small florets

1/2 cup whole milk

2 tablespoons butter or olive oil

1 heaping tablespoon all-
    purpose flour

Salt and black pepper

1 cup grated Gruyère or other
    sharp cheese

Place a steamer basket over water in a small pot with a lid and set over high heat. Steam the cauliflower for 10 to 12 minutes, until just tender. Drain and return to the hot pot with a cover on top to keep it warm while you make the sauce.

Scald the milk in a small saucepan and set aside. Heat the butter in a sauté pan set over medium heat. When the butter is hot, whisk in the flour and then slowly whisk in the warm milk along with a pinch of salt and plenty of black pepper. To avoid lumps, work vigorously and don't add the milk too fast. When the sauce is a nice smooth paste, remove it from the heat and stir in the grated cheese.

Put the cauliflower in a gratin dish and pour the béchamel on top. Place the dish under the broiler for 1 to 2 minutes, until the top is lightly browned. Serve hot right in the gratin dish.

ONION TART
Tarte à l'Oignon

My family lived for many years in the Jura, in eastern France. Because so many recipes from the region were mostly about all the cheese they contained, we ate a great deal of Comté, the region's best and most famous cheese. My mother had access to the very best Comté as my father was an agronomist who specialized in milk production, quality control, and sourcing. (He even helped to develop and sell the Laughing Cow cheese that was so ubiquitous in the United States during the 1970s.) This simple tart is a lighter version of the classic quiche Lorraine: The onions are blanched and the cream is replaced by milk. If you prefer a little less fat with plenty of good cheese and onions, this might be a recipe for you. Serve with lightly dressed garden lettuce. —JEAN-PIERRE

Serves 8

Tart dough (see page 157) or
    1 (10-ounce) sheet puff
    pastry

8 onions, thinly sliced

Salt

1 bay leaf

2 sprigs thyme

4 thick slices smoked bacon,
    cut into lardons

3 eggs

2 cups whole milk

4 ounces Comté cheese, grated

Black pepper

Nutmeg

Preheat the oven to 400°F. Roll out the dough and press it into a 9-inch tart form; place in the refrigerator for at least 30 minutes. Use a fork to prick holes in the bottom of the tart shell and blind bake it for 12 to 15 minutes, until lightly brown and slightly puffy. Set aside.

In plenty of boiling salted water, cook the sliced onions with the bay leaf and thyme sprigs until tender, 10 to 12 minutes. Drain and set aside to cool. Refill the pot with water and return it to the stove set over high heat. When the water boils, add the bacon lardons and blanch for 3 minutes before draining and setting aside with the onions to cool.

Mix together the eggs, milk, grated cheese, and a pinch of salt, a grind of pepper, and the tiniest pinch of nutmeg in a mixing bowl, then add the onions and lardons.

Pour the egg-onion mixture into the tart shell and bake for 30 to 40 minutes, until the edges of the tart are deep brown and the custard is fairly firm (it should reach 160°F). Remove the tart to a rack to cool for a few minutes before cutting. The tart can be served warm, at room temperature, or cold.

SWISS CHARD FRITTATA
Frittata aux Blettes

I frequently make this simple frittata or an omelet, often with vegetables from the garden, to serve alongside a green salad and cheese for the lunch that Jean-Pierre and I share each day. If you want a heartier dish, you can sauté some thinly sliced potatoes in olive oil until they're soft and then add them to the eggs as they cook with the other vegetables and herbs. A frittata is versatile, which makes it ideal for those days when there's nothing much left in the refrigerator other than eggs and a bit of cheese. Serve with a simply dressed green salad. —DENISE

Serves 6

4 eggs

1/2 cup milk

1/2 cup grated Gruyère or Comté cheese

1 teaspoon salt

Black pepper

1 bunch rainbow chard

2 tablespoons olive oil

1 onion, thinly sliced

Preheat the oven to 375°F.

In a large mixing bowl, beat together the eggs, milk, cheese, salt, and a grind of black pepper. Set aside.

Cut the stems into thin slices and blanch them along with the leaves, cut into 1-inch ribbons, in boiling water for 5 minutes. Drain immediately and squeeze with your hands when cool enough to handle.

Combine the olive oil and onion in a large (14-inch) frying pan and cook over medium heat until soft and golden, 10 to 12 minutes. Add the chard to the pan and sauté for another 6 to 8 minutes; combine the chard with the egg mixture in its bowl.

Scrape the bottom of the frying pan but do not wash it. If it's dry, add a splash of olive oil before pouring the egg-chard mixture into the sauté pan. Bake for 20 to 25 minutes, until the frittata is golden and puffy. Let it rest on the counter for 15 minutes, then run a paring knife around the edges before inverting it out onto a serving plate. Leave it bottom side up and cut into wedges as you would a pie. Serve at room temperature.

LEEK SALAD WITH MUSTARD VINAIGRETTE AND EGG

Salade de Poireaux, Sauce Moutarde

Leeks are a staple in France. All vegetable gardens have leeks planted and French farmers' markets offer beautiful, tall, firm leeks throughout the fall and winter. As common and as inexpensive as potatoes, leeks are used throughout the long French winters to make soup (the sentimental equivalent of chicken soup in America) and to complement hearty meat stews. This is a traditional preparation that shows off the subtle complexity of the leek. —DENISE

Serves 4 to 6

5 leeks

1 tablespoon Dijon mustard

1 tablespoon white wine vinegar

3 tablespoons olive oil

Salt and black pepper

3 hard-boiled egg yolks, coarsely grated

2 sprigs parsley or chives, chopped

To prepare the leeks, trim away the rough bottom on the root end and the tough dark green stalks at the top. Starting 1^1/$_2$ inches from the root end, cut the leek in half lengthwise all the way to the green tips. Turn the leek a quarter of a turn and repeat step one. (The leek will still be intact but the top will be quartered). Briefly soak the leek in a bowl of cold water, swishing it around and rubbing to remove any dirt. Finish by rinsing the leek under cold running water, taking care to flush away the hidden grit between the layers at the root end.

Set up a steamer basket over water in a pot with a tight-fitting lid and set over high heat; bring the water to a boil. Steam the leeks for 10 to 15 minutes, until tender and fully cooked. Drain and set aside to cool.

Whisk together the mustard, vinegar, olive oil, a pinch of salt, and plenty of black pepper in a small mixing bowl. Place the leeks on a platter or in a large dish and coat thoroughly with the dressing, gently working it in and over the leeks without destroying them and finish by scattering the egg yolks and parsley or chives over the top.

LEEK AND POTATO SOUP

Soupe de Poireaux et de Pommes de Terre

A good soup isn't challenging, but the details need attention. Here, to highlight the pure taste of the leeks, nothing extra is added (you probably could skip the bay leaf if you don't have a fresh one. The slow careful sweating of the leeks is important, as you don't want them to color. Covering the pan traps the flavors, but since you won't be able to see the leeks, you'll need to keep the heat moderate to prevent browning. I use butter instead of olive oil to bring a little roundness to the soup and to keep the flavors as pure as possible. The potatoes are added toward the end of the cooking process to thicken the soup and give it body, but I have made leek soups without them by doubling the amount of leeks. Feel free to try this here—the result is an intensely flavorful soup with a slightly lighter feel. —DENISE

Serves 4 to 6

2 tablespoons butter

2 onions, diced

5 large leeks, tender parts,
    cut into 1-inch rounds

1 bay leaf

4 cups cold water

Salt

2 Yellow Finn potatoes, peeled
    and sliced 1/2 inch thick

2 tablespoons crème fraîche

1 tablespoon minced chives

Melt the butter in a soup pot over medium-low heat. Add the onions, leeks, and bay leaf and cook, covered but stirring occasionally, for 12 to 15 minutes, until the leeks and onions are soft. Add the water and a pinch of salt. Turn the heat to high and bring the liquid to a boil. Add the potatoes and cook for 20 to 25 minutes, until the potatoes are tender when tested with a paring knife. Remove the bay leaf and puree the soup in a blender, working in small batches. Taste, adding more salt as needed. Serve in hot soup bowls with a little crème fraîche and with chives sprinkled on top.

wild mushrooms

ONE OF THE UNBENDING RULES OF MUSHROOMING: Never give away your spots. You may not need my help in any case—when the first rain arrives, at least in California, mushrooms (and foragers) are everywhere. You'll see that porcinis are hard to find, but easy to recognize while chanterelles and morels are both abundant and fairly simple to identify. However easy to find or abundant, it's extremely dangerous to pick and eat any wild mushroom unless you are absolutely certain of its identity. I can say this from experience: I ended up in the emergency room one evening after eating a wild mushroom. I confess this incident only because I didn't pick the mushroom that made me ill—it was served to me by a supposed expert. Beware! —JEAN-PIERRE

PORCINI OMELET
Omelette aux Cêpes

In Bordeaux in the summer and fall, we gather basket upon basket of wild mushrooms. Jean-Pierre loves walking in the woods scanning the ground for signs of mushrooms no matter what the weather. When we came to Berkeley in the seventies, we found plenty of mushrooms, mostly chanterelles, in the hills above Berkeley. At the time, few people knew anything about wild mushrooms. We had so many we wanted to share them, but even our friends were afraid of being poisoned. Now mushrooming is fashionable, with clubs, groups, and classes devoted to studying and foraging for wild mushrooms. Their popularity, combined with the fungus's ordinary whims of location, temperature, and weather, means mushrooms are harder than ever to find these days. Whenever we're fortunate enough to find plenty of wild mushrooms, especially boletus (porcinis), we make this omelet. Because eggs let the mushroom flavor really shine, this omelet is served everywhere in France during mushroom season—even in some of the best restaurants. Serve with a simple green salad on the side. —DENISE

Serves 6

1 pound porcini mushrooms (substitute chanterelles, morels, or a mix of wild mushrooms)

1 tablespoon olive oil

3 tablespoons butter

2 cloves garlic, minced

8 eggs

Salt and black pepper

2 tablespoons water

1 tablespoon chopped parsley

Trim the bottoms of the mushroom stems, separate the stems from the caps, and clean both stems and caps with a paper towel (don't rinse them as they will absorb the water). Coarsely slice the mushrooms and sauté them over medium heat in the olive oil and 1 tablespoon of the butter, along with a pinch of salt, for 8 to 10 minutes, until nicely browned. Add the garlic, stirring to combine it with the mushrooms and then remove it from the heat.

Beat the eggs in a mixing bowl with a pinch of salt, black pepper, and the water (this will make the omlelet fluffy).

Melt the remaining 2 tablespoons of butter in a sauté pan set over medium-low heat. Add the eggs and turn the heat up. Stir very fast with a spatula for 30 seconds before turning the heat down to medium-low. Add the mushrooms, spreading them evenly over the surface of the egg. Cook for another 2 or 3 minutes, roll, and flip the omelet over a warm platter. The omelet should be served right away.

CLAFOUTIS WITH GARDEN FRUITS

Clafoutis aux Fruits du Jardin

In France, we never remove the cherry stones before baking a clafoutis; they add depth and distinction to the dessert's delicate flavor. When you serve the clafoutis, just be sure to warn your guests of your method. They will savor each bite—carefully. Depending on the season, you may substitute plums, pears, peaches, nectarines, or raspberries to make this clafoutis. The only fruit I don't like to use are strawberries, which are watery and flavorless when cooked this way. —DENISE

Serves 6

1 pound fresh cherries or peaches

1 heaping tablespoon cornstarch

1/2 cup whole milk

4 eggs

1/2 cup packed dark brown sugar

1 teaspoon kirsch or pure vanilla extract

Preheat the oven to 400°F. Stem, wash, and dry the cherries but don't remove the pits. If using peaches, peel and slice thinly. Line the bottom of an oval or round ovenproof clay or ceramic baking dish (10 by 14-inches) with the fruit. Cast iron pans work well too.

Make a slurry by mixing the cornstarch and milk together. In a separate mixing bowl, beat together the eggs, brown sugar, and kirsch. When the egg mixture turns bright yellow, glossy, and smooth, slowly add the cornstarch-milk mixture to the batter.

Pour the batter on top of the fruit and bake for 30 to 40 minutes, until the top is golden and the clafoutis has pulled away from the pan. Set to cool at room temperature; do not refrigerate—it spoils the dessert's delicate flavor.

APRICOT CRISP
"Crisp" aux Abricots

When apricots are plentiful in mid- to late July, this dessert appears often at our family table. In truth, I make it all summer long and well into the fall, starting with cherries in the early summer, moving to apricots, plums, and peaches midsummer, and to raspberries and blackberries in mid-August. By fall it's appearing on the table with pears, apples, quince, or all three. Very ripe, juicy fruits like peaches and plums will make a looser crisp, but there's nothing wrong with serving this dessert in a bowl with a scoop of Lemon Verbena Ice Cream (page 128) or a dollop of whipped cream with the merest hint of vanilla to set it off. —DENISE

Serves 6

2 pounds ripe, soft apricots, pitted

1/2 cup butter, melted

1/2 cup packed brown sugar

1/2 cup all-purpose flour

1/2 cup almond flour or finely ground blanched almonds

Pinch of salt

Preheat the oven to 375°F. Place the apricots in an 8 by 10-inch clay, glass, or ceramic casserole dish. Mix together the butter and brown sugar in a mixing bowl before adding the flour, almond flour, and salt. Pour the mixture evenly over the apricots. Bake for 30 minutes, or until the top is just beginning to brown and the juices are bubbling up on the edges. Cool and serve lukewarm.

ELSA'S RASPBERRY CRUMBLE
"Crumble" aux Framboises d'Elsa

Like a crisp, crumbles can be made with a variety of fruit, depending on the season. My daughter Elsa often pairs two complementary fruits together, giving her crisp a little more complexity. She likes the classics—apple and pear, peach and raspberry, strawberry and rhubarb, plum and apricot. You can also just make this crisp, as she often does, as a way to use any fruit in danger of overripening on the counter or on the tree. It won't much matter what you put together—it will not disappoint. If you're buying your granola, look for wholesome ingredients rather than buying sugar- or corn syrup–sweetened oats with nothing more than the name to recommend them. You can, of course, easily make your own granola with whole oats, honey, nuts, seeds, coconut, flaxseeds, and a little oil. Your crisp will be all the better for it. —DENISE

Serves 4 to 6

2 pounds raspberries or other fruit (cut larger fruit into bite-size chunks)

1 to 2 tablespoons sugar (optional, depending on how sweet the fruit and granola are)

1¹/₄ cups all-purpose flour

6 tablespoons packed brown sugar

¹/₄ teaspoon salt

¹/₂ cup granola

12 tablespoons cold butter, cut into ¹/₂-inch cubes

Preheat the oven to 375°F. If the raspberries or other fruit are not quite ripe or less sweet than you'd like, toss them with a tablespoon or two of sugar and place in a glass or ceramic baking dish (8 by 10 inches). Combine the flour, brown sugar, salt, and granola in a mixing bowl, working the butter into the flour mixture with your fingers or a pastry cutter. When you're finished, the mixture should have a crumbly, not sandy, texture. Sprinkle the mixture over the raspberries, covering the fruit completely. Bake for 35 to 45 minutes, until the crumble topping is golden brown and the fruit juices are bubbling up at the edges.

ALMOND TEA CAKE WITH CANDIED ORANGE PEEL

Gâteau d'Amandes à l'Orange Confit

In France, we have tea time—not quite British high tea, but a pause in the afternoon to stop the work of the day, gather, chat or maybe gossip, drink a cup of tea, and indulge in a special pastry. Many foreigners imagine that the wine-loving French take a glass of wine in the afternoon. We do, but the *salon de thé*, which you'll find throughout France, arose to satisfy an alternative ritual. *Salons*, many of which evolved into pâtisseries, serve tea, coffee, hot chocolate, and elaborate pastries like those that made Ladurée and Dalloyau in Paris so famous. (Sadly, both of these are now so well known that it's impossible have a peaceful cup of tea unless you're prepared to stand in line with hordes of eager tourists.)

Wherever you go, the vast display of immaculate pastries, cookies, tarts, and cakes should match the decadent feel of the elaborate space. Like the classic pastries they sell, many pâtisseries date back to the eighteenth and nineteenth centuries. Part of the pleasure of going is feeling oneself in another world, or at least another century.

Living in Berkeley and raising my girls there, I kept the ritual of tea time. It was a treasured habit for us to stop in at a little bakery or café after school or, for a real treat, to indulge in high tea at the Ritz Carlton in San Francisco. Often we simply went home to prepare our own little "tea time" with hot chocolate for the girls and a bite of something sweet I'd baked that day.

These were never elaborate pastries; I'm a baker who prefers to improvise by adding stray ingredients I have on hand rather than following a precise recipe. That's how I first came up with this cake. Because Jean-Pierre doesn't waste anything (really!), we usually have a confit of orange, lemon, or grapefruit peels in the refrigerator. I cut these preserved rinds into minuscule pieces and added them to the batter along with a handful of almonds. They brought brightness and acidity while giving the cake an appealing, slightly chewy texture that's made this a beloved standard at our house. —DENISE

Serves 4

1 cup almond flour or finely ground blanched almonds

1/4 cup all-purpose flour

1/2 cup Candied Orange Peels (recipe follows), cut into 1/4-inch cubes

Salt

2 eggs, at room temperature

1/4 cup milk

4 tablespoons butter, melted

1/4 cup packed brown sugar

Preheat the oven to 350°F. Mix together the almond flour, all-purpose flour, candied orange peels, and a pinch of salt in a mixing bowl and set aside. In another bowl, beat together the eggs, milk, butter, and brown sugar. Add the flour mixture to the egg mixture and mix just until smooth; don't overwork. Pour the batter into a loaf cake pan (5 by 9 inches) and bake for 45 to 55 minutes, until a toothpick inserted in the center of the cake comes out dry.

Allow the cake to cool for 10 to 15 minutes before turning it out of the pan onto a wire rack to finish cooling. Do not refrigerate, as it dulls the cake's delicate flavors; simply wrap tightly in plastic wrap and store at room temperature. The cake lasts 3 to 4 days this way, if it doesn't get eaten first.

CANDIED ORANGE PEELS
Confit d'Orange

When I candy peels this way, I usually cook a mix of citrus—often it's whatever I have left over. In season I use our own fruit and some from friends who have a grapefruit tree in their backyard. We have some orange trees and a Meyer lemon tree. It all works beautifully together as a mix. The various, multicolored mix of peel goes into the same pot while we drink the juice that's left over. You can cook and recook the peels several times over a few days if you find them bitter. If the peels you begin with are very bitter—let's say Seville oranges or thick-skinned grapefruit—then you might start the process using less sugar and then add a bit more every day. —DENISE

Makes 40 to 50 peels, 2 cups

5 oranges or 3 grapefruits or
  6 Meyer lemons

3 cups water

2¹/₂ cups sugar

Remove the peels from the orange with a sharp knife, both the zest and the white pith. Put the peels in a pot of cold water over high heat, bring to a boil, reduce the heat, and simmer for 30 minutes. Drain and cut the peels into thin strips, about ¹/₄ inch wide. Mix together the water and 1¹/₂ cups of the sugar in a saucepan and bring to a boil over high heat. Add the peels, reduce the heat to low, and cook very gently until most of the syrup has been absorbed. Remove from the heat, cover, and let the peels rest in the syrup overnight. The following day, reheat the peels and their syrup, bringing to a simmer once again over very low heat. Cook gently for 10 to 15 minutes and drain the peels into a colander set over a bowl to catch the syrup. Let the peels dry and cool for at least 20 minutes.

Spread the remaining 1 cup of sugar on a tray lined with parchment paper and roll the peels in the sugar, turning to coat them on all sides. Set the peels on a tray or platter and leave overnight, uncovered. They are ready to be used or stored when they are completely dry. Store in an airtight container with some of the remaining sugar to prevent them from sticking together. They will keep for 2 to 3 months.

FLOATING ISLAND
Île Flottante

Americans have a tendancy to exaggerate—everything is "gorgeous," you're a "genius," you're "terribly depressed," you "adore" this and "just love" that. The French are more negative and restrained; excess of this sort can be seen as very American and somewhat vulgar. If you serve a delicious dish to a French guest, it's never *delicieux* or *magnifique*. High praise would be *pas mal* (not bad). Well, I'm going to be very American (I often am) about this classic French dessert: floating island. I adore it because it's so light after a big dinner and yet beautiful and profoundly impressive when presented in an oversize glass bowl. I love the soft, white peaks of cooked meringue floating like mini icebergs in the rich, yellow crème anglaise. If you've never made it, have no fear; I make it so often that I've developed a quick, simple method. By cooking the meringue in the same milk that's used to make the crème anglaise, the fussiest steps can be eliminated. Omit the vanilla bean if you don't plan to use the milk to make crème anglaise. Keep in mind, any trouble you take with this nearly perfect expression of French elegance is worth it. —DENISE

Serves 6

4 cups whole milk

1 vanilla bean, split lengthwise (optional)

1³/4 cups sugar

6 eggs, separated

Pinch of salt

3 cups crème anglaise (recipe follows), cool or at room temperature

1/4 cup water

In a large saucepan, gently warm the milk over medium-low heat. It should not boil. (If using a vanilla bean, add the vanilla bean before you heat the milk and leave it in the pot the whole time.)

Beat ³/4 cup of the sugar and the egg yolks in a mixing bowl until lighter yellow in color. Set aside. In a separate bowl, beat the whites with a pinch of salt until they form soft, rounded peaks that retain their shape. (Don't beat beyond this point, or they will be stiff and dry.)

When the milk is warm, take a large scoop of egg white and put it on top of the milk, then add another scoop and another, depending on the space you have on the surface of your pot; work in as many batches as necessary. The meringues should float on top of the milk without being pressed together. Gently turn them over after 3 to 4 minutes and cook for another 3 to 4 minutes; they should be just firm. (If you plan to serve them with cold crème anglaise, they should be cooked on each side for another minute until they are quite firm.) After cooking each side, scoop them out and place them on a large, cool plate or tray. (You may reserve 2 cups of the milk to make crème anglaise, page 179.)

When you're ready to serve, pour the crème anglaise into a wide bowl. You want as much space as possible to float the meringues on top. Place each meringue carefully on the surface of the crème anglaise until it looks like you have a sea of little icebergs floating on the crème anglaise.

—continued—

An hour before serving, make a dark caramel. To make the caramel set a small pot on low heat with the remaining 1 cup of sugar and the water. Cook without stirring, until the mixture becomes quite dark. Stop the cooking process by dipping the bottom of the pot in cold water before you smell burnt sugar. Drizzle the hot caramel over the islands in long streaks. The caramel looks pretty and solidifies as it hits the cold islands and crème anglaise, giving the dessert a sugary crunch.

CRÈME ANGLAISE

Crème anglaise is the base for most ice creams and for many French and American desserts, including classic Floating Island (page 177). I prefer to add less sugar to this decadent sauce than most recipes call for, so you may find my version lighter and more versatile than you expect. Served with fresh berries, stewed fruit, a crisp, or a crumble, it makes even the most rustic dessert elegant. If you are making Floating Island, use milk from that recipe and omit the vanilla here. —DENISE

Makes about 3 cups

2 cups whole milk

1 vanilla bean, split lengthwise, or 2 teaspoons pure vanilla extract

8 eggs, separated

1/2 cup sugar

In a small pot set over medium heat, scald the milk along with the vanilla bean. Set aside to steep. In a separate bowl, whisk together the yolks and sugar until mixed but not beaten. When the milk has cooled off a bit, pour a little of it into the egg mixture, whisking vigorously as you pour. Add this sugar-egg mixture to the remaining milk in the pan, whisking all the while. Cook over very low heat, mixing continually with a silicone spatula or wooden spoon until the custard thickens enough to coat the back of the spatula or spoon, 8 to 10 minutes. Strain through a fine-mesh sieve into a bowl set over ice, stirring occasionally. Serve warm or at room temperature. Refrigerate in a tightly sealed container for up to a week.

CAT'S TONGUE
Langues de Chat

These very popular French cookies are quite obviously called cat's tongue because of their thin, fine shape. I rely on them to garnish desserts that need a little something extra on the side. I particularly like their elemental good looks and the gentle crispness they add to simple desserts. From unadorned ice cream in a bowl to fresh fruit with crème anglaise, their understated neutrality is bolstered by the scent of vanilla and butter. —DENISE

Makes 25 small cookies

3 tablespoons butter, melted and cooled

7 tablespoons sugar

1 teaspoon pure vanilla extract

1/2 cup all-purpose flour

2 egg whites

Salt

Preheat the oven to 350°F.

Mix together the butter, sugar, and vanilla extract in a mixing bowl. Add the flour and mix it in without overworking.

In a separate bowl or in a stand mixer with the whisk attachment, beat the egg whites with a tiny pinch of salt until stiff peaks form. Fold the egg whites into the flour mixture until the batter is smooth.

Fill a pastry bag fitted with a flat, fairly wide tip with the batter. Pipe broad bands of batter onto a buttered or parchment covered baking sheet. They should be about the size and shape of your thumb and very thin. Bake the cookies for 8 to 10 minutes, until lightly brown around the edges. Remove them from the baking sheet after they have cooled for a minute or two and place them on a cooling rack. Once they're thoroughly cool, store the cookies in an airtight container on the counter to keep them from losing their shape and texture.

recipes

IN THE KITCHEN
AT CHEZ PANISSE

Dans la Cuisine de Chez Panisse

Looking back with the perspective and insight forty years brings, I see how much Chez Panisse shaped me. Without question, my first few years there, during the seventies, were the most formative for me. At that time, the air in the ad hoc kitchen was filled with new ideas, overgrown passion, and a fair dose of craziness. From the day I arrived I entered into a space of organized chaos. I was working with people who had no background in the restaurant business, no experience cooking, and no real goal other than to serve some sort of dinner each night. Despite this lack of purpose, skill, and organization, it had its own magic and miraculously—it worked! Once the early days passed and the restaurant gained recognition and success, the level of creativity and excitement in the kitchen was never again quite the same. The unity we shared in those years, the fun, and the crazy youthful antics, couldn't be duplicated. As I often reminded my interns, if you don't have the energy and passion for food when you're young and fresh, do something else.

In those early years, of course, the restaurant was not famous as it is today: no professional cooks, no articles in the newspaper, no celebrity. We worked twelve-hour days together, more often than not serving innovative food that pushed the boundaries of the customers'—and sometimes even our own—expectations. For me, this was the best time of my career. I already had learned the technical skills in school that I need to anchor my ambition as a chef; what was missing was creativity and my willingness to trust my own impulses. During those early years I worked to unlearn the formal kitchen rules I had been taught and to put my knowledge to use in innovative ways. As I explored the unfettered possibilities of cooking, the freedom and excitement I felt fueled the adventure. As I collapsed more and more of the rules, I discovered how much I loved cooking without limitations. Heavy sauces, classic combinatons, set methods of building a plate—all of it went out, to be replaced by a sense of food and cooking as a nearly unlimited opportunity to explore the pleasures of flavor, texture, and method.

I was very young when I became responsible for running the kitchen at Chez Panisse. It so happened that the chef left right around the time the restaurant began to get some serious notice. Suddenly a small place in Berkeley became a mecca for gourmets from all over the Bay Area and soon from all over the state and beyond. Suddenly our little experiment had become something rather more serious—something we had to keep going night after night, with the expectations we put on ourselves, and those the diners and critics put on us, growing apace.

What is the end of an era? I'm not sure. For me, looking back, those early years when the sheer fun and excitement of creating something new each night, never knowing where we were going or how it would all turn out in the end, was a powerful attraction. The stakes weren't all that high and if they were, we didn't know or care. Caught up in our little revolution, it all seemed possible. Were we cooking better then? I don't think so, but the unassuming ambiance of that kitchen and dining room can never be recreated. That innocence was part of its charm for all of us.

I often wanted to create more complicated dishes back then; maybe it was my ego, or maybe I just wanted to be challenged. In the end, though, simplicity won out, becoming the philosophy that guided everything I did in the kitchen. A simple dish is far harder to make than a complicated one, because you can't afford any mistakes—the dish has to be pure. Achieving that purity involves a certain amount of skill, but more than anything, the success relies on impeccable ingredients. To really achieve simplicity you have pass through complication and come out the other side.

In the early days, a dish started with the quest for good produce. This took time. Not much was out there back then, but as word got out that we were buying, people just started showing up at the back door offering us their backyard fruits and vegetables. One day a guy connected with a bunch of fishermen showed up, the next week it was a forager who wanted to sell us wild mushrooms. After many years of ad hoc sourcing, the constellations of small connections like this became a network of farms, ranches, and orchards.

Later, my challenge wasn't finding ingredients, qualified staff, or creating a menu, but a different set of challenges: making sure the fish for a dish was on the green list and that the catch method was sustainable; ensuring that the chicken was fed 100 percent organic feed, but also that the organic feed did not originate in China; it was double checking that the olive oil truly was local; that the beef was grass-fed and not finished with corn; and that the chocolate was fair trade. Not only did you have to be a chef—what you served had to also be politically correct down to the finest detail. In some ways, the early difficulty of finding a decent peach or a backyard chicken seems easier, and certainly more innocent.

My kitchen team was always exceptional. The selection seemed to work out naturally—if you didn't fit in on the team, you didn't survive. I never ran the kitchen like a typical top down operation as many chefs do. I never saw us as an orchestra with a maestro in command—we were a loose and rangy jazz band, each one playing his part, with just the right balance of discipline and freedom for improvisation to keep the food lively. I didn't just have to organize this ensemble, I had to be one of its members. Ultimately we worked to please the customers, just as you might work to please the tastes of your guests at a dinner party. The restaurant, its city, its staff, and its chef—me—changed and evolved, but one constant over the years was that I was inspired and pushed to work harder and be better by food critics, guests, and friends. It is and always has been a pleasure to cook for people who love to eat and for those who take the time to really taste and appreciate the meal for what it is—an attempt to attain perfection through simplicity.

—*Jean-Pierre*

A BRAISED PORK SHOULDER
WITH SAVOY CABBAGE
Épaule de Porc Braisée aux Choux

Braised meat is comfort food I never grow tired of. I like the subtle flavors the vegetables, herbs, and meat form as they come together, bubbling quietly in the oven while slowly working their magic. Here I call for straining the meat juices and the vegetables through a sieve to make a more refined sauce, but you can serve both as they are, if you prefer. For a fall or winter dinner party, this is an ideal choice if you prefer enjoying your guests to remaining chained to the stove. If you do cook ahead, very gently reheat the meat, liquid, and vegetables in a covered braising dish before delivering the giant steaming pot of aromatic meat to the center of the table. Then sit back and let your guests help themselves. —JEAN-PIERRE

Serves 6 to 8

1 (3- to 4-pound) pork shoulder, bone-in or boneless

Salt and black pepper

1 onion, cut into large chunks

2 carrots, peeled and cut into large chunks

2 tablespoons olive oil

1 head garlic, peeled

1 sprig rosemary

2 sprigs thyme

4 or 5 sage leaves

3 bay leaves

1/2 cup white wine

2 cups chicken stock (see page 24) or water

1 small savoy cabbage, cut into wedges

2 tablespoons butter, melted

Preheat the oven to 375°F. If using a pork shoulder with the bone in, trim a little bit of the fat, if necessary. If working with a boned shoulder, simply tie it with kitchen string. Season the meat generously with salt and black pepper 1 hour before cooking and set the meat out to temper at room temperature.

In a large sauté pan set over medium-high heat, cook the onion and carrots with 1 tablespoon of the olive oil for 10 to 12 minutes. Transfer them to a heavy baking dish. Add the remaining 1 tablespoon of olive oil to the same sauté pan, brown the shoulder slightly, turning it frequently to give it a little color all over. This may take 10 to 15 minutes, depending on your stove. When the meat is browned, place it fat side up on top of the carrots and onions along with the garlic, rosemary, thyme, sage, and bay. Deglaze the sauté pan with the white wine, scraping the pan to loosen the browned bits. Add the liquid to the pot with the meat along with the chicken stock. Braise, uncovered, for 45 minutes before turning the meat over to cook for another 30 minutes. Check for doneness by inserting a skewer into the meat—if it slides in easily, the meat is probably done. If you have a thermometer, the temperature should read no less than 145°F at the center. Cook the meat longer as needed and remove it from the oven when tender. Transfer the roast to a platter, skim the extra fat off the braising liquid, and then pass the liquid and vegetables through a strainer to make the sauce.

Cook the cabbage wedges in plenty of salted boiling water, drain well, and toss with the melted butter. Slice the meat and arrange it and the cabbage on a platter. To serve, reheat the sauce and pour it over.

PAN-FRIED BASS WITH LEEKS
IN CABERNET SAUCE
Bar aux Poireaux Sauce au Vin Rouge

Although I can't very well explain why, the combination of fish, leeks, and red wine is at the top of my list of favorite dishes. The sweet leeks and the robust red wine sauce might seem a strange combination with delicate fish but trust me, it works! The success of the dish depends entirely on achieving the right balance between acidity and sweetness in the sauce. —JEAN-PIERRE

Serves 4 to 6

2 tablespoons olive oil

1 onion, coarsely chopped

1 carrot, peeled and coarsely chopped

1 leek, tender parts, washed and sliced into thick rounds

1 stalk celery, sliced into chunks

1 pound fish bones from nonoily fish like cod, halibut, or sea bass

Bouquet garni: 1 leek, green part only, 6 to 8 parsley stems, 1 (4-inch) celery stalk, 2 bay leaves, 3 sprigs thyme (see page 21)

1/2 (750 ml) bottle red wine

1 tomato, diced

Water

3 shallots, finely diced

4 tablespoons butter

6 to 8 young leeks

2 pounds sea bass or striped bass fillets, cut into 4 or 6 portions

Salt and black pepper

1 tablespoon chopped chives

Heat 1 tablespoon of the olive oil in a large stockpot or Dutch oven. Add the onion, carrot, sliced leek, and celery; cover and cook over medium heat for 6 minutes. Add the fish bones and bouquet garni and cook, covered, for 5 to 6 minutes before adding half of the red wine and the tomato. Bring the liquid to a boil and then add enough water to just cover the fish bones. Simmer, uncovered, for 30 minutes.

Strain the liquid through a fine-mesh sieve, discarding the solids. Pour the strained liquid into a small saucepan and reduce by half over medium heat. In a separate sauté pan, combine the remaining red wine and shallots and cook over medium heat until the pan is nearly dry.

Combine the fish reduction and the shallot reduction and reduce until you have 4 to 6 tablespoons of sauce, 5 to 8 minutes. (You could strain it at this point but I often leave the shallots in.) Reduce the heat to low and whisk 2 tablespoons of the butter into the remaining liquid. Set aside on or near the stove and keep warm.

Trim the young leeks, cut in half lengthwise, and cut into large chunks. Cook for 5 to 8 minutes in a large pot of salted boiling water. Drain and set aside.

Season the fish with salt and pepper and sauté it in the remaining 1 tablespoon of olive oil in a nonstick pan, 4 to 5 minutes on each side. Transfer the cooked fish to a paper towel and set aside.

In a small pot, rewarm the leeks in the remaining 2 tablespoons of butter mixed with a little water. Arrange the leeks (discard the juices) in the middle of four hot plates, place the fish on top, and pour the reduced red wine sauce in a circle around it. Finish with a sprinkle of chives, black pepper, and a pinch of salt.

WARM OYSTERS IN THEIR SHELLS WITH LEEKS AND CHAMPAGNE BUTTER

Huitres Chaudes au Champagne

One of my favorite outings during the late 1960s was our family trip to the oyster farm near Marennes. My father had hired the son of an *ostréiculteur* who lived by the ocean, and after a few months, we were invited to come and taste a few oysters on the farm. The spot wasn't so special—a flat area by the mouth of the river, La Seudre, with a swamp, channels, and estuaries. It was always windy, but it smelled and tasted of the sea, with that hint of iodine and salt.

The somewhat desolate landscape contained a complex water system that mixed salt water from the ocean with the fresh river water. A dozen manmade shallow pools spotted the ground. The pools, called *claires*, were used to finish the oysters before they were sent to the market. At Marennes, they finish the oysters by placing them in the shallow pools where the oysters feed on special algae which give them their distinctive taste—of hazelnuts!—and that unmistakable green color.

Our family had many fine picnics there over the years, our time spent diving into the surprisingly warm water, coating our bodies in beautiful soft mud, fishing, and sunning ourselves on the big rocks. I can still feel the anticipation as we drove toward the sea—the car packed with children, the trunk crowded with nets, and the cooler full of Muscadet. The picnic basket was packed and the wine was chilled and ready to be swallowed down with some of the finest oysters I've ever tasted. —JEAN-PIERRE

Serves 4

2 dozen oysters, shucked, with liquid reserved and shells washed and reserved

2 leeks, all but the tough leaves, julienned

2 shallots, finely diced

1/2 cup plus 2 tablespoons Champagne or dry sparkling white wine

8 tablespoons butter, cut into small pieces

Salt

1 tablespoon chopped chives

Preheat the oven to 180°F. Refrigerate the oysters in their liquid and place the shells on a baking sheet. Cook the leeks in a pot of boiling salted water for 4 to 5 minutes, until tender. Drain and cool on a towel.

In a small pot set over medium heat, combine the shallots and 2 tablespoons champagne, cooking until the liquid is reduced to almost nothing. Over very low heat, slowly whisk pieces of butter into the nearly dry pan, one at a time. The mixture should thicken as you whisk. Thin the sauce with the remaining 1/2 cup of Champagne and taste for salt, adding little if any; the sauce should be only lightly salted (the oysters are already salty).

Place the oyster shells in the oven. In a small pot set over low heat, gently simmer the oysters in their liquid until they begin to curl up ever so slightly. Remove the shells from the oven and arrange them on a serving platter lined with rock salt. Fill each shell with a spoon of cooked leeks and a warm oyster and finish with the Champagne butter and a sprinkle of chives.

SEAFOOD SAUERKRAUT
Choucroute de Poisson et Crustacés

An alternative to authentic choucroute, this preparation makes a lighter dish, appropriate for all seasons. The combination of cabbage and fish work well, and the butter brings each component together.

It's not at all difficult to make your own sauerkraut, and the homemade is always preferable to store-bought. Take a green cabbage, slice it thinly, and in a stone crock or a large glass container, put a layer of cabbage, lots of salt, another layer of cabbage, more salt, and so on. Cover the container and leave it out at room temperature for a day or two. Once it starts to ferment, put a weight on the cabbage to keep it below the level of the liquid it's putting out, and refrigerate or keep it in a cool spot for a couple of weeks. —JEAN-PIERRE

Makes 4 to 6 sevings

2 pounds halibut or Pacific wild
    salmon fillets

Salt and black pepper

8 scallops

12 mussels

Fish and Shellfish Terrine
    (see page 206), uncooked

4 pounds sauerkraut, packed in
    brine

4 tablespoons duck fat, melted

1 onion, sliced

1 fennel bulb, trimmed and
    sliced

1 carrot, peeled and cut into
    sticks

8 to 10 juniper berries

2 cloves

2 cloves garlic, sliced

2 cups white wine or Champagne

1 cup cold water

2 bay leaves

8 ounces smoked cod
    (see page 195)

About 3/4 cup Beurre Blanc
    (see page 25)

1 tablespoon minced chives

1 tablespoon chopped chervil

Cut the halibut or salmon into four portions and season with salt and pepper. If they're still attached, remove the foot from the scallops and the beards from the mussels; scrub the mussels.

Roll the fish terrine mixture in plastic film and shape it as a large sausage. Set aside. Bring a pot of water with a steamer basket and a tight-fitting lid to a simmer over high heat. Steam the terrine for 20 to 25 minutes to cook. It should be relatively firm and warm throughout.

Preheat the oven to 350°F. Drain the sauerkraut, rinse in plenty of cold water, and squeeze to remove as much moisture as you can. Set aside.

In a large casserole with a lid, combine the duck fat and the onion, fennel, carrot, and half of the sauerkraut. Sprinkle with the juniper berries, cloves, and garlic. Add the remaining sauerkraut and pour the white wine and water over the top. Cover the casserole with parchment paper and place the lid over the parchment to seal. Bake for 30 minutes, then remove from the oven and arrange the fish fillets and shellfish on top. Bake, uncovered, for another 10 minutes. Finally, slice the fish sausage and the smoked cod and lay the slices on top. Return to the oven and reheat for 5 minutes.

To serve, spoon a portion of the sauerkraut on a platter and arrange the salmon, smoked cod, scallops, mussels, and fish sausage. Pour the beurre blanc over the top and sprinkle with chives and chervil.

SEA SCALLOP AND ENDIVE SALAD WITH MEYER LEMON SALSA

Coquilles Saint-Jacques et Endives, Vinaigrette au Citron

The magical combination of scallops, endives, and lemon works beautifully; it's as if the three ingredients were created to be eaten together. You won't stray from the brilliant flavors if you make the recipe with cooked scallops and warm Meyer lemon butter. The lemon vinaigrette can be too sharp; I use a little mustard to cut it and to give the dressing a well-rounded, almost unnoticeable heat. If you can't get the right balance or if you taste so much acidity that the sweetness of the scallops is lost, simply add a splash of sweet wine. —JEAN-PIERRE

Serves 4

1 pound sea scallops,
    feet removed

Salt

Piment d'Espelette

1 head frisée

4 small Belgian endives

Juice and zest of 1 lemon

2 tablespoons sweet white
    wine vinegar

1 tablespoon Dijon mustard
    (optional)

1/2 cup olive oil

2 small Meyer lemons

2 shallots, minced

1 tablespoon chopped parsley

1 tablespoon minced chives

Season the scallops with salt and piment d'Espelette and set aside. Trim the greener outer leaves of the frisée and then wash, rinse, and dry the remainder. Tear the leaves into small pieces. Remove and discard any brown outer leaves of the endives, then cut the endives in half lengthwise and cut again in strips.

To make the vinaigrette, combine the lemon juice and zest, white wine vinegar, mustard, and a pinch of salt in a bowl before whisking in 1/4 cup of the olive oil.

Make the salsa by slicing the Meyer lemons, peel and all, into very thin rounds. Lay the slices on the cutting surface and cut them into 1/8-inch cubes. Put the cubes in a bowl with the shallots, parsley, chives, and 2 tablespoons of the olive oil. Taste for salt.

Coat the scallops with the remaining 2 tablespoons of olive oil and cook over medium-high heat in a nonstick pan for 2 or 3 minutes on each side, until lightly brown.

Toss the frisée and endive with the vinaigrette in a mixing bowl and arrange the salad on plates. Place the scallops around the greens and drizzle the salsa over the top before serving.

SPRING GRILLED LEG OF LAMB
Gigot d'Agneau de Pré-Salé à la Ficelle

This rustic dish is ideal if you have a fireplace to cook in, a Tuscan grill, for example. When I don't have a wood-fired oven, I roast this lamb in a conventional oven. The principle of melding the juices of the lamb, the potent herbs, and the soft, starchy potatoes has delightful results however you cook it.

If you do have a fire to work over, the spinning of the lamb leg on a string is similar to spit roasting, but when the lamb leg is hung vertically the texture and flavor of the meat is improved. A whole leg of lamb is pear-shaped, which means that when hung from the foot at the narrow end, the largest, thickest portion of meat is closest to the fire. As the juices drip down the leg, the spinning distributes the juices, resulting in a juicy, evenly cooked piece of meat.

When working with a string, I soak the string in water ahead of time. Be sure to hang the string in place at the correct height before you start your fire so that when your fire is ready all you need to do is attach the leg. —JEAN-PIERRE

Serves 6

1 leg spring lamb (5 to 6 pounds)

2 tablespoons olive oil

Salt and black pepper

6 to 8 heads new garlic

2 sprigs thyme

1 pound small, new potatoes, skin on and blanched

Prepare a fire 1 hour before cooking and allow it to burn down to medium-hot coals, or turn the gas grill on to medium-high (see Grilling, pages 27–28).

Tie the leg of lamb with butcher's or heavy household string in order for it to keep its shape while cooking—and also, if possible, to hang it in the fireplace. If the leg will hang to cook, tie another piece of string between the bone and tendon of the shank, hang the leg upside down, spinning every 5 to 10 minutes. Rub the meat with the olive oil and season with salt and pepper.

Once the fire has reached the right heat, hang the leg of lamb in front of it, placing a roasting pan underneath the leg with the garlic, thyme, and potatoes. Start twisting the leg clockwise on itself and then release and let the string unwind. The lamb will spin by itself for 5 to 10 minutes. Repeat the operation until the leg is fully cooked to your taste, somewhere between 45 minutes and 1 hour.

While the leg is cooking, keep stirring the garlic and potatoes into the juices and fat of the lamb. Let the lamb leg rest for 10 minutes before carving. Serve the potatoes and garlic with the sliced lamb on top.

If you cook the leg on the grill, use a low, soft fire and baste the lamb with olive oil or as they do in Morroco with salty water to get a crispy skin. To check for doneness, use a thermometer (135°F) or insert a finger between the bone and the meat, it should be warm to the touch for medium-rare and hot for well done.

SMOKED FISH SALAD
WITH SALMON CAVIAR

Salade de Poisson Fumé au Caviar de Saumon

Smoking fish produces excellent flavor and makes an outstanding base for a first-course salad. Depending on the season, I use different salad mixes and various kinds of fish, including salmon, black cod, eel, and trout. I also vary the liquid—using verjus rather than vinegar gives the salad a subtle flavor. This makes it an ideal pairing for better wines that you may not wish to overwhelm with the marked acidity of lemon juice or vinegar. The addition of crème fraîche drizzled on top, a few croutons, and a dollop of salmon caviar make a more complex dish. You will need wood chips and a smoker (either stovetop or outdoor) to cook the cod. —JEAN-PIERRE

Serves 4

¼ cup kosher or rock salt

1 pound fillet Atlantic cod or ling cod, carefully boned

2 shallots, diced

1 tablespoon Dijon mustard

1 tablespoon white wine vinegar

Salt and black pepper

Juice of ½ lemon

½ cup olive oil

¼ cup Beaumes-de-Venise or Sauternes, or use 1 tablespoon honey dissolved in 3 tablespoons hot water

4 heads Belgian endive

1 head frisée

1 bunch watercress

2 tablespoons chopped chives

4 tablespoons salmon caviar

Salt the fish heavily and refrigerate for 1 hour. Soak a couple of large handfuls of hardwood chips in water. Build a fairly large fire and allow it to burn down to medium-hot coals, or turn your gas grill to medium (see Grilling, pages 27–28). Be sure the grate is clean and well oiled.

Remove the fish from the refrigerator, brush away any excess salt, rinse, and smoke for 35 to 45 minutes according to the instructions for your smoker. When finished smoking, the cod will be fairly firm with beads of sweat on the surface, and the flesh will be a light caramel color. Let the fish cool briefly before using a fork to flake it.

In a large bowl, whisk together the shallots, mustard, vinegar, salt, pepper, and lemon juice. Let the mixture sit for 5 minutes before adding the olive oil and correcting the acidity with the Beaumes-de-Venise. Remove and discard the coarse outer leaves of the endives. Slice the endives lengthwise (core them if they are very large) and combine with the frisée and watercress in the bowl; toss to lightly coat with vinaigrette. Arrange the salad mixture in the center of the plates with the cod on top, and finish with the salmon caviar and a sprinkle of chives.

GRILLED QUAIL WITH BRAISED
RED CABBAGE AND CHESTNUTS
Caille Grillée au Chou Rouge et Châtaignes

Pheasant or partridge can take the place of quail in this recipe—for that matter, you could use chicken or rabbit, but the flavor of the game birds with the cabbage, a classic combination, is particularly good. Red wine can be used instead of white if you're cooking a stronger-tasting bird. If it's the dead of winter, the birds can be browned briefly in oil in a frying pan on the stovetop and then added to the cabbage. Although you will not have the crispy, smoky skin of a grilled bird, the juices from the bird will make the cabbage even more succulent. —JEAN-PIERRE

Serves 4

4 quail, cleaned

Salt and black pepper

2 sprigs thyme

2 bay leaves

6 garlic cloves, sliced

1 bunch parsley stems

2 shallots, sliced

4 juniper berries, crushed

2 tablespoons olive oil

2 tablespoons duck fat

1 carrot, peeled and sliced

1 onion, sliced

1 small head red cabbage, cored
    and quartered

1/4 cup sweet white wine

1/2 cup water

2 dozen chestnuts

2 tablespoons butter

Remove any excess fat or flaps of skin from the quail and cut off the wing tips. Season with salt and black pepper. In a glass baking dish or fairly large mixing bowl, mix together the thyme, bay leaves, 4 of the garlic cloves, parsley stems, shallots, juniper berries, and olive oil. Place the birds in the marinade, turning over several times to coat them all over. Cover and refrigerate for a couple of hours.

Preheat the oven to 325°F.

Heat the duck fat in a heavy pan over medium heat and then add the carrot, onion, and the 2 remaining garlic cloves. Cook gently until just soft, 10 to 12 minutes, then add the cabbage, breaking it apart to separate the layers as you do. Season with a pinch of salt and add the white wine and water. Turn the heat to high and bring to a boil, then reduce the heat to medium and cover. Transfer to the oven and braise for 20 to 25 minutes, until the cabbage is fully cooked and tender.

Split the chestnuts with a small paring knife and blanch in plenty of boiling water for 4 to 5 minutes. Remove the pot from the heat and set aside for a few minutes, leaving the chestnuts in the water. When they're still hot but cool enough to handle, peel away the outer skins and the inside membranes. Set aside in a small bowl.

Remove the quails from the marinade and let them sit at room temperature for 30 minutes to temper before going on the grill. Build a large fire and allow it to burn down to very hot coals (see Grilling, pages 27–28). Grill over a medium-hot fire for 8 to 10 minutes on each side, until the skin is lightly browned and crispy and the thickest spot on the thigh has reached 160°F. Place the birds on a plate and set them in a warm spot to rest for 3 to 5 minutes. While the birds rest, break the chestnuts into large pieces and heat them with the butter in a small sauté pan set over medium heat. Shake the pan frequently to cook on all sides. They're done when they're very hot and lightly browned on the outside. Season with a pinch of salt. To serve, arrange the braised cabbage on a platter and place the grilled quail on top of it along with any juices from the plate. Finish by scattering the crispy chestnuts over the top.

GRILLED SCALLOP SKEWERS
WITH PANCETTA AND HERB BUTTER

*Brochettes de Coquilles Saint-Jacques Grillées
aux Lardons et Beurre d'Herbes*

Rinsing scallops with water subtracts from their flavor. If you must, drop them into a small bowl of milk or white wine for a second or two to remove any sand. This quick herb butter recipe is one of my favorites for a last-minute sauce. Lighter than a traditional beurre blanc and somewhat easier to master, it will break if not served soon after it's made. If you have one, a milk frother—that little battery-driven wand whisk for frothing milk—works nicely to lighten the sauce, incorporating the butter into the hot liquid along with a little air. —JEAN-PIERRE

Serves 4

1 pound scallops, feet removed

Salt

Piment d'Espelette

4 slices pancetta or bacon,
    cut into 1¹/₂-inch pieces

1 tablespoon olive oil

2 tablespoons white wine

¹/₄ cup water

¹/₂ cup butter, cubed

Lemon juice

¹/₄ cup mixed chopped herbs
    such as tarragon, parsley,
    chives, and chervil

Season the scallops with salt and a pinch of piment d'Espelette and thread them, alternating with the pancetta, onto four to six metal or wooden skewers (soak wooden ones in water for half an hour before using). Brush with the olive oil.

In a small saucepan set over high heat, bring the white wine and water to a boil. Turn the heat to low and vigorously whisk in the butter, one piece at a time. Turn off the heat and stir in a pinch of salt and a squeeze of lemon.

Prepare a large fire and let it burn down to medium-hot coals (see Grilling, pages 27–28). Be sure the grate is clean and well oiled. Grill the scallops for 4 to 5 minutes on each side, until lightly brown and hot all to the way to the center. Just before serving, add the chopped herbs to the butter sauce and pour over the scallop skewers.

FRESH CORN SOUP WITH ROASTED RED AND GREEN BELL PEPPERS

Soupe de Maïs aux Poivrons

This recipe is fairly basic, but if you have the chance to buy extremely fresh sweet corn, the soup tastes like a dessert. You can finish it with a dollop of crème fraîche for a richer soup or vary its look and texture by serving the peppers as a puree spooned over the surface before serving.

I can't help thinking of my mother when I make this soup. She used to say, "Corn is good for nothing but feeding livestock." The French, I need not point out, do not consider corn a worthy ingredient. Whatever I did to convince her of its virtues, she never changed her opinion on this weighty matter. I remember one dinner together in the dining room at Chez Panisse at the height of summer vegetable season. The sweet corn on her plate, picked only hours before from a local farm, could not have been sweeter or more tender. Never mind that I'd supervised its preparation and verified its quality. She was not about to eat it, as I observed with great amusement when it ended up on shoved to the side of her plate along with other vegetables she deemed unworthy of consumption. How typically French! I thought to myself. —JEAN-PIERRE

Serves 4 to 6

1 red pepper

1 green pepper

2 tablespoons butter

2 onions, diced

Freshly shaved kernels from
    6 ears white corn

Salt

4 cups cold water

Preheat the oven to 450°F. Place the peppers on a baking sheet and roast for 20 to 25 minutes, turning frequently, until the skin blackens or turns dark brown. Place the peppers in a plastic bag or other sealed container and allow them to cool before peeling away the skin. Seed and slice the peppers lengthwise into 1/4-inch strips. Set aside.

Heat 1 tablespoon of the butter in a pot set over medium heat. Add the onion and sauté for 10 to 12 minutes, until soft. Add the corn kernels, season with a pinch of salt and sauté for another 2 to 3 minutes, until the corn is coated with butter and heated through. Cover with the water, turn the heat to high, and bring to a boil. Turn down the heat and simmer gently for 6 to 10 minutes, depending on the freshness of the corn. Very fresh corn will take less time. Puree in a blender or food processor and then pass through a strainer back into the pot you began with. Set over low heat just to be sure the soup is hot before serving, add the remaining 1 tablespoon of butter, and taste for salt. Serve hot with the green and red pepper strips arranged on top.

SPRING VEGETABLE RAGOÛT
Ragoût de Légumes Printanier

This is the spring version of the vegetable ragoût. You can, of course, use any vegetable you like. In summer, zucchini, green beans, tomatoes, or corn will work. The most important part of the recipe is to add the different vegetables according to their cooking time. Working with the shape and color of the vegetables will also make your ragoût more attractive. I like to add a little bit of butter at the end as a liaison for the broth; it gives a necessary richness to the dish. If you prefer, finish the ragoût with a drizzle of good olive oil instead. —JEAN-PIERRE

Serves 4 to 6

2 tablespoons olive oil

4 small new onions, sliced

2 stalks green garlic, sliced

2 young carrots, peeled and
    cut into batons

2 young turnips, peeled and
    cut into wedges

2 stalks asparagus, peeled and
    cut into 2-inch lengths

Salt

¹/₂ cup water

4 ounces shelled English peas

8 ounces fava beans, shelled,
    blanched, and peeled

2 tablespoons butter

1 tablespoon chopped parsley

Combine the olive oil, onions, and garlic in a sauté pan set over medium heat. Cook for 5 to 7 minutes, until soft, before adding the carrots, turnips, and asparagus. Season with a pinch of salt and add the water. Cook for another 8 minutes before adding the peas. When all the vegetables are tender and more than half of the water has evaporated, add the fava beans and finish the ragoût with the butter. Taste for salt and serve right away in hot soup plates or bowls, finished with a sprinkle of parsley.

BAKED RICOTTA WITH PEA SHOOTS AND GREEN GARLIC

Ricotta Gratiné aux Pousses de Petits Pois et d'Ail Nouveau

This is the quintessential spring dish. It's simple enough to make but does require locating pea shoots and green garlic. A farmers' market is certainly your best bet. If you have a garden with garlic and peas, pick the pea shoots when they are young and tender—they have the beautiful aroma of fresh peas and are very sweet. —JEAN-PIERRE

Serves 4

8 ounces ricotta cheese

Salt and black pepper

1 teaspoon fresh thyme leaves

3 tablespoons olive oil

2 handfuls pea shoots

8 green garlic stems, thinly sliced

Preheat the oven to 400°F. Mix the ricotta with a pinch of salt, a generous grind of black pepper, thyme, and 1 tablespoon of the olive oil. Coat a small terra-cotta dish or a terrine with a teaspoon or so of the olive oil. Pack the cheese into the dish and bake for 30 to 35 minutes, until lightly brown on top.

In a sauté pan set over medium heat, combine the remaining olive oil with the pea shoots and green garlic. Sauté, stirring frequently, until the pea shoots are wilted and the garlic is tender, 10 to 12 minutes, adding a spoonful or two of water if the pan gets too dry. Season with a pinch of salt and serve by placing a scoop of the baked ricotta on each plate and surrounding it with the greens.

CREAM OF YOUNG TURNIP AND TURNIP GREENS WITH CURED HAM

Crème de Navet et Leurs Fanes,

Jambon de Bayonne

This soup is a model of purity when made from very fresh turnips from either your garden or a local farm. Where your turnips come from matters because the full and hearty taste of freshly picked turnips is the real focus of this soup. Older turnips have a much stronger flavor and aren't particularly sweet. The turnip greens balance the flavor of the bulbs, rounding out their flavor while giving the soup a beautiful pale green hue. To really taste the essence of the vegetables themselves, I now make many of my soups with water—not stock. I also tend to leave out the customary potato for a lighter, cleaner result. The smoky, salty prosciutto is there to bring out the flavor of the root and to provide a contrasting texture. —JEAN-PIERRE

Serves 4

3 bunches young turnips
    with greens

2 tablespoons olive oil

2 white onions, sliced

1 large leek, washed, white part
    sliced, green part reserved
    for bouquet garni

Salt

Bouquet garni, 1 leek, green
    part only, 6 to 8 parsley
    stems, 1 (4-inch) celery
    stalk, 2 bay leaves, 3 sprigs
    thyme (see page 21)

1 potato, peeled and cut into
    chunks (optional)

2 tablespoons butter or
    crème fraîche

2 slices prosciutto, cut
    into strips

Cut the greens off the turnips. Remove the stems from the leaves and wash the leaves. When the leaves are young, there's no need blanch them; if the leaves are very mature, blanch them for a minute, shock them, and drain them. Reserve four of the nicest leaves to line the soup bowls and coarsely chop the remainder. Peel the turnips and cut into large cubes.

Combine the olive oil, onions, and leek in a large soup pot set over medium heat. Cook for 8 to 10 minutes, stirring occasionally, until the onions and leeks are soft. Add just enough water to cover, turn the heat to high, and bring to a boil before adding the turnips, salt, bouquet garni, and potato. Add more water if needed. Cook for 10 minutes before adding the chopped turnip greens. Cook for another 5 minutes before transferring the mixture to a food processor. Process until smooth and strain only if necessary. Reheat briefly as you stir in the butter or crème fraîche and a pinch of salt. Taste, and adjust the seasoning before serving by placing the reserved blanched greens in warmed soup bowls and pouring the soup over top of them. To finish, sprinkle the julienne of prosciutto on top.

FISH AND SHELLFISH TERRINE
Terrine de Fruits de Mer

This is a base for a fish mousse. You can fold in anything, making it as exotic or quotidian as you like—lobster claws and tails, smoked trout, and even diced cooked vegetables, such as fennel, carrots, or celery. Passing the mousse through a sieve can be frustrating, and it takes time, but the result will be smoother and much more pleasing. Serve the terrine hot with a lobster sauce or cold with a saffron mayonnaise or lemon vinaigrette. —JEAN-PIERRE

Serves 4

1 pound sole or halibut fillets, diced into 1/2-inch cubes

8 ounces scallops, cut into 1/2-inch cubes

1 egg

1/2 cup heavy cream

Salt

Cayenne pepper

2 tablespoons chopped fresh herbs such as chives, chervil, and tarragon

Pulse the fish and scallops in a food processor until the mixture is almost a puree but still has a little texture. Scrape down the sides of the bowl with a spatula before adding the egg. Pulse for another 30 seconds before adding the cream, a pinch of salt, and the tiniest pinch of cayenne. Pulse briefly just until mixed, then force the mousse through a fine-mesh sieve into a bowl set over ice. Mix in the herbs, cover tightly, and refrigerate for 30 minutes.

Preheat the oven to 375°F. To cook the terrine, set up a bain-marie in the oven by pouring hot water into a baking dish to a depth of 1 to 2 inches. To correct the seasoning before cooking the whole terrine, put a spoonful of the raw mixture in a buttered ramekin and place the ramekin in the simmering bain-marie for 8 to 10 minutes, until just firm. Allow to cool slightly before tasting. Adjust the seasoning as necessary before generously buttering a full-size terrine (about 8 by 4 inches and 3 inches deep). Fill the terrine, smoothing the surface with a rubber spatula before placing it in the bain-marie. Bake for 20 to 25 minutes. Check for doneness with a wooden skewer inserted into the center of the terrine. If the skewer comes out clean, the terrine is done. The mousse should be set but still soft to the touch. Allow the terrine to cool for 10 minutes or so before unmolding by running a paring knife around the edge and then inverting the terrine onto a platter. Covered tightly in the refrigerator, the terrine will keep for 2 to 3 days.

CHOCOLATE SOUFFLÉ
Soufflé au Chocolat

Denise loves this recipe. She is a huge chocolate lover but not a fan of desserts because they are often too rich and sweet for her taste. She appreciates the appearance of this soufflé because it's very chocolaty yet extremely light and fluffy. I usually serve it with a raspberry coulis, which cuts through the dark chocolate while giving it a bright, refreshing appeal. —JEAN-PIERRE

Serves 4

1 tablespoons butter

8 ounces high-quality dark chocolate, chopped

1/4 cup plus 4 teaspoons sugar

3 tablespoons milk

2 egg yolks

3 eggs whites

Salt

Confectioners' sugar

Preheat the oven to 350°F. Butter and sugar a 2 quart soufflé dish (about 7 inches round and 4 inches high), shaking off any excess sugar. In a double boiler, melt the chocolate and then whisk in the 1/2 cup of the sugar and the milk. Let the mixture cool before beating in the egg yolks.

Beat the egg white with the remaining 4 teaspoons of the sugar and a pinch of salt until soft peaks form. Fold the egg white into the chocolate mixture. Bake the soufflé for about 20 minutes, or until the soufflé rises above the rim of the baking dish and a skewer inserted into the center comes out clean. Dust with confectioners' sugar and serve immediately.

Wine

LE VIN

As the firstborn of seven children in the Lurton family, I witnessed many births. Each time my father heard the news that my mother had safely delivered at the hospital in Bordeaux, he set out to the vast wine cellar where he aged both the wines he made and those he acquired. Confronting the racks, he would choose an old, treasured bottle and carry it back to the kitchen. Once in the kitchen, he carefully decanted the wine, pouring very slowly so as not to disturb the sediment settled at the bottom of the bottle from the unclouded wine on top. You might expect he would then bring this lovely, decanted wine to my mother, who had heroically survived another long labor. No. He delivered the sediment to the hospital, offering the rather unpleasant sludge to her as a restorative potion. She didn't seem to mind.

I'm told that each time she took it willingly. I guess she drank it because the lees are reputed to be rich in minerals and excellent for restoring the blood. I suspect she also drank it to indoctrinate each child into the life of the vineyard through this sacred winemaker's ritual—as if the very blood of her children as she fed them with her own milk for the first time would be infused with the concentrated essence of the best wine my father had to offer and all that it represented.

Whether his mother was offered the lees at his birth or not, my father seems to have been born with wine in his blood. In any case, he has made a life of it and little else. From a young age, few things have mattered to him beyond land, soil, weather, vines, cultivation, harvest, production, aging—anything that affects the grapes and the ultimate quality of the wines he makes. Knowing this about him, you can better understand that opening a treasured bottle of wine from his cellar was not simply a generous gesture—it's was his way of offering the essence of himself.

⁓

The Lurton family—my family—has been making wine since 1880. My great-grandfather Léonce Récapet purchased Château Bonnet in 1897 after the vineyards were destroyed by phylloxera. Virtually all the European vineyards were destroyed by this pest and had to be replanted on resistant American rootstock. The vineyards decimated and the future of French wine uncertain, it was an opportune but risky time to buy property at a bargain.

My resourceful great-grandfather slowly bought many properties around Bonnet in the Entre-Deux-Mers, a wine appellation not far from St. Emilion, famous for producing white, red, and rosés. Brave and adventurous in his will to expand, he ventured as far as the Médoc, which at that time was considered quite a distance from Bonnet. There he bought Brane Cantenac, which was already classified as a second growth in the Bordeaux Classification. He also had the foresight to acquire half of Château Margaux, a prestigious property classified as a first growth.

Even though he owned these respected vineyards and the châteaux that went with them, he was a relatively humble, hardworking farmer. Despite his vast holdings he would have been the first to agree that he was a peasant in the sense that, like a peasant, his life work was tending the land and contending with the vagaries of nature. The weather was everything for him, as it was for any farmer, particularly when the quality of a single crop each year determines that year's success. Nature set the outcome of a bountiful crop or one annihilated in one day by hail or frost.

I was raised with the greatest respect for the power and importance of nature. Not a meal passed when my father wasn't complaining about the weather—future, past, or present. It was always too cold, too hot, too rainy, too dry, too windy. If it wasn't the weather, it was the vines—they were not flowering properly, the clusters were small or unevenly distributed, the grapes were slow to ripen, the flavor of the grapes was off. Like most people who depend on the land, he was rarely satisfied with nature's whimsy.

My grandmother, Denise Récapet, inherited the estate when her father, Léonce, died. She and her husband, François Lurton, took over the vineyards; she bore four children, and my father, as the firstborn, inherited Château Bonnet. He then went on to buy seven additional properties. In the course of this ambitious expansion, he was instrumental in improving properties in the northern portion of the Graves. He was convinced that the area's wines deserved to be distinguished from those of the southern Graves with an appellation of its own, and in 1987 his effort paid off with the creation of a new *Appellation Controllé* as Pessac-Léognan.

Not only is my father an outstanding winemaker, he's a savvy businessman who has survived some very difficult times, all the while taking advantage of the availability of land, and the attached noble houses, when any came up for sale. At Château Bonnet, he survived difficult times—particularly in the wake of World War II when the vineyards were still recovering from neglect and damage, and grapes weren't selling—by rotating crops, cultivating clover, and designing a machine to dry it into pellets for animal feed, growing feed corn for animals, and, at some point, making a go of raising cattle. All the while he made some wine, and very slowly the vineyards returned to normal as Bordeaux regained its markets, mostly in France and England. Finally, in the seventies, his winemaking became profitable. As the American market expanded and the region's reputation for outstanding wine grew, land values soared as vineyards in the region became highly profitable. The days of hay, clover, and cattle were over.

Bordeaux today is a wealthy wine-producing region defined by vineyards that stretch in every direction, interrupted only by stone farmhouses and incredibly beautiful eighteenth-century châteaux, many of them restored to their former glory. Foreign investors and aspiring winemakers have sought land in Bordeaux in the past decade, and slowly the older generations are disappearing as improvement and modernization makes its way into the closed, highly traditional society. Innovations affecting soil, vines, cultivation, harvest, and vinification have had mixed results. The wine made today is more consistent in quality and often excellent—possibly better than ever. In some cases though, modernization has been poorly managed, stripping the wine of its distinctive character and leaving it with a sterile, almost generic quality.

&

At Château Bonnet when I was growing up, my father entertained *négociants*, journalists, and other winemakers regularly. He poured new and old wines from his cellar, and talked a great deal about them at the table. I would have had to try hard not to learn about wine; as it was, I loved wine and greedily took it all in. When my siblings and I were very young, we were not allowed to taste wine—or at least we weren't encouraged to do so. After our ninth or tenth birthday that all changed. We then had no choice but to join in the family business—we tasted, discussed the properties of a wide range of wines, and helped in the vineyard and cellars when we could.

At first I didn't like the taste of wine—or perhaps I simply didn't like the taste of the alcohol in the wine. Slowly, it grew on me. Learning about wine and acquiring opinions about it was a duty as well as a privilege in the Lurton family. I learned early that participation in this culture at the table, in the vineyard, and in the cellar was the surest way to belong. Like anyone who grows up learning a trade, I knew more about wine than I realized when I arrived in Berkeley in the late seventies. At the time most people in the United States had fairly limited knowledge of wine. Aside from a handful of wine aficionados with incredible (mostly French) cellars, Americans didn't drink much wine and if they did it tended to be sweet. Remember Lambrusco? This was the climate I entered when I began buying wine for Prima in Walnut Creek, just outside of San Francisco. I was in my late twenties and excited to be given the opportunity in an industry that was then, as now, dominated by men.

It was a good time to enter the business, as it began changing and expanding at an unbelievable pace. In those innocent years, owning a vineyard in California was a relatively humble pursuit for those willing to work hard and quite literally get their hands dirty. It was agricultural work just as it had been in France for so many years; it definitely didn't have the glamour to be an attractive hobby for those looking for a place to play at winemaking. Finding my way into the industry in California was easy. There wasn't nearly the interest there is today in the wine, and producers were happy to speak with someone who could talk knowledgeably about it. They were even more open to someone like me, given my family credentials as the daughter of a respected Bordeaux producer. Those were exciting years for me. I knew quite a bit about the wines of Bordeaux, but much of California, as well as the other wine-producing regions of France including Burgundy, Alsace, Champagne, Loire, and the Rhone were new to me. I was eager to learn.

As you probably know, the only way to really learn about wine—whether you're a beginner or an expert—is to taste, taste, and taste some more. I certainly sampled an incredible quantity of wine during that period. I didn't limit myself to France and California; I tasted at cellars in Spain, Italy, Portugal, Germany, Australia, Chile, and Argentina. I covered a great deal of ground and got to know most of the decent wines produced at the time, a feat that would be impossible today, as there are now at least ten times as many producers making palatable wine as there were then.

My work as a buyer brought me attention and a favorable reputation in the industry. Word of my expertise in the United States eventually reached my father. With limited opportunities for selling his wines in the United States, he asked me to represent the family's wines. We formed a company and called it Grand Domaine de Bordeaux. I was the boss—well, my father was probably still the boss, but I ran the company. My job was to develop a market for the Lurton family wines by locating distributors and publicizing the family's various brands. By that time, my father owned seven properties and produced nearly four million bottles of wine each year. The French market was saturated and to get the prices he wanted, he needed to tap the American market; that's precisely what I did for him. I worked tirelessly—traveling across the country, teaching, holding tastings, and working the media to gain a reputation and expand the market for the Lurton brand. Those were heady, frantic, memorable years for me.

—Denise

The Wines of Bordeaux

The Bordeaux region is the largest wine producing region in France and one of the largest in the world as measured by total sales. There aren't many places that can compete with Bordeaux's heritage as a wine-producing region, which reaches back to the second century CE, when the Romans occupied the land. Vestiges of the stone villas and wine cellars from that period remain to this day, reminders of just how long the people of the region have pressed grapes for juice to ferment into wine.

Blessed by fine gravel soil heavy in limestone, with well-drained hillsides and temperate weather, Bordeaux boasts the terrain and the climate to grow healthy grapes characterized by their complexity—the *terroir* that makes Bordeaux wines distinctive, including the region's proximity to the ocean and the effect of the tidal Dordogne and Garonne rivers. The varieties are truly remarkable. There are the inexpensive wines from Entre-Deux-Mers and smaller appellations like Côtes de Bordeaux, Côtes de Castillon, Côtes de Bourg, and Blaye. There are midrange wines produced throughout the region, and then there are the wines most closely identified with Bordeaux, including Saint-Émilion, Médoc, and Graves. These fine, extremely elegant wines produced by extraordinarily talented, dedicated winemakers on special *terroirs* are expensive and age beautifully. Finally, there are the sweet wines of Sauternes and Barsac, with their satellites producing less expensive wines. The region's great range and diversity is one of its charms.

Reds

For centuries the best red wines from Bordeaux served as the benchmark for judging the quality of red wine from around the world.

For years, Bordeaux reds held a virtual monopoly on the highest end of the international wine market. In those days, serious wine collectors wouldn't think twice about filling their cellars with classified-growth Bordeaux. Things have changed: Many countries now produce outstanding wines. Still, no other region can copy Bordeaux's particular *terroir* or its lengthy pedigree.

Most of the more expensive Bordeaux reds are rich wines with some tannins and aging potential, although red wine in the region is always made from one, two, or all of the following varieties: Cabernet Sauvignon, Cabernet Franc, Merlot, and Petit Verdot. In their youth, richer red wines can be difficult to appreciate; they need time in the bottle to develop their complexity and soften—in short, to become great. In this fast world, Bordeaux reds can have a difficult time finding their place. They are for people who appreciate the effects of age and recognize the value of waiting for these wines to grow into themselves. Many young sommeliers these days don't much like Bordeaux red. They are used to bigger wines, full of fruit and high in alcohol because they're produced in warm-weather areas. These wines cater to a particular taste and, in most cases, show well young. A Bordeaux will never be this sort of wine, nor will it aspire to be. The Bordeaux climate does not allow the grapes to reach the super maturity found in other parts of the world. Lots of sugar in the grape yields more alcohol and overwhelming fruit, which does happen on rare occasion to vintages in Bordeaux. Most Bordeaux wines, however, remain delicate, subtle, and complex, with some gentle tannins (depending on the age) and a balanced acidity.

Whites

When you think of Bordeaux, white wine is not the first thing that comes to mind. But Bordeaux produces a large quantity of white wine in a range of styles. There are light, easy to drink wines from Entre-Deux-Mers, an appellation named for its place between the Garonne and the Dordogne rivers. These tidal rivers carry the waters of the Atlantic deep inland, hence the name in French, which translates to "between two seas." These wines are made of Sauvignon Blanc, Sémillon, and Muscadelle (a rare grape found almost exclusively in Bordeaux). They are very light wines with only 12 to 12.5 pecent alcohol. They are as easy to drink as an aperitif, as they are to pair with raw oysters, or fish.

Some of the most elaborate white wines in Bordeaux come from the Pessac-Léognan appellation. This area was called Graves for centuries, as it is characterized by the alluvial flow of the Garonne River. The vines are planted in deep beds of gravel, giving a special flinty taste to the wines while providing excellent drainage. The soil is extremely poor. Looking at it, it's hard to believe that anything can grow in it. Nothing much does grow there except grapevines and pine trees, both of which seem to thrive from the harsh struggle required to grow there. Thirty years ago, these beautiful terroirs were under threat by the expansion of Bordeaux—the acreage where a vine might grow in such an unusual terroir was being sold to build condominiums.

This area in the northern part of Graves has proved to produce very delicate and elegant white wines with excellent aging potential. My father, André Lurton, was instrumental in both protecting the area and in bringing it to prominence as a producer of outstanding whites. He spent a great deal of his own money to hire geologists and other experts to prove to the government that the special soil deserved protection. After years of fighting, in 1987 he managed to have the area protected by law through its own appellation, Pessac-Léognan.

Pessac-Léognan today produces mostly red and a little bit of highly respected white wine from Sauvignon Blanc and Sémillon grapes. These wines are rich, flinty, and delicate. They can age for fifty years or more but more often than not they're opened too young, before they've fully developed their potential.

Of course, the most famous white wine in Bordeaux are the sweet wines of Sauternes and Barsac. This part of the Bordeaux region, south of Graves, is also planted on deep, gravelly, poor soils. The microclimate there allows the development of botrytis, a fungus that attacks the grape, puncturing the skin and leading to evaporation and withering of the fruit. At harvest time, which is usually later than in the rest of Bordeaux, the effects of this fungus (often referred to as "noble rot") is highly sought after.

This area produces the most respected and delicate sweet wines in the world, including the revered Château d'Yquem. These wines have an incredible aging potential—as much as a hundred years. When properly aged, their bouquet is extremely complex and floral; drunk young, they can be too sweet. Praised as the "nectar of the gods," these sumptuous wines fetch high prices because they are produced in such minuscule quantities. It's often said that a vine in Bordeaux produces a bottle of wine and a vine in Sauternes and Barsac produces a glass of wine.

Rosés

Bordeaux has never been known for its rosés. In fact, until quite recently rosé in France was only produced in Provence. Rosé also didn't have much of a reputation—it was seen as inexpensive wine to be quaffed in the heat of summer. Just in the last ten years, the popularity of rosé has taken off, and fine rosé is now produced everywhere in the world, including Bordeaux. Some of these are very lovely, unassuming wines, made to be drunk young and fresh with light meals, on picnics, or as aperitifs.

Rosé is made from red grapes using a couple of different methods. The red grapes can be pressed right after sitting on their skins for twenty-four to thirty hours, depending on the maturity of the grapes. It is, of course, the skins that give the color to the juice, producing a pink juice that is then fermented. The end result is a rosé that is made like a white but with red grapes.

Most of the Bordeaux rosés are made another way. When the red grapes are brought to the cellar, ready for fermentation, a *saignée* is made: some of the juice is taken away from the vat before fermentation. This reduces the quantity of must in contact with the skins to make deeper, more concentrated red wine. This *saignée* is a pink juice that is fermented separately in its own vat or in barrels, producing more refined rosé. The color of the wine varies; some are very light while others have a deep pink-orange tint. The grapes may be Cabernet Sauvignon, Cabernet Franc, or Merlot, or a blend of the three. Some winemakers make their rosé more complex by aging it in oak barrels. Most Bordeaux rosés are a way to make a better red by reducing the must. They also bring fast and easy cash flow to the business because they are released soon after they are produced, whereas red wine is aged in barrels for months and only released two years or more after harvest.

Wine and Food

When I married Jean-Pierre and he became part of the family, he was already an accomplished chef. From the beginning, he was asked to cook for special occasions. Despite my father's respect for the excellent food he knew Jean-Pierre would prepare, he made it clear early on that, at his table, the wine came first. In a wine family, it is the wine that is given top priority: The chef is presented with the wines and designs the menu around them, doing his best to set them off to their best advantage. In many houses—and certainly in Jean-Pierre's own mind—the food comes first. The wine is naturally chosen to bring out the best qualities in the food.

The reversal was humbling, but Jean-Pierre took it in excellent humor, despite some early stumbles when his magnificent food stole the show, distracting from the attention my father wanted directed at his old, special wines. It's been an education all around. When Jean-Pierre cooks today, we strike a balance between the food and the wine, aiming to let the two work together as much as possible without necessarily showcasing one or the other. Wine and food are best shared with a focus on the totality of pleasures the table offers—not just food and wine, but conversation, friendship, and knowledge of all kinds. Flexibility, including surprising combinations of food, wine, people, and places, leads to unexpected results.

There are no firm rules when it comes pairing wine and food. Personal preference is the most essential factor and not one that should be overlooked for the sake of propriety based on abstract rules. If you mostly enjoy red wine, then drink red wine. Explore lighter and heavier reds, wines with more and less alcohol, older wines and wines made to be drunk young and fresh: Just because you prefer red wine doesn't mean there aren't choices to make. The same goes for white wine, which varies greatly from heavy and sweet to bitingly acidic to soft and rich. Although you might be fairly hard pressed to find a white wine that will really complement a rare steak or lamb, you can certainly find an excellent white wine for most foods, if that's what you prefer to drink.

Regional Food, Regional Wine

Traditionally, white wines are served with fish, lighter meats such as pork, poultry, and eggs, while reds go with cheese, red meats, and some game. But it doesn't always work this way. To my mind it's more useful to think about regional wine accompanied by traditional dishes of the region. Take Alsatian Gewürztraminer. It goes beautifully with a classic Alsatian dish, quiche: The richness cuts the taste of the egg yolk. Similarly, no other wine would fit as well as an Alsatian Gewürztraminer or Riesling with choucroute, another dish famous in the region, because its sweetness stands up to the potent fermented cabbage and sausage. In Bordeaux, where red wines dominate, the gastronomy is based on duck, lamb, and steaks. Unsurprisingly, the typical Bordeaux red goes very well with these heavier meats. And white wines from the Loire Valley, including Vouvray, Sancerre, or Pouilly, perfectly complement the famous fresh Loire goat cheeses, such as Sainte-Maure.

Wine with Cheese

Most cheeses are overwhelmed by big red wines, as much as the wine is thrown off by the cheese. As counterintuitive as it might seem, fresh milk cheeses are best with a Sauvignon Blanc rather than a potent Cabernet. Then again, a Cabernet or another fairly dense red is excellent with older, hard cheese, such as sheep's milk Pyrenees and aged Gouda from Denmark. Surprisingly, an aged Comté from the Jura or a redolent Époisses from Burgundy will be best complemented by a sweet wine, whereas a red wine paired with these two cheeses would show neither the wine nor the cheese to advantage. In Bordeaux, where the top sweet wines of the world are produced at places like Château d'Yquem in Sauternes and Climens in Barsac, these wines are served with cheeses after the main course and can be continued on into the dessert course.

Wine with Fish and Shellfish

When one thinks of fish, one does not think of red wine, but fish like monkfish and eel are excellent with a red wine sauce and a light red wine to complement the dish at the table. Conversely, fresh oysters will be overwhelmed by a rich white, but a light white wine like an Entre-Deux-Mers will protect the delicacy of the sea in the oyster without distracting the palate from the subtle essence of the mollusk. Sweet white from Bordeaux can provide a balance in particularly acidic dishes, such as sea scallops with Meyer lemon salsa (page 191), skate poached in vinegar (page 83), or monkfish with spicy tomato sauce (page 56). When a dish is heavier, with lots of cream and butter, it is better served with a rich white wine, like a Chardonnay or a rich Sauvignon Blanc. I'm thinking of grilled scallops with herb butter (page 198), poached halibut with hollandaise sauce (page 54), and baked mussels with saffron and cream (page 53). A light Pinot Noir could go well with a fish dish like grilled eel skewers with pancetta (page 117).

Wine with Poultry and Game Birds

Sweet wines can be served during a meal to accompany a chicken cooked with a touch of vinegar or with a chicken salad if it's more rich than salty. (Sweet wines don't show as well with salty foods.) Sauvignon Blanc can have herbaceous notes that go well with bell peppers or a strong taste like cauliflower with eggs and anchovies; it is also good with egg dishes like quiche and frittatas because the acidity in the wine cuts the richness flavor of the egg yolk.

Wine with Vegetables and Salads

If one eats only vegetables, the choice of wine depends more than ever on preference. For example, a light red as well as a rich white wine can go well with a tian, or a ratatouille, or a cauliflower salad.

Salads with highly acidic dressing are tricky when it comes to wine. If you're serious about drinking wine with a salad or another dish dominated by vinegar, it's best to moderate the strength of the acidity in the dressing as much as possible. You can do this by using better, lower acid vinegars; by using a little less vinegar or just a squeeze of lemon juice; or by substituting verjus for the vinegar in your dressing (see page 20).

Wine with Meat, Confit, and Braised Meats

With rustic dishes like confit, rich meat sauces, and grilled meat, red is the preference. The strength of the meat will be matched by the richness of a Cabernet, Merlot, Syrah, or Zinfandel. I'm thinking of dishes like grilled duck breast with cassis (page 103), *entrecôte bordelaise* (page 107), and leg of lamb in the fireplace (page 193). The big red wines produced in California can carry enough alcohol to complement these rustic dishes. A Pinot Noir could be good also, but only if it is rich and round—a light Pinot Noir will not stand up to the strength of the meat and meat sauces but is often excellent with pork.

recipes

APERITIFS AND TOASTS

Aperitifs et Canapés

The French *aperitif* doesn't exactly translate into English. In French the word refers to the sacred part of the day that begins around six or six-thirty and extends until dinner is served, around eight or eight-thirty, as well as to the drinks consumed during this hour—usually white wine or rosé, Champagne, or a splash of crème de cassis mixed with Champagne (a Kir Royale), or perhaps a glass of Pernod, Lillet, or homemade liqueur, mixed or not. The ritual of the aperitif closely resembles the American cocktail hour, with a few key differences; for example, "aperitif," in the sense of a drink, doesn't translate to "cocktail," of course, since American cocktails are mixed drinks made with hard liquor. But in either case, the ritual marks the end of the day and the beginning of the evening as we gather, shedding whatever work and worries have kept us occupied and separated. Gratefully we let the day fall away in the company of friends and family, drink in hand to aid the transition.

In French cities and towns the ritual of the aperitif is practiced in cafés where friends meet, often stopping on the way home at the same café at the same hour each day for years on end. In the country, Jean-Pierre and I observe it with the same near-religious consistency—we would never move to the table for a meal without pausing first for an *aperitif*. Sometimes it's marked by nothing more than opening a bottle of wine, setting out two glasses, and sharing a few olives as dinner cooks. If we're having guests, the toasts and other small snacks we put out mark the beginning of the menu for the evening. Because we eat late in France, this drinking and light snacking can go on for hours.

At Peyraut, where we spend our summers, the end of the day is the time when neighbors and family stop by uninvited to have a drink, chat, gossip, and catch up. Anyone who knows us can be certain of a welcome at this hour; we will be glad of the company and eager to share a glass of wine or Jean-Pierre's homemade walnut, orange, or raspberry liqueur (see page 241 and page 242). In France there's no implied obligation to extend the invitation to dinner when friends drop by for a drink; but in the United States, it feels a little impolite not to at least offer dinner to a guest if we're sharing a drink at this hour.

After so many years in the United States I'm still negotiating the differences between the French and American rituals—one, the venerable "cocktail hour" with its hard liquor, mixed drinks, beer, red or white wine, and cheese. In France, you would be looked at quite strangely if you offered cheese and crackers before the meal—or if you drank red wine or beer before the meal. Perhaps in this, as in other matters, Americans are simply more flexible. Perhaps at least some of the differences can be written up to history. The French, after all, never endured Prohibition, a period in American history conducive to the quiet consumption of the boozy gin cocktail, washed down in hushed tones in a darkened speakeasy. Our drinking was never forced underground, and to this day the French aperitif remains lighter, more open, less apologetic than either the American cocktail or the hour that's named for it. In France, there are few bars—only cafés where the light and mood have little in common with the dimly lit mysteries of the classic American bar.

I doubt I need to point out that the French are not abstemious. Far from it. If anything, we've defined luxury and overindulgence for centuries. It's simply that the "hard stuff" often emerges later, after the meal in the form of Cognac, Armagnac, or port. Mostly we simply drink our wine, and plenty of it, over the course of the evening—or even over the course of the day. A glass of wine or even two with the midday meal is natural and civilized. In France, wine is not lumped in with all kinds of other alcohol, as it is in the United States. Rather, wine is seen as food, and drinking it with lunch or dinner, or for several hours as an aperitif, is not a sign of indulgence or excess. It's simply a glass of wine—an unmistakable marker of French culture.

Although nuts are rarely served for the aperitif, olives, sliced salami, pâté, radishes, brandade, and tapenade are common. When we have guests, the aperitif menu takes more care and planning; the food offered will be prepared in advance to complement the dinner to follow. Gougères, fish or rabbit rillettes, and marinated sardines or fava beans on toasts are a few of the hors d'oeuvres you'll find here. Jean-Pierre might serve a *pissaladière* for the aperitif, but not if there's a course on the dinner menu that has any sort of a crust, be it a meat pie or a fruit tart. If we serve pâté or another potted appetizer containing liver, we offer it when we don't have foie gras on the menu. Even olive tapenade would not appear if there were olives in the first or main courses. In short, we are careful that the planning of the menu begins not with the first course, but with the food offered during the hour or two before we sit down. It's all of a piece.

—Denise

respecting time

IN FRANCE, it's most impolite to arrive on time. The first few times I invited guests for dinner in the United States, I think I was still in the shower when they knocked at the door. In France, guests are at least fifteen minutes late—granting the hosts an extra half an hour is simply more polite from the perspective of the French host. It has taken me some time to get used to American ideas on this point. I'm sure I thought my guests were incredibly rude at first. I've learned—and now I school my French friends and relatives that many Americans will think them rude for arriving more than ten minutes late. *Vive la difference!* **—DENISE**

DENISE'S OLIVE TAPENADE

La Tapenade Façon Denise

Store-bought tapenade is nothing like this homemade version. I make it often, keeping a jar on hand to smear on toast for a last minute aperitif, as a simple sauce with poultry, and to add to salad dressing. Depending on how fat and juicy your olives are, you may not need much oil at all, so add it slowly. The tapenade, of course, does not need salt, as the olives are already quite salty. —DENISE

Makes about 2 1/2 cups

3 cups black niçoise or Greek
olives, not pitted

4 anchovy fillets, canned in
olive oil, coarsely chopped

3 tablespoons almond flour or
very finely ground blanched
almonds

1 clove garlic, sliced

1/4 to 1/2 cup olive oil

Pit the olives and put them in the bowl of a food processor along with the anchovies, almond flour, garlic, and 1/4 cup of the olive oil. Pulse until smooth and spreadable; if the mixture is too stiff, slowly add up to another 1/4 cup of olive oil. Store the tapenade in a jar in the refrigerator, where it will it keep for several weeks.

picnics

JEAN-PIERRE AND I ADORE PICNICS. The pleasures of eating and drinking in a entirely new setting, a place chosen for some natural beauty—perhaps a stream, a distant view, a forest canopy, or a meadow—are always worth taking the trouble of preparing and packing a complete meal for. The beauty of a picnic is that once you're out in the wild, your work is done. Without a kitchen handy, your only job is to unpack and enjoy the outdoors. Something about the unfamiliar gives picnics their elemental appeal. Perhaps eating while sitting on the ground in a new spot is all it takes to bring a fresh taste to food and drink. I use a cotton tablecloth to spread on the ground (or picnic table if there is one). We always bring real silverware, never plastic, and more often than not we use sturdy china or wooden boards rather than paper plates to serve the food. As much as rustic charm is at the core of a picnic, taking the indoors outdoors gives the experience its particular appeal. —DENISE

MARINATED SARDINES
Sardines Marinées

This recipe works best with oilier fish—not just sardines but mackerel and anchovies—but I've also tried it with halibut and ling cod with excellent results. The simplicity of chilled raw marinated fish served with a bright sauce is an ideal appetizer or a canapé for the summer months. If you prefer, in winter, serve the fish hot on a slice of toasted bread by putting the fully marinated fillets in a hot oven just long enough to warm them without actually cooking them. —JEAN-PIERRE

Serves 4 to 6

12 sardines, scaled and filleted
Salt
1 small lemon, thinly sliced
2 shallots, thinly sliced
1 tablespoon coriander seeds
1 tablespoon fennel seeds
1 small bunch parsley stems
3 sprigs thyme
1 bay leaf
3 tablespoons olive oil
¼ cup white wine
1 tablespoon chopped chervil
1 tablespoon chopped parsley
1 tablespoon chopped chives
Black pepper or piment
   d'Espelette

Arrange the fish fillets in a dish and season with salt. Cover with plastic wrap and refrigerate for 2 to 3 hours. Remove from the refrigerator, rinse well, and then pat dry with a towel. Put the fillets back in the dish and add the lemon, shallots, coriander, fennel seeds, parsley stems, thyme, bay leaf, olive oil, and white wine. Cover, refrigerate, and marinate for 12 hours, or overnight.

To serve, strain the marinade, put the sardines on a platter, and cover with the strained marinade. (For a more informal dish, you can serve this dish without staining the marinade.) Finally, sprinkle the fish with the chervil, parsley, chives, and pepper.

SALT COD BRANDADE
Brandade de Morue

This popular dish from the Atlantic Coast is one of Denise's favorite appetizers—never mind the toast we usually serve with it: Given the chance she laps it up with a spoon (she claims this is really the only proper way to eat it). Brandade makes regular appearances on the hors d'oeuvre table both at Peyraut and in Healdsburg when we gather for an aperitif before dinner. If you can't find salt cod, buy fresh Atlantic cod and cover it with salt for a few days. The potato to fish ratio is important to balance the saltiness of the dish. Do not salt the water when you cook the fish or the potatoes. The real brandade calls for cream, but I usually use either milk or a mix of cream and milk for a lighter, more flavorful result. If you find your brandade too salty despite all that soaking, add a drop or two of lemon juice. It works wonders. Serve the brandade in a bowl with toasted bread lightly smeared with raw garlic or with plain, crispy toast rounds. —JEAN-PIERRE

Serves 4 to 6

1 pound salt cod

2 cups water

1/2 cup milk

2 bay leaves

1 sprig thyme

1 tablespoon peppercorns

2 potatoes, peeled

1/2 cup half-and-half

1/2 cup olive oil

5 cloves garlic

Cayenne pepper

Salt, if needed

Lemon juice, if needed

Soak the cod in cold water 1 to 2 days in advance, changing the water twice a day, keeping the fish in the refrigerator during the soaking period.

In a medium saucepan set over high heat, combine the water, milk, bay leaves, thyme, and peppercorns; bring to a simmer. Rinse the cod one last time, discard the water, add the cod to the pan, and simmer the fish for 8 to 10 minutes. Boil the potatoes in plenty of water using a separate pot set over high heat. Cook for 15 to 20 minutes, until soft. Drain well and set aside to dry, then mash roughly with a fork.

Heat the half-and-half with the oil in a small saucepan set over medium heat. Set aside. In a mortar and pestle, pound the garlic cloves into a paste. (If you don't have a mortar and pestle, mince until very fine and then mash with a fork.)

Remove the fish and drain, discarding the cooking liquid. When the fish is cool enough to handle, break up the fish, flaking it as you discard any skin or bones. Combine the fish, mashed potato, and garlic paste in the bowl of a stand mixer (or a regular mixing bowl if you're using a hand mixer). Using the paddle attachment with the mixer set on low, slowly add the half-and-half mixture, mixing until smooth. Taste the brandade, adding a pinch of cayenne pepper and salt, if needed. If it's too salty, add a few drops of lemon juice.

WILD KING SALMON RILLETTES
Rillettes de Saumon

At Chez Panisse, one of the pleasures of the weekend was the addition of hors d'oeuvre and an aperitif to the regular five-course menu. Since everyone on the team of five chefs already had their tasks set for the night, I took charge of creating the extra course. Because the usual produce, fish, and meat deliveries for the day often didn't account for the extra course, I had the fun of ransacking the walk-in for inspiration—and the ingredients to make it. Often we had plenty of lightly salted end pieces of fish left over from service the night before. Depending on the fish, I could quickly and easily create fish rillettes, fish tartare, deep-fried fish accra (similar to beignet), fish mousse, brandade, and more. In the spirit of making do with what's fresh and available, black cod or even sardines will work nicely if king salmon is out of season. Either is preferable to farmed Atlantic salmon. Serve with grilled bread as an aperitif or as a first course with lightly dressed greens. —JEAN-PIERRE

Serves 4 to 6

1 pound fillet wild king salmon
 or coho salmon

Salt

4 ounces smoked salmon,
 finely diced

1 large shallot, finely diced

2 tablespoons olive oil

3 tablespoons butter, softened

2 tablespoons plain yogurt

1 tablespoon chopped chives

1 tablespoon chopped chervil

1 tablespoon chopped parsley

Juice of 1/2 lemon

Black pepper

Set up a steamer basket in a pot with a lid. Season the salmon with salt and steam for 6 to 8 minutes, until the fish is medium-rare. It should still be translucent in the center. Transfer the fish to a mixing bowl and set aside to cool for 5 to 10 minutes before flaking into pieces with a fork. Add the smoked salmon to the steamed salmon, along with the olive oil, butter, yogurt, chives, chervil, parsley, and half of the lemon juice. Blend until smooth, but do not overmix. You should still have chunky pieces. Taste and season with salt and pepper, adding additional lemon juice as needed. Pack the mixture in a terrine and set to rest and cool in the refrigerator for 2 hours to firm up.

FRESH YELLOWFIN TUNA TARTARE WITH HERBS ON TOASTS

Canapés de Rilletes de Thon

The fish is eaten raw in this recipe or very lightly "cooked" in the acid of the lemon juice. Whenever you're eating raw fish you must be certain, of course, that it is extremely fresh and generally in excellent condition. I like to make this recipe with tuna, but other fish such as salmon, halibut, or even mackerel work as well. Capers or small-diced hot peppers can be added to this dish for an extra kick. Do not keep this raw fish tartare in the refrigerator for more than 24 hours; if you do keep it beyond the day it's made, make sure the bowl is placed on ice and positioned in the coldest part of the refrigerator—generally at the bottom in the back. —JEAN-PIERRE

Serves 4

8 ounces yellowfin or fresh
   albacore tuna

1 lemon

2 shallots, finely diced

2 tablespoons chopped mixed
   herbs, such as parsley,
   chives, and chervil

2 tablespoons olive oil

Salt

Piment d'Espelette

8 slices white bread, such as
   pain de mie, toasted and cut
   into quarters

Using a very sharp knife, cut the fish into thin slices, then cut the slices into a julienne and then into small dice. Refrigerate in a covered bowl. Zest half of the lemon and chop it; squeeze the juice from the lemon and set it aside.

In a bowl, mix together the diced fish, shallots, lemon zest, herbs, and olive oil and season with a pinch of salt and piment d'Espelette.

Before serving, add the lemon juice and taste to adjust the salt and the acidity. Serve on the toasted pain de mie as an appetizer.

RABBIT RILLETTES WITH ROSEMARY

Rillettes de Lapin au Romarin

One well-fed wild or domesticated rabbit will yield more rillettes than you might expect. And rilletes keep well: if you don't need much, you could roast the loins and back legs and use the remaining, slightly skimpier parts for rillettes. If you have a real butcher, you might also buy just a few pieces rather than a whole rabbit. Depending on how much you make, removing the meat from the bones after it's been slowly cooked is time-consuming, but the flavors are much better. I prefer duck fat to pork fat because it's somewhat sweeter. I sometimes add fresh minced rosemary directly to the rillettes before I pot them, but the impurity of the herb in the fat prevents it from keeping quite as long. Instead, I usually serve a tiny bit of chopped rosemary on the side. —JEAN-PIERRE

Serves 4 to 6

1 small rabbit, skinned and cleaned

Salt and black pepper

2 bay leaves

1 sprig thyme

1 sprig rosemary

1 tablespoon juniper berries

10 cloves garlic

1/2 bottle dry white wine

1 cup rendered duck fat or pork fat

1 tablespoon Armagnac or Cognac

Toasted bread, for serving

Rosemary, for serving

Cornichons, for serving

Cut the rabbit into small pieces. First cut off the legs, front and back, then cut the rear legs into two pieces. Next, remove the saddle, the large fillet that runs down each side of the rib cage. Once removed, cut each side into three pieces. Reserve the ribs. Season the pieces heavily with salt and pepper and place them in a mixing bowl with the bay leaves, thyme, rosemary, juniper berries, and garlic. Add the wine, cover, and refrigerate for 24 hours, or overnight.

Preheat the oven to 325°F. Pour the duck fat into a large pot with a lid set over medium heat and bring to a simmer. Add the rabbit to the pot along with the marinade, cover, and roast for about 2 hours. Stir occasionally to prevent the rabbit from sticking to the bottom of the pot. The rabbit is done when all the liquid has evaporated and the meat is lightly colored. Uncover the pot and set it to cool for 1 hour before straining out the fat (reserve the fat) and removing the bay leaves, rosemary, and juniper berries. Use your hands to pull the meat from bones and place it in a mixing bowl. Add the cooked garlic from the pot and 2 to 3 tablespoons of the reserved fat. Mash the rabbit with a wooden pestle or some other blunt instrument until the meat is incorporated into the fat. If the mixture is too dry to stick together, add a little more fat. Taste and correct the seasoning with salt, black pepper, and Armagnac. Pack the rillettes into a glass container or a terra-cotta dish. Cover with a thin layer of the reserved fat and lay parchment paper over the fat. Refrigerate for at least 1 week before using. Properly sealed, rillettes will keep for at least a month.

To serve, bring the meat you'll be using to room temperature and spread it on toasted bread. Serve with a pinch of fresh minced rosemary and cornichons.

CHEESE PUFFS WITH COMTÉ CHEESE
Gougères au Comté

This is a very common appetizer in France, especially in the eastern part of the country. If you visit the vineyards of Burgundy, Savoie, or Jura, you will almost certainly taste their wines with a homemade cheese puff. All the ingredients are relatively inexpensive with the exception of the cheese. Because its quality determines the flavor of the puffs, try to buy the best quality Comté or Beaufort you can find. —DENISE

Makes 40 puffs

1/2 cup water

1/2 cup milk

Pinch of salt

Pinch of sugar

1/2 cup butter, cut into small cubes

1 cup all-purpose flour

5 or 6 eggs

1/2 cup grated Comté or Gruyère cheese

Preheat the oven to 400°F. In a saucepan, combine the water, milk, salt, sugar, and butter. Bring to a boil over high heat. Remove from the heat and add the flour at once, mixing well with a wooden spoon until the mixture forms a smooth, sticky dough. Return the pot to the heat, this time set low, and stir for another 5 minutes to dry the dough.

Transfer to the mixing bowl of a stand mixer with the paddle attachment. Add one egg and mix on low speed until it's incorporated into the dough before adding the next, and so on until you have a smooth mixture. It should be soft but not runny—use your best judgment in deciding if the dough needs the moisture of the final egg. Add the grated cheese and spoon the dough into a pastry bag fitted with a 1/2-inch tube.

Line a baking sheet with parchment paper or prepare a nonstick silicone sheet. Pipe the dough into 1 1/2-inch mounds, spacing them about 2 inches apart. Bake for 25 minutes, until golden brown. They are best served right out of the oven, hot and crispy on the outside and soft in the center.

SPRING FAVA BEAN TOAST

Croûtons aux Fèves de Printemps

Cooking fava beans takes time and patience. The beans have to be shelled first, cooked, and then shelled a second time to remove the skins of the beans. All the effort is worthwhile because fava beans are unusually delicious. This recipe works best when the season runs to the end and the beans are bigger and starchier. —DENISE

Serves 4 to 6

2 pounds fava beans

2 cloves garlic, sliced

1 sprig savory

1 tablespoon water

Salt

2 tablespoons olive oil

3 tablespoons butter (optional)

8 slices baguette, toasted

Prepare the fava beans by shelling them, then parboil for 2 minutes in boiling water. Plunge the fava beans in ice water to stop the cooking. Once they're cool enough to handle, pop each one out of the outer skin and reserve in a bowl.

In a saucepan set over medium heat, cook the fava beans with the garlic, savory, and the water until tender. Taste for salt and add the olive oil and butter. Serve the beans at room temperature on toasted bread.

ONION TART WITH ANCHOVIES, OLIVES, AND THYME

Pissaladière

If there's one dish I return to over and over, it's *pissaladière*! Anchovies and black olives are always in our refrigerator the way most Americans always keep ketchup, mustard, and mayonnaise in theirs. The tart can be an appetizer cut into small pieces or a first course with a garden salad. It can be served all year-round, with a garden salad—everyone always has a few onions somewhere in the kitchen. Recently, Denise and I were deciding on the menu for a dinner at home, and I mentioned the onion tart. "Not again!" she said. Our friends had come to our house twice and both times we'd served them the tart! Note that the Pizza Dough recipe on page 240 must be doubled to make plenty of dough for the *pissaladière*. —JEAN-PIERRE

Serves 8

1/4 cup olive oil

6 onions, sliced

3 sprigs thyme

Pinch of salt

10 to 12 ounces pizza dough (recipe follows) or 11 ounce pie dough or puff pastry

1 egg, beaten (optional)

2 tablespoons milk (optional)

Anchovy fillets, cut in half lengthwise

Black olives, pitted

Combine the olive oil, onions, and thyme in a low-sided heavy pan set over medium heat until the onions are soft but not browned, 20 to 30 minutes. Add the salt and cook for a few minutes more, stirring frequently. Pour the onions into a strainer set over a bowl to drain, reserving the liquid.

Preheat the oven to 400°F. Roll out the dough into a 14-inch circle. Brush off the excess flour, transfer the dough to a baking sheet lined with parchment paper, and let it firm up in the refrigerator for 10 minutes. (If using puff pastry, cut and then cool in the same way.) Spread the cooled onions over the dough (remove the thyme), leaving a 1 1/2-inch border at the edge. Fold the border up over the onions. For a shiny, more finished look, brush the folded dough with the egg beaten together with the milk.

Top the onions with as many anchovies as you like, and plenty of black olives. Try to arrange the anchovy in a nice "checkers" pattern.

Bake the tart on the bottom rack of the oven for 15 to 20 minutes, until the crust is golden brown on the bottom and the edges are dark brown and crispy. (Puff pastry cooks faster than pizza dough—check the tart after 15 minutes or so, depending on your oven. It should be very crisp and well browned.) Slide the tart off the pan onto a rack to cool; serve warm or at room temperature.

—continued—

PIZZA DOUGH

Pâte á Pizza

Evan Shively helped Elsa become a great pizza maker. Here is her recipe. Top this flatbread with any variety of savory—or sweet— ingredients. Keep it simple, with just olive oil and fresh herbs, including rosemary, thyme, or sage. You might also add virtually any cheese, olives, sardines, cherry tomatoes, or thinly sliced vegetables. For a dessert, top the dough with a thin layer of fresh fruit sprinkled with raw sugar. When the tart comes out of the oven, finish with a gloss of melted butter, toasted slivered almonds, and a sprinkling of thyme leaves. Feel free to double or triple this versatile recipe as you like; freeze any extra before the bench proof.

Makes about 6 ounces, enough for 1 (10-inch) round flatbread rolled 1¼ inches thick

1½ tablespoons warm water
½ tablespoon honey
1 teaspoon active dry yeast
1 tablespoon olive oil
½ cup all-purpose flour
1 teaspoon salt

Whisk together the warm water, honey, and yeast in a small mixing bowl. Add the olive oil to the bowl but don't mix it in. Set aside to proof for 15 to 30 minutes. It should foam slightly. Mix together the flour and salt in a large mixing bowl and pour the liquid yeast mixture evenly over the flour mixture. Fold the flour and liquid together gently with a wooden spoon until just mixed. Do not overwork or try to make the dough smooth.

Gather the dough and place it on a lightly floured surface. Fold and press once or twice to bring the dough together into a loose ball. Do not knead. Clean the large mixing bowl and coat with oil. Place the dough in the bowl, flip it over once to coat both sides, and cover the surface of the dough with plastic wrap. Set the dough to rise at room temperature for 12 hours (18 hours maximum).

Turn the dough onto a lightly floured work surface and form one or two balls with the dough. Set on a lightly floured baking sheet, cover with plastic wrap, and set aside to rise for 2 hours.

Preheat the oven to 400°F. Flatten the balls with your hands or very gently roll the dough into a rectangle or circle about 1¼ inch thick. Place on an oiled baking sheet. Add your toppings and bake for 10 to 15 minutes, until the crust is nicely browned on the edges.

WALNUT WINE
Vin de Noix

This is an old recipe from the French countryside, from a time when everyone made at least one home-made aperitif from the nuts or fruit freely available to them on their own property. Walnut wine is one of the most of commonly made liqueurs because the trees grow everywhere in France, producing an abundant crop each season. Some traditions call for the addition of walnut leaves, while others add the sugar at the beginning. Everyone in the country has his or her own secret recipe for making the best version—some real old-timers even insist on the exact day to pick the green walnuts according to the waxing and waning of the moon. Whenever they're picked, it is important to harvest them before the nut inside is fully formed, otherwise they're too hard and difficult to remove with a knife—in Bordeaux, this is usually at the end of June or in early July. I've had excellent success trying many variations of this recipe using this same basic ratio of ingredients. Peach leaves or sour cherry leaves in place of the green walnuts makes an extraordinary liqueur. *A votre santé!* —JEAN-PIERRE

Makes about six (750-ml) bottles

20 green walnuts

4 (750-ml) bottles red wine

1 (750-ml) bottle white wine

1 (750-ml) bottle eau-de-vie or vodka

1 vanilla bean

4 cloves

2 pounds sugar

Wash and cut the green walnuts into halves or quarters. In a large glass container with a lid, cover the walnuts with the red and white wine, eau-de-vie, vanilla, and cloves. Close the container and keep it in a dark, cool place for 40 days. Strain the liquid and add the sugar. Return it to the glass container and shake it once a day until, after several weeks, all the sugar dissolves. Pour into bottles, seal with a cork, and let the liquor age for at least 6 months. The walnut wine is best when aged for a full year. Serve chilled or on ice.

SEVILLE ORANGE APERITIF
Vin d'Orange

Some produce is so specifically seasonal that you simply have to buy it when it appears. This was true at Chez Panisse of the hard-to-find bitter Seville oranges. Once a year, usually in late January or early February, cases of Seville oranges would appear in the walk-in. The first time this happened no one really seemed to be using them, so I began to play with some ideas, and this is one of the recipes I came up with. Over the years, many friends asked me about the recipe, which I happily shared—I think by now it must have spread quite far. At the restaurant, we served aperitifs on weekends as part of the menu. This *vin d'orange* made a terrific base for the wild mixes of herbs, fruits, and spices I concocted for this portion of the menu. Some of these were completely crazy, but they were always very much appreciated. —JEAN-PIERRE

Makes 8 (750-ml) bottles

5 (750-ml) bottles Sauvignon Blanc

1 (750-ml) bottle vodka

1¹/₂ to 2 cups packed brown sugar

6 Seville oranges, sliced into thin rounds

1 orange, sliced into thin rounds

1 lemon, sliced into thin rounds

1 vanilla bean, split

In several large canning jars, combine the wine, vodka, brown sugar, Seville oranges, orange, and lemon, distributing the ingredients evenly as needed, depending on how many jars you're using. Cut the vanilla bean into as many pieces as you have jars and add a piece to each jar. Close the jars tightly, turn the containers upside down, and store for 3 weeks in a cool, dark place.

Strain the liquid through a sieve lined with cheesecloth into a bowl; taste for balance. The wine should be neither too sweet nor too bitter. Adjust with additional sugar or dilute with additional wine. Using a funnel, fill clean wine bottles with the *vin d'orange*. Cork the bottles and set them to rest in a cool, dark spot for at least 3 months or for up to 1 year. As the wine ages, the flavors will mellow. It can be kept for over a year, but as it ages beyond that point, it will begin to darken, losing its bright flavor. Serve chilled or over ice as an aperitif.

ARMAGNAC WITH PRESERVED PRUNES

Pruneaux à l'Armagnac

Every autumn I make a few jars of these prunes to tuck away in the wine cellar—some remain there for many years, improving as they age. The alcohol level drops over the course of the year, and the prunes become sweeter and smoother. The Agen prune, named for the town of Agen in southwestern France, is an oval plum covered by deep purple skin. As the fruit ripens in August, the prunes in and around Agen are dried on racks in the sun or on vast trays in wood ovens. The town is not far from our house in Bordeaux, so I look for the prunes at farmers' markets at the end of summer and in the early fall. I buy all I can when I see them. Because they aren't fully dried, the prunes have a softer texture and more pronounced flavor than conventionally dried prunes. Those dried in wood ovens have a distinctive, lightly smoky flavor.

When preserving the prunes in liquor, as I do here, I use a white Armagnac (young and very strong) that a friend gave me more than fifteen years ago. You can also make this recipe with a neutral spirit like vodka. When we don't cook with them or use them in ice cream (page 127), we serve these prunes whole with a little of their liquor. They're a perfect complement to a strong espresso after a meal. —JEAN-PIERRE

Makes 1 (1-quart) jar

2 pounds unpitted prunes

1 cup Armagnac

1/2 cup sugar

2 cups dry white wine

If you are using conventionally dried prunes from a package, soak the prunes in warm water overnight. Place the prunes in a large canning jar and pour over the Armagnac, sugar, and wine. Cover tightly and shake the jar every day for a week to dissolve the sugar. Store in a cool, dark place for 6 months to 10 years.

PICKLED VEGETABLES OR CORNICHONS

Légumes au Vinaigre ou Cornichons

Pickling in vinegar is a basic method for preserving vegetables and fruit, though the French don't use it as much as Americans do. I most often use it to put up white onions and cornichons, as described here. —JEAN-PIERRE

Makes about 4 (8-ounce) jars

2 pounds cornichons or "gherkin" cucumbers, brushed clean

1 cup coarse salt

3 cups distilled spirits

2 sprigs tarragon

10 pearl onions, blanched, drained, and peeled

Black peppercorns

2 tablespoons coriander seeds

3 cups white wine vinegar

Mix together the cornichons and salt, cover, and set aside at room temperature for 24 hours. Remove the cornichons from the salt, rinse under cold water, and place them in a clean canning jar along with the spirits, tarragon, onions, black peppercorns, and coriander seeds. Close tightly and keep it in a cool and dark place for 1 month.

Drain the spirits from the jar and replace it with the wine vinegar. Transfer to 4 8-ounce sterilized jars, cover tightly and set aside in a cool, dark place for an additional 2 months before using.

cherries

IN THE JUNE CHERRY SEASON, all the trees produce fruit at the same time and we find ourselves with too many cherries.

Since this is one of the first fruits of the summer, we get very excited the first few days of the cherry season. We eat them directly from the trees while walking through the garden and what we manage to bring back to the house we eat for lunch and dinner. As the days pass by and the weather warms, the fruit matures. That's when I begin to cook with them—baking clafoutis, a fresh cherry tart, or just briefly cooking them with a little water and sugar to eat on toast or with ice cream or yogurt.

No matter how much baking I do, with all our cherry trees producing fruit in sync, we quickly find ourselves overwhelmed. That's when we begin to give them away, arriving at dinner parties with a giant bowl full as a gift or sending our own dinner guests home with a big bag of them. But the cherries just keep coming, and the limbs of the trees begin to bend at dangerous angles from the weight of all the unpicked fruit. Happy as the birds seem to be to gobble their share, they don't make much of a dent in the total volume.

This is when I begin to make my preserves. I prefer to use the small, bitter cherries, which are less sweet and do well for canning. I remove the stems and wash them but leave the pits in. I then pack them in pint-size glass jars, adding 2 tablespoons of sugar and 1 tablespoon of water before closing and sealing the jar with a rubber seal and a lid. I then sterilize the jars for 30 minutes.

During the winter we start to crave fresh fruit. This is when my preserves are greatly appreciated, and we open them up and serve the cherries for dessert with a cake or ice cream.

I preserve many of the other cherries whole, stems on, in pure white Armagnac (vodka is fine, too). I close them up and keep them covered in the liquor for at least 6 months. They make an excellent digestive served after meals with coffee.

I make more traditional jam with the darkest, ripest cherries. The rest I put in my four-fruit jam, which has raspberries, strawberries, red currants, and cherries. It's a delicious temptation if you have a weakness for jam on buttered toast.

There's an old peasant song from the country around the Jura where I grew up about *le temps des cerises*, which translates as "the time of the cherries" or, most literally, "cherry season." The song is about romance, sultry weather, and the long sunny days in late June when cherry season is at its peak. It captures some of the more subtle reasons for the popularity of and enthusiasm for cherries that seems nearly universal, linking them with the welcome days when summer weather begins and the endless pleasures and promises of the warm days and nights to come. —JEAN PIERRE

CANNED ROASTED TOMATOES
Tomates Cuites au Four Mises en Conserve

About a year ago I agreed to help my parents take care of their new "ranch" in Healdsburg while they were in France, busy with their summer culinary tours for Two Bordelais. Diligently, I walked the property each day, counting the cows (making sure the night hadn't swallowed one up), checking the fences for holes, watering fragile trees, and, most important, tending my father's garden. Before leaving for Europe he had tilled, dug, and planted his large fenced plot with, what seemed, any seed he could get his hands on. By the time he left for Bordeaux that summer the results of his hard work were starting to be visible, the neat stripes of soft green seedlings patiently pushing through the dirt.

Two months later it was a very different scene. In an effort to test the varieties that would grow best in his new garden, my father had in fact cultivated every seed he could find, including heritage varieties of pepper, eggplant, zucchini, tomato, and cherry tomato. By mid-summer, I had a garden gone wild on my hands. I spent hours every day tending, picking, and eating nothing but vegetables—but the plants just kept on giving. Of all the challenges of taking care of such a garden, the five-dozen tomato plants were especially difficult to keep up with. After eating tomatoes for breakfast on toast (page 253), for lunch sliced with mozzarella and in salads of all kinds, and for dinner hot, cold, and in-between, I still had baskets of them sitting on the kitchen counter. Gathering as many canning jars as I could manage to carry, I began to can—partly to save my sanity and partly so I would have the incredible tomatoes as a treat for later, filling my pantry for the cold months of winter. —MAUD MOULLÉ

Makes 4 (8-ounce) jars

2 pounds tomatoes, any single variety or a mix, washed and dried

2 tablespoons olive oil

4 garlic cloves (optional)

Salt (optional)

2 teaspoons lemon juice

Preheat the oven to 375°F. Core the tomatoes, if necessary, and then cut them in quarters. Leave cherry tomatoes whole and slice small or medium-size tomatoes in half. Arrange the tomatoes skin side up in one or two large, shallow ceramic or glass baking dishes. Whatever you use, squeeze the tomatoes in tightly; they will shrink as they cook. Drizzle the tomatoes with the olive oil. If you're using garlic, tuck the cloves in among the tomatoes now. Generously sprinkle with salt and bake for 1 to 1 1/2 hours or until the skins begin to turn very dark.

Prepare the water to sterilize the canning jars by placing a large pot full of water over high heat. Bring the water to a boil, turn off the heat ,and set aside until you're ready to sterilize the jars.

Just before removing the tomatoes from the oven, sterilize the mason jars and their lids by immersing them in boiling water and leaving them there for several minutes. Remove the jars with tongs and place them with their lids on a sterile surface, such as a clean paper towel or an immaculate dishcloth. Divide the hot tomatoes between the two jars along with all their juices. Add 1 teaspoon of lemon juice to each jar to keep the tomatoes from discoloring. Stir the tomatoes gently with a sterile chopstick to release any trapped air bubbles. Close the jars with the sterilized lids. If the mason jars are piping hot and the tomatoes have come straight from the oven, the tops will seal. If you're uncertain, you can submerge the tightly sealed jars in boiling water for 10 to 15 minutes. Jars that seal have a concave shape at their center and will not move or pop when you press on the center of the lid. Any jars that do not seal, or that you're uncertain of, should be refrigerated and used within a week.

MORNING TOMATO TOAST
WITH FRESH RICOTTA
Tartine de Tomate et Fromage Frais

This is a recipe for late July and August when the tomatoes are as juicy and flavorful as they are plentiful. As you may have guessed, there's no point in making this dish unless you have stellar tomatoes, and if you are lucky enough to have different varieties, mix them up in this recipe. Keep things simple as possible by tearing the herbs and roughly chopping the tomatoes—it's morning, after all. On those mornings when I'm wide awake and have plenty of time, I poach an egg and slide it on top of the toast. If I'm rushed, I'll drizzle a little olive oil over a slice of fresh ricotta to eat alongside my toast. —MAUD MOULLÉ

Makes 1 toast

2 tomatoes, roughly chopped

4 leaves basil or 4 sprigs
    parsley, chopped or torn

Salt and black pepper

Olive oil

1 garlic clove

1 large slice Levain bread,
    toasted

Mix the tomatoes, herbs, a pinch of salt, a grind of pepper, and a drizzle of olive oil together in a mixing bowl. Rub the toast with garlic before topping with the tomato mixture.

INDEX

Ten Speed Press and the Ten Speed Press
colophon are registered trademarks of
Random House LLC

All photographs by Jan Baldwin with the
exception of the following: pages 129, 185,
and 251 by Dan Hicks.

Library of Congress Cataloging-in-
Publication Data is on file with
the publisher

Hardcover ISBN: 978-1-60774-547-1
eBook ISBN: 978-1-60774-548-8

Printed in China

Design by Toni Tajima
Food Styling by Alice Hart

10 9 8 7 6 5 4 3 2 1

First Edition